IF I'M NOT BACK BY WEDNESDAY

ADVANCE PRAISE FOR *IF I'M NOT BACK BY WEDNESDAY*

If I'm Not Back by Wednesday is poignant and enthralling. A story of suffering, misery, fear, adventure, survival and youthful naïveté, told with admirable candour.

—*Paul Williams, The Daily Gleaner*

A great, great read; attention-holding and accurate. I would unhesitatingly urge Jamaicans in the Diaspora—and we are everywhere in this world—to read the book. It is a necessary historical document.

—*Philip Mascoll, OD, founding member, Jamaican Diaspora Advisory Board*

Indeed a remarkable recollection and meticulously documented autobiographical memoir.

—*Hon. R. Danvers 'Danny' Williams, OJ, CD, JP,*
Chairman, Jamaica College Foundation

Thrilling and thoroughly intriguing. A well researched and recorded piece of a previously undocumented historic event in Jamaica.

—*Montgomery 'Monty' Alexander, CD, internationally acclaimed jazz pianist*

It was a great privilege for me to read Geoffrey's new book *If I'm Not Back by Wednesday*—and, yes, from cover to cover. It is a masterpiece. Excellent and exciting reading with a wonderful collage of photographs…well prepared and beautifully written; it is also intertwined with historical information of Geoffrey's family, his life at Jamaica College and, among other things, the worried families and general public back home. Well done, Geoffrey. I wish you all the success, and I am very proud of you.

—*W. Donald Soutar, sole living survivor of the 1939 expedition*

Gripping, fluid and engaging. A thrilling trek through the jungle ends up being a race for survival.

—*Nicola Cunningham-Williams, Buzz Magazine*

One family's worst nightmare in Jamaica's history. For the worried parents and all of concerned Jamaica, Christmas came early.

—*Carlysle Hudson, Managing Director, Mother's Enterprises*

An interesting read for the Blue Mountain odyssey…pulled in by the memories it brought back to life.

—*G. Raymond Chang OJ, OC, Chancellor Emeritus at Ryerson University*

A dramatic and descriptive story…fright-stricken as the boys were, they were determined and never gave up. It is impossible to describe the dangerous parameters I faced. A great book has been written and I'm sure you will enjoy it as much as I did.

—*Colonel Anthony 'Bunny' Stern, OD, helicopter rescue pilot*

Geoffrey Haddad's account *If I'm Not back by Wednesday* has captured the essence and intrigue of the Blue Mountains, the spirit and traditions of the Jamaica College schoolboy, and the never-say-die will of our Jamaican people. That the boys got the breaks in the weather, allowing them to be found, is the greatest miracle of all. Climbing out of the valley was the best thing they could have done, leading them to the other miracle, the only grass patch in the area. We at Whitfield Hall have had to search for and rescue many lost hikers; some, including wild pig hunters, have died here too.

—*John Allgrove, PE, owner, Whitfield Hall Hostel in the Blue Mountains*

 FriesenPress

Suite 300 - 990 Fort St
Victoria, BC, V8V 3K2
Canada

www.friesenpress.com

Haddad, Geoffrey B., 1950

If I'm Not Back By Wednesday – Trapped in Jamaica's Blue Mountains, 1967,
Blue Mountains, Jamaica – Trapped – Lost – True Stories – Survival -Search &
Rescue – Jamaica – Blue Mountains – Geoffrey Haddad – Geoffrey B Haddad –
Jamaica College – Helicopter Rescues – Army Searches – Police Searches

ISBN
978-1-4602-7438-5 (Hardcover)
978-1-4602-7439-2 (Paperback)
978-1-4602-7440-8 (eBook)

1. Biography & Autobiography

Distributed to the trade by The Ingram Book Company

IF I'M NOT
BACK BY
WEDNESDAY

Trapped in Jamaica's Blue Mountains

A TRUE STORY

GEOFFREY B. HADDAD

The author (at right)
at the Trig Station
Blue Mountain Peak
December 1969

IF I'M NOT BACK BY WEDNESDAY

Trapped in Jamaica's Blue Mountains

A TRUE STORY

GEOFFREY B. HADDAD

In loving memory of my father, Badia 'B. S.' Haddad
(1911–2001) who gave me everything, including his heritage and his good name; I also dedicate this book to Isabella
Rachel, Julianna, Evelyn, and Jonah—the joys of my life.

With good perspective of history, we can have a better understanding of the past and present, and thus a clear vision of the future.

—*Carlos Slim, son of Khalil Salim Haddad of Lebanon and Linda Helú of Mexico.*

TABLE OF CONTENTS

PERILOUS ASCENT

On December 16, 1967, five adventurous boys from one of the island's elite high schools, Jamaica College, set out into the majestic Blue Mountains in search of a mythical trail, endeavouring to reach its highest point, the Peak, at elevation 7402 feet. They never made it.

After almost ten days in heavily forested terrain described as "inaccessible as any place in the world, and perhaps where no man has ever trodden," they found themselves hopelessly lost, trapped, and far from a living soul. Cold and starving, they probably only had hours to live.

A platoon of soldiers dispatched to the area where it was believed that the boys began their hike along the Blue Mountain Ridge reported that they were never there or had vanished into the jungle. The soldiers turned back.

This is the story of the harrowing journey that would make headlines and test the character of five boys as they faced down death on their way to manhood. Using eyewitness accounts, maps, and never-before-seen photographs, the author tracks the action from an innocent plan hatched during Christmas break to the dramatic, last-ditch efforts to rescue the boys.

In 1967, Geoffrey Haddad was a curious Jamaica College student with a passion for the outdoors. He was one of the five

AUTHOR'S NOTE

This account reflects perceptions of the years before, during, and after the adventure. Events depicted in this book are true and accurate, and where not previously documented, are recounted from the best of my memory. Whenever it was impossible to document conversations verbatim, they have been recreated almost entirely from memory and/or in conjunction with at least one of the participants, which means that it may not be word for word.

Some persons were asked to review certain sections for accuracy. This does not mean, however, that they liked or agreed with everything they read. But this is my story, not theirs.

In an effort to safeguard the privacy of certain few people, some individual names and identifying characteristics have been changed. In any event, although those figures were peripheral to the overall story, they deserve their privacy.

PREFACE

DÉJÀ VU: FIVE JAMAICA COLLEGE BOYS
TRAPPED IN THE MOUNTAINS

Being at the summit of the Blue Mountain range always gives me that feeling of accomplishment, even if it's never quite the satisfaction of conquest. Maybe it's because the Peak is so unassuming, just wind-ravaged scrubland rising a bit higher than the nearby trig-station pyramid, the one climbers often assume to be the highest point on the island. I guess it's one final ironic misconception about Blue Mountain Peak that helps preserve the mystique of the place. This was my third trip to Jamaica's highest point, all the way to 7402 feet, and though it felt thoroughly manageable in 1969, this mountain wasn't always that way for me.

As I stood atop the trig-station, my gaze out yonder was not random, but very focused. Two miles away to the west, I could see the very top of Mossman's Peak, approximately 700 feet below where I stood. The entire ridge to the north and below was engulfed in the densest mass of cloud one could ever imagine. Not a single ray of sunlight permeated the mass, reminding me of the distant past—ominous, frightening, dark, cold, fraught with hunger, parched throat, pain and suffering with nowhere to go. The names and faces of Jackie, David, Robin, another David, Victor, Roderic and Pedro flashed through my mind. I had visions of my parents, the newspapers, television cameras, helicopters and aeroplanes, the popping of the rotors and the drone of engines overhead. Police and soldiers, family and friends going crazy, horrible things and times filling my thoughts.

Trying to concentrate on more pleasant topics, my mind drifted to model planes, badminton, soccer and cricket, *Stranger and Goliath**, a childhood triumph. Then I remembered the words I'd left with my good friend, the casual statement that would pull me from the jaws of death. But I hadn't been there alone. How about my newfound and newly bonded friends, George, Gordon, Cecil, and Roger? They had been somewhere down there as well, below that sea of miserable cloud and fog, yelling for help, praying that someone would hear or see them. There were no cell phones, GPS or Emergency Locator Transmitter (ELT) back then; any one of them would have helped—even telepathy.

Then the picture in my mind got clearer. Almost two years earlier, on December 24, 1967, a party of teenage climbers, somewhere in the vast expanse of the jungle below, comparable to the densest in the world, a tiny fern patch, a fifty-foot tree and five lost souls, afraid to move, not that they had any strength to go anywhere; trapped at elevation 4000. Fearful, not knowing what lay beyond and just about to lose faith. Would anyone be found, and if so, alive?

Standing there at the Peak in 1969, I felt compelled to recount to fellow climbers, Charles and John Royes, the detailed memories of those nine tortuous days. As I did so, the desire grew even stronger within me to record those memories so that the winds of time would not blow them away completely.

★ ★ ★

---

* Stranger and Goliath was the first of many 8mm productions by the boys and girls of Windsor Avenue. Its final version was just over seven minutes long, spliced together with sections from at least four three-minute reels of film. Complete with professionally designed costumes, make-up artists, true-to-life settings and a script, it became the standard by which future productions would be judged. Robin and Roderic Crawford were the producers and directors. Their senior siblings, Janet and Denis acted in supervisory roles and to a lesser extent, as actors, our 'movie stars'. I was one of the scriptwriters, photographers and actors for this premiere event. It was about this time that the gang, now numbering about thirteen, had begun meeting daily at my home for afternoon soccer and cricket matches. This was the highlight of our teenage activities. There and then began a bond among us all, the feeling of a true club. The last production, Room 13, was filmed in 1968.

This is the story that has burned inside me for nearly fifty years.

I had done the research, meticulously collecting and cataloguing every bit of information I could, including memorabilia related to the trip. That process should have, I suppose, served as a kind of catharsis, a way to purge the demons. Yet, every year—especially on the anniversary—I am still haunted by the events of my 1967 Christmas season; in fact, I had nightmares about this ordeal every December for twenty years. I've told the story to myself and others many times over, always arriving at the same conclusion: I really shouldn't be alive.

The story begins simply enough: Five adventurous boys set out to blaze a trail through uncharted territory in the Blue Mountains without sharing the finer details of their plan, hatched one afternoon at school. The adventure went horribly awry. What transpired is recounted here, compiled from the notes, photographs, and memories of those who went to the brink of death, and the recollections of the brave souls who went in search of them.

During the intervening years, I have spent more time dreaming about this story than planning an actual book. Yes, I had committed my memories to paper, and I had notes that constituted the skeleton of the story, but it had rested for far too long. Then, I stumbled upon a column written by Hartley Neita in an edition of Jamaica's *Daily Gleaner*. Neita, then one of the island's prominent historians and communications consultants, had chronicled the misadventure of five teenagers—from my old high school, Jamaica College (JC)—who had dared to challenge the wilds[1] of Jamaica's Blue Mountains in 1939. This gave me the inspiration, finally, to put the book together.

The newspaper excerpt from his book, *The Search,* had me spellbound as I read how the boys had taken only enough rations for four or five days, but survived after being lost for almost two weeks. An intensive five-day search—which, at its height, included the military, police, the Forest and Public Works departments, their headmaster/scoutmaster, boy scouts, concerned businessmen, family and friends—had not found them, and they had been presumed dead. Then miraculously, they simply emerged from the bush, back to civilization, without having ever been spotted from the air. Once again, five JC boys would tackle the hostile and ravenous environment of the Blue Mountains.

★ ★ ★

There was, I think, something symbiotic about Jamaica College and the Blue Mountains, some cosmic connection between the school's barracks survivalism and those misty Peaks. JC boys, you see, were known to have lived a tough, martial existence in the early years of the school. Because of this hard heritage, they studied and played hard, expecting to win national academic prizes or excel in all the inter-school sports. Accustomed to rigid discipline, many would march off to both world wars to suffer and die when the Empire beckoned. Others, following family customs or guided by the challenging traditions of the school, routinely took off into the bush for hunting, picnicking, and nature treks. A favourite reward for good JC boys was a hike into the mountains, with the Peak as the blue ribbon.

Not surprisingly, Reginald Murray, the school's headmaster from 1933–1941 (himself a JC man and Rhodes scholar), was one of the first hikers to cross the Blue Mountain range from its south side to the island's north coast, accomplishing the feat in 1928 after gaining experience over eleven years of trips into those heights. Those who knew him declared him tough as iron. Without a doubt, his reputation helped to marshal the committed response that came from a diverse cross-section of Jamaicans, who gave their financial support, time, and technical expertise when the first 'Blue Mountain Five' went missing in 1939.

Supporting the tactical mission then was an amphibious Pan American aircraft given a special waiver to fly as low as 1,000 feet above the treacherous terrain.

"The thick undergrowth of the forest prevented our seeing any trace of the missing lads," one of the pilots remarked. "It would have been dangerous to fly lower because of the fear of air pockets. We flew round and round for one-and-a-half hours."

The crisis was made worse by scant communications facilities. In 1939, few homes had telephones or the luxury of a daily newspaper delivered to the door. Without the benefit of commercial radio or television service, messages had to be conveyed primarily by carrier pigeon and the few ham radio operators active on the island.

The boys' notes were compiled and put into a chronological account by their leader, DG Hall, in his book, *Lost in the Blue Mountains of Jamaica*, and it is upon Hall's account that Hartley Neita based his book, *The Search*. As I read it, Neita's writing powerfully inspired me to tell my own story. Much of what the 1939 hikers experienced was frighteningly familiar, but so much is different about the 1967 hiking drama that it deserves its own telling.

In addition to addressing some of the questions I've been asked over the years, the account is designed to encourage future hikers and explorers to take every precaution whenever planning an expedition without marked trails. Be sure to take at least the following: an ELT, cell phone, GPS, flares, radio, appropriate clothing, and protection from the weather (sleeping bags, rain coats, tents, etc.), and enough food and extra water. Mark your way, advise a knowledgeable person about your plans, and, most importantly, make sure that you at least have a reliable connection to home base.

END NOTES

[1]   Newspaper reports during the 1939 crisis had carried sensational headlines such as: WIDE JUNGLE SEARCH FOR FIVE LOST HIKERS—DRAMATIC SEARCH. An excerpt from one of the many reports is reproduced here from Hartley Neita's book, *The Search* (p. 38) describing the inhospitable deep interior of the mountains:

It is no exaggeration to say that there are places in the island that the foot of man has never trodden, and are as inaccessible as any place in the world.

Strange at it may seem, in a tropical island, these places so high up in the hills have a climate that is as near as it is possible for one to get in comparison to the colder regions of the world and when one adds to it almost incessant rain and mist of terrifying density one should be able to see what any one getting lost in there is up against.

First of all, there is no food of any kind to be found at that altitude. You can see water and cannot get it and it means cutting your way through moss-covered vegetation from which moisture is always dripping even at high noon. It is never dry. The sun appears only for a few seconds and then it is gone, might be, never to appear for the remainder of the day.

Then there comes the backbreaking nature of each step that must be made before one can get anywhere. This is the type of thing that the lost fellows are up against, also their would-be rescuers. It is no place for the unfit or the tyro, no matter how willing they might be, and the search parties themselves must proceed with the greatest of care as one mistake and you will have to search for them and perhaps bring in a severely injured man thus wrecking their usefulness right away.

PROLOGUE

A NINETY-MINUTE WINDOW

December 24, 1967, 8:42 a.m.

The weather that morning was reasonably clear with only light cloud cover. Tiny against the sky, a 230-horsepower Cessna 180 with identification characters 6Y-JDY was making tight circles above Jamaica's Blue Mountain range. From Earth, the aeroplane must have seemed slow and lazy way up there, as if it hadn't a care in the world. The pilot, J. S. Tyndale-Biscoe—the island's best-known pilot and aerial photographer, a remarkable man who had been a mechanic, refrigeration technician, bottling plant manager and musician—was at the stick. With his experience in the air, if anyone could find a person somewhere more than a mile below in thick and unremarkable vegetation, it was Jack.

The flight so far was mostly routine for him, and there was hardly anything of interest to report since he had been airborne.

"Palisadoes Tower, Juliet Delta Yankee," Tyndale-Biscoe droned over the radio.

"Palisadoes Tower, Delta Yankee," came the matter-of-fact reply from the tower.

"Delta Yankee at 9500 feet, north Blue Mountain slopes Portland," the pilot came back, "returning Palisadoes, no sign of boys, over."

"Roger, Delta Yankee, report fifteen miles out, runway in use two-nine, wind 110 at 10 QNH 29.98, over."

"Delta Yankee, roger."

Three minutes later, Tyndale-Biscoe was heading due east, descending now from 8,300 ft. Beside him, glued to his binoculars, was his close friend and mentee, David du Mont, who was serving as Jack's spotter and searcher.

"Jackie," du Mont said, injecting some urgency into the mission as he used his binoculars to peer through the window, "go below those clouds and turn right, more…more…down…down…hold and level…I think I see some smoke down there!"

"No way, David, not again—much too risky, too much turbulence. Remember what happened fifteen minutes ago?" Biscoe asked, referring to an earlier near-mishap during the flight when they entered a gorge to investigate what they thought was smoke, only to discover that it was merely localized fog.

The risk made Jack adamant. "I'm not taking that chance again. The weather is closing in. No more time to search today. We're heading for terra firma, my friend, back to Kingston!"

At that moment, the men in the little plane had given the outing their best shot, spending more than an hour in ideal morning conditions. The decision to abort had to be made before the early sunny morning conditions turned bleak, or dwindling fuel levels could conspire and ground them. All they could see for certain were treetops—tall, thick, endless greenery that clung to the steep ridges and ravines in the search area.

As he got ready to aim his highly manoeuvrable craft back to Kingston, Jack Tyndale-Biscoe's heart was sinking. He felt he was out of time and good skies; in a little while, he'd have to land with no news of the year's five most wanted persons in Jamaica.

CHAPTER 1

BLUE MOUNTAIN MYSTIQUE

Jamaica is truly a 'land of wood and water' (as Columbus got it from the Tainos), but also of fun-loving people, old sugar plantations, rum, coffee, spices, aluminium ore (bauxite), alumina, reggae music and world-class athletes. There are also mountainous regions, which hold their own among the most dense and dangerous jungle terrain anywhere in the world. Because of the inhospitable, sometimes impassable terrain, these parts of Jamaica remain virtually unexplored.

North of the capital city, Kingston, and rising to 7402 feet in just ten miles on the southern side stands Blue Mountain Peak, the crown of a range that serves as Jamaica's most imposing geographical feature. Internationally famous Blue Mountain Coffee, a necessary ingredient for the world-renowned Tia Maria liqueur, and perhaps the best cup of java anywhere, grows in abundance on the southern slopes (compared to the uninhabited, rain-soaked and ruggedly forested slopes to the north).

The Blue Mountains are named after their rich palette of blues, viewed from a distance through the Caribbean light that plays on its misty forests. The range runs west-east for a distance of approximately twenty-five miles and towers over the mid-east section of the island; yet Blue Mountain Peak, unlike many other famous mountains that are located more remotely, rises from foothills that stand just at the edge of Kingston, the capital. The mountains are so steep and compact that they soar from the plains to nearly a mile in the air after less than an hour's travel by road.

The Peak can be reached from Kingston by way of Irish Town or Guava Ridge on one road that meets at the village of Section, then continues to Buff Bay on the north eastern coast. On the south side of the mountains, there exists a well-defined and much-travelled trail. The last three to four hours of the fourteen-and-a-half-mile trip on foot, which begins at Mavis Bank on the Yallahs River, involves a very steep climb, featuring numerous 'S' bends and switchbacks, about a mile below the Peak, known as 'Jacob's Ladder'.

The upper slopes on the northern side stretch halfway to the north coast, the part of Jamaica that boasts some of the most beautiful beaches on the island. The Blue Mountain and John Crow Mountain National Park[1] covers six per cent of the entire mass of Jamaica and serves to preserve the island's most important remaining natural forests and watershed. These mountains are home to a diverse collection of 800 species of plants, the world's second largest butterfly (the Jamaican giant swallowtail *Papilo homerus*), and 200 kinds of resident and migrant birds. The area is one of the largest migratory habitats in the Americas. Fully half of the more than 500 flowering plant species are uniquely Jamaican, including the Jamaican bamboo grass and the shy *Chusquea abietifolia* that takes more than three decades to flower.

Only the fittest[2] and most determined of hikers will reach Blue Mountain Peak in a day. To break up the journey, climbers can stay at a decades-old, traditional overnight spot, set on forty acres of an old coffee estate. The rustic charm of the hostel at Whitfield Hall has retained much of the appeal of years past, though nowadays, hikers arrive there as much on foot as, more luxuriously, by rough-and-tumble jeep ride. The building's low ceilings hover closely over the old planked floors, while Tilley kerosene pressure lamps and the fireplace in the large drawing room warm visitors as deep night and cold fall over the property.

Having rested for the night, hikers wanting to greet the sunrise will wake in the wee hours to begin the expedition to the Peak, via Portland Gap, from Whitfield Hall. The trek from here can be risky without a guide and proper lighting from a good flashlight because there are many steep precipices along the way.

Annual rainfall can be as much as 275 inches in the hills above Buff Bay and Port Antonio. In 1937, 21.7 inches were recorded in a single day. This is due to the region's sharp relief and saturated north-east cloud formations. A diurnal range of more than 30°F can exist, usually between October and March. Then and there, the climate has no tropical characteristics. Temperatures drop radically on the ridge, and there have been reports of the odd dusting of snow at the Peak, sometimes even hail. I vividly remember being there in December of 1969, and experiencing 28°F (-2°C). It was so cold that there was a thin layer of ice on top of the forty-five-gallon drums that contained our only source of water.

One never gets used to witnessing sunrise at the Peak. Seasoned hikers will say that it is a new thrill every time; there a ray, another, one more, and voilà, up she comes, an exhilarating and treasured moment.

In sharp contrast, the northern slopes consist of dense thickets of trees—an essentially impenetrable forest with an undergrowth of tight-knit bamboo grass, sometimes underlain with loose shale. Mud and rock slides are not uncommon, and in most of these areas, daylight hardly penetrates through the trees, even on the sunniest of days. According to Jack Tyndale-Biscoe, on the northern slopes of these areas, no less than seven rivers rise, all with numerous tributaries; and due to the terrain, these rivers are a continuous series of cataracts and waterfalls. To follow them to the sea and civilization would be virtually impossible as they often fall through deep gorges with vertical sides, past ridges running up into the heights. The upper reaches of these valleys are usually cloud filled, and the surrounding terrain invisible beyond a few feet, making it more than easy to wander endlessly and never get anywhere.

Unlike its southern counterpart, virtually no trails exist on this side of the Blue Mountain Ridge, and the lower foothills of these northern slopes pose a real danger to the most experienced wild-boar hunter. Steep slopes—some of them greater than 75°, bordered by deadly ravines, and intersected by fast-flowing streams—are commonplace.

END NOTES

[1]   The Union for Conservation of Nature (IUCN) is an international organization working in the field of nature conservation and sustainable use of natural resources. Excerpts from one of its articles entitled 'Five protected areas to see before you die' dated May 28, 2015, lists the Blue and John Crow Mountains as "one of five of the best kept protected area secrets on the planet:

The Blue and John Crow Mountains National Park (BJCMNP)Jamaica was designated in 1993 under the Natural Resources Conservation Authority Act, on the boundary of the Blue Mountain Forest Reserve and a group of adjoining forest reserves, designated between 1945 and 1965. The government agency responsible for national parks is the National Environment and Planning Agency, who have delegated management to the Jamaica Conservation and Development Trust (JCDT)—a non-government organisation. These two have a collaborative agreement with the Forestry Department, and JCDT is recognised as responsible for the Park's operational management, and more recently, Jamaica's lush Blue and John Crow Mountains have become the island's first UNESCO World Heritage site.

Source: https://www.iucn.org/news_homepage/news_by_date/?18943/ Five-protected-areas-to-see-before-you-die

[2]   According to *Jamaica Insight Guide*, p. 217 'Scaling the Blue Mountain Peak', Discovery Channel, APA Publications, 2004:

Only the hardy will succeed in reaching the summit of the Blue Mountain Peak, a three hour scramble up a rough track [beginning at Whitfield Hall]. The climb begins in a montane mist forest, a rare remnant of Jamaica's forests. Its name derives from the characteristic mist which often lies on the Peaks between 10am and 4pm. This reduces the incidental sunlight immensely, which affects the flora.

The Elfin Woodlands finally starts at about 1,677 metres (5500 ft.), petering out in windswept scrub on the summit. It is open and eerie woodland, consisting mainly of short, twisted, gnarled trees, often laden with lichens, mosses and ferns. A dwarf species of orchids grows here in the swirling mist. The flowers that grow well are honeysuckle, rhododendron, ginger lilies and the lesser known merianias (called 'Jamaica Rose'), whose hanging rose-like blossoms appear to be lit from within when bathed with sunlight.

CHAPTER 2

JAMAICA COLLEGE—SCHOOL FOR WINNERS

I spent my high school years at Jamaica College, one of the island's oldest and most respected institutions. Then, as now, Jamaica's top grammar schools produced a disproportionate number of star athletes and renowned academics, as well as leaders in the business and government spheres.

JC is the fourth oldest high school in Jamaica. It was founded in the late 18th century by an Englishman, the planter Charles Drax, who stipulated in his Will that a charity school be built in his working parish of St. Ann. The school began as Drax Free School, and though it went through three relocations and name changes, it maintained a carefully privileged status through the generations until establishing itself in Kingston on July 9, 1885.

Separatism was inherent in the colonial structure of society, and in the early years of the school, its doors were intended to admit only the children of 'free people', or rather, the landed gentry. Slowly, the school broadened its base to allow entrance to those who could comfortably afford tuition. Under economic pressure to justify the high cost of running the school, it was obliged to then consider accommodating any who would strive to afford the tuition and, finally, to the brightest young academic potential.

In the late 1950s, a new government mandate and system saw all high schools awarding placement based on merit rather than family heritage. The emphasis placed on academics and the moulding of good character was consistent and of an extraordinarily high standard. Jamaica College alums often said their school was the 'national college' and routinely lay claim to an exemplary record of academic and athletic successes, with many of its graduates having played larger-than-life roles in steering the country towards independent nationhood. Many others continue to lead Jamaica in every sphere of private and public life.

JC remained the island's most respected and accomplished high school for generations. There was an expectation, away from the campus, that its boys upheld high standards of decorum. Students were also required to stand whenever a teacher entered the classroom. On Sundays and on jaunts to the movies, they wore suits, giving them special attention from the cinema cashiers, who sometimes let them in for free.

By the start of World War II, JC had won the national athletics championships ten times, more than any other school; the football crowns (Manning Cup and Olivier Shield) ten and eleven times, respectively; the rifle championship thirteen times, and top cricket honours on nine occasions. One can imagine the average JC boy, therefore, as having the confidence (sometimes, even the blind arrogance) to take on anything.

The disciplined culture and social graces of the Jamaican school in the 1960s were highly valued. Caning was not unusual.* Academic standards were high and many British expatriates were happy to have their children educated in the West Indies.

Youngsters were expected to gain a rounded, British-based education while living in the agreeable tropical climate, but the advantages did not stop there. Indeed, one of the most valued aspects of the system at the time was a devotion to discipline. In the case of Jamaica College, the headmaster presided over every hallowed room and corridor, and

---

* The cane was a slender piece of bamboo or rattan about three to four feet in length with a rigid 'u' handle at one end. The straight end was very flexible and whistled through the air to the point of impact, the buttocks. It was sometimes soaked in water or a low viscosity oil in order to preserve its flexibility and to prevent it from splitting due to dryness. A caner without much compassion would mark his victim's pants with a horizontal line, using chalk, to ensure that each strike was delivered in the same position. This guaranteed maximum pain. Sometimes a student was made to bend over to ensure that the cane did not strike above his belt. 'Six of the best' was not unusual.

he invariably cut a fearsome figure. Austere and highly principled, he presided over the school as if it were a royal domain. To him, the structure of its small world was symbolic of the wider society, and he was uncompromising where discipline was concerned.[1] In his absence, the Deputy Headmaster would preside.

While it is true that a confrontation with either of the two senior masters was not a desirable thing, it is equally true that their minions, the prefects, were not to be taken lightly. These were senior students who had distinguished themselves in school life and been elected to the leadership body. Wherever masters were not on hand to impose law and order in the school, these eager young men saw to discipline. Topping the list would be the head boy, his deputy and the captains of the senior and junior houses into which the school population was divided.

Other final-year students, known as monitors and who had been recognised for any laudable achievement, supported them on the basis of their academic excellence, leadership skill, social awareness or the like. These monitors had the privilege of imposing punishment as they thought appropriate, and there was a fine reservoir of disciplinary measures from which to select.

Before enrolling at JC, I attended a Roman Catholic prep school, Campion Hall Preparatory, which was run by Jesuits. The school had strict codes of dress, punctuality, attendance, work compliance and sports. Being Jewish, I was exempt from Catechism class. Up until then, I had led a very sheltered life, during a time when children were supposed to be seen and not heard. I was fairly studious, and regularly finished third in all my classes (Junior A in 1959, Middle school in 1960 and Senior in 1961), behind S. Michael McLaughlin, retired from Deloitte Consulting LLP (an actuary who I understand is said to have 'written the book' for the life insurance industry, and who is a co-founder of the internationally acclaimed Trees that Feed Foundation, of which the Clinton Foundation is a donor), and Robert Figueroa, son of a prominent professor at the University of the West Indies.

Very quiet and somewhat shy, I was never any trouble at school and was perhaps a favourite of the priests. The corporal punishment there was carried out with a bamboo ruler referred to as a 'stick', approximately one inch in width and three feet long. Luckily, I never came close to experiencing the hand of Fathers Coleman, Delaney, or Krim.

So when I arrived at JC, I only knew three students, yet was very conspicuous, with some of the boys assuming my family was wealthy because of my skin colour. I hadn't done very well in the Common Entrance (high school placement) Exam, and it took me three years, nearly half my high school career, to enter the 'A' stream.

My father was very protective of me, and since I was the first-born male of a Lebanese father and was expected to do better than my father had, I could do no wrong, except when I didn't prevent my sisters from getting into trouble—but I'll come back to that. B. S. Haddad did all my talking for me, so much so that he enjoyed telling everyone that I was the captain of my school house (Gonzaga) and represented my school at cricket and football at Campion Hall. During holidays he took me to all his Monday meetings with lawyers and bankers, and I was a regular guest at his side at luncheons when he would dine with some of his past contemporaries from R. Hanna & Sons Ltd. I guess having me there with him was to teach me about business at an early age and to keep his company. I also remember him buying me a plastic model plane at Woolworth's (an early incentive for going along on Mondays)—a gift that would lead to an obsession of mine.

My father took me to and from school in his 1948 V8-Ford up until my last days in high school. I felt so embarrassed every time he would enter the school gate and blow the horn at 6:00 p.m., even though I was ready from 3:00.

B. S. Haddad's beloved
1948 Ford V8

"Haddad boy," someone would always jeer, "the old man is here, yu nuh see the hearse coming through the gate. A money man like you, how yu ol' man so stingy?" That went on for quite a while.

What had escaped me all along was that my father was observing and listening to the ridicule, but said nothing until 1963, when Old Hope Road ran with Hurricane Flora flood rains.

The main culprit (a fellow with an almost perfectly round head, brilliant white eyeballs and dark complexion), who came from a well-to-do family, made the mistake of flagging us down at the stop in front of the school. Wet, cold, and alone, he needed rescuing. I was shocked by what followed. In response to the boy's signal, my father stopped the car the way a Samaritan would.

"What is it you want, Moon Head?" he asked.

"Is a lift me begging to go a Matty (Matilda's) Corner, sir," the round-headed boy replied.

"Well, Moon Head," my father told him, "dis hearse only carry dead people. Wait on the Number Six bus. By the way, no more buses running today!"

Once I got involved in badminton and became interested in girls, my grades fell again, but later, once I got the hang of university studies, I would finish second in my class in my final year, gradu-

The Jamaica Omnibus Service (JOS) provided a municipal bus service for the Kingston Metropolitan Area, from 1953 until it was wound up in 1983. The buses were referred to as the 'Jolly Joseph'. The Number Six was the most direct route and hence the one I rode most of the time. Very conveniently, it stopped along Old Hope Road just opposite Windsor Avenue and Bundy Lane, bypassing the well known, 'Matilda's (Matty) Corner'.

ating with first-class honours. I was selected spokesperson for engineering students—particularly to get professors to reduce the number, length and types of assignments—and haven't shut up since then!

★ ★ ★

By the time I arrived at Jamaica College in the 1960s, the punishments must have become rather entrenched and comfortable to the ones dispensing them, because the prefects were quite practised in the corporal arts.

Line punishment (also known as imposition and penance) might have been more severe in the 60s than it was back in 1939. The worst was being made to write

PERSISTENT PERVERSITY PROVOKES THE

PATIENT PEDAGOGUE PRODUCING

PARTICULARLY PAINFUL PUNISHMENT

between 100 and 500 times, alternately using red, blue, black, and green ink for each new sentence, and with perfect accuracy in the set order. This punishment was not uncommon.

There were also some demeaning physical punishments, which one could earn by not obeying orders from senior students. The call to sing, for example, was commonly required of first formers by older students. 'Not singing', therefore, was an infraction. What ensued in such a case would be considered barbaric by today's standards; the offending student could be subjected to a 'candle-waxing' or a 'crack toe'. To be candle-waxed, the offender would stand still while the wax of a burning candle was dripped onto his head. The 'crack toe' meant that his toe would be hit with a wooden club. One surefire way of wrangling himself out of this was to let it be known that he had a pretty sister and that he was willing to furnish her name and contact information.

It was January 1962 when I had my own intimate encounter with the disciplinary code. Jamaica was to gain independence in August of that year, and perhaps ugly memories of the colonial past had re-emerged. Although I had never witnessed any class or racial conflicts in the past, it quickly became reality for my present. Those who appeared to be well-off, or sons of 'gentry'—either by skin colour or by virtue of higher academic standing—were ridiculed, made to carry books for others, and buy them lunch. I remember being called 'Shylock' (after Shakespeare's money-lending villain), 'Jew boy', 'whitey', and 'money boy'.

On my very first day in high school, I refused when they bid me sing. Guilty of non-compliance, I was sentenced to a classic 'candle waxing' and then a 'crack toe'. Older boys made me stand on a spot they chose, with both arms extended at my sides, each holding heavy textbooks. While I was bearing this load, upper-school boys held thorny branches under my armpits.

The candle waxing and the toe-bashing were expected, and though barbaric, were well within the unwritten letter of the law. The business of the 'macca bush' at my armpits, however, was something else altogether. That was totally uncalled for, and so there were institutional repercussions.

Distraught and frightened, I told my father about my first-day ordeal. For a few weeks after that, he would not let me return to school. News spread on campus that parents and the police had been called in. The older students were suspended.

My stay at JC was rather protected after that incident. It became known (likely through me) that the minister of education at the time, the Honourable Florizel Glasspole, was a friend of my father.*

It was also whispered that a cousin of mine who attended St. George's College, a particular fellow 'respected' by the boys for his toughness, was the other influence that proved quite handy in keeping me safe for the duration. After that, I was left alone well enough to pursue my studies in peace. As I recall, between 1962 and 1967, no similar incident took place.

Prior to my altercation, there was a notable incident involving seniors and a stubborn first-former and now infamous jazz pianist 'Monty' Alexander who also refused to sing. This, however, had a much different outcome.[2]

Although very little had changed through the years in the matter of discipline, the infrastructure of the school itself was changing. Its boarding facilities were being phased out over my time there, and Jamaica College was on its way to becoming a day school. Since then, however, its population has steadily increased, and by 2010, there was an enrolment of approximately 1800 boys and a staff complement of a hundred. With the gaining of political independence from England in August 1962, there were also proud post-colonial changes in curricula. Albeit small, they were reflected in the studies of history and geography, where students were now being introduced to topics more related to their own country and region. They learned of natural resources, exports, the history and principal figures of slavery and colonialism; the Maroons, the abolitionists and other fighters for emancipation. It was an exciting period, in which former 'shadows', previously suppressed by English governance, would emerge, claim their proper name and humanity, and become leaders in society.

---

* A classmate of my father's at Wolmer's Boys School later became Sir Florizel Glasspole, governor general of Jamaica. He toasted the bridesmaids at my wedding in 1974.

END NOTES

[1]   An excerpt from Charles Levy's book *Hash and Roast Beef* (4th edition, 2013) gives a good example of the all-powerful Jamaican grammar school principal:

No One Above the Law (an account of Jamaica College in the 1949s)

It was established that a student M, had "thrown a book at a master, and that the Headmaster was intent on punishing him with 'six of the best' despite his age and status as a prefect….[a] meeting with M's father had not changed the Head's decision…I found myself in company with the whole student body, deserting the class room in the middle of class and joining a mass march towards…the gate. M had been expelled, and we were seeing him on his way. Not silently, but loud cheers!"

"The next day, Chapel was held as usual, and as the morning service progressed in normal fashion, we began to entertain hopes that 'the event' would pass off without retribution being taken. Fat chance! When the time arrived for the daily announcements to be made, the Head went to the lectern, and his face suddenly assumed the appearance of Nemesis."

"The Head went on to say that we were mistaken if we thought that he was unable to punish the entire school. If memory serves me correctly, he then suspended all sports activity for a fortnight, and inflicted what amounted to an hour's detention for all boys, to be served every day after school for one week."

"M later served in the Royal Canadian Air Force, was a popular labour leader and politician, and served as Prime Minister of Jamaica on two occasions."

[2]   The happy side of what can come from a confrontation between senior and junior students is the story of someone who preceded me at the school:

'Monty' Alexander, world-renowned jazz pianist, was also convicted of 'not singing' when he started at JC. Thinking fast before his sentence could be carried out, he asked his captors, "Do you have a piano? Take me to a piano!" The ensuing musical interlude was, by all accounts, a joyous affair. Monty played mentos, calypsos, hymns and jazz. After that day, he would be recaptured by the music teacher, Barry Davies, to play regularly in the chapel until his last days at school. Shortly before leaving for Miami, Florida with his family, Monty started his first entrepreneurial venture, that of forming a band known as 'Monty and the Cyclones'. By 1959 they had produced a number of records at the studios of Federal Records featuring a variety of music including a number of Rock 'N' Roll classics.

Growing up in Jamaica, where he was born on D-Day, June 6, 1944, he was named Montgomery Alexander, a name fashioned after General Bernard Montgomery who was in overall command of the ground forces with Supreme Commander of the Allied Expeditionary Forces, General Dwight D. Eisenhower.

Monty was hugely inspired as a teenager by seeing performances of Frank ('Ol' Blue Eyes') Sinatra and Nathaniel 'Nat' King Cole at the island's Carib Theatre. He nurtured an innate musical skill and continued, largely self-taught, to develop a style which, after his arrival overseas, captured the attention of some of the best in the business. As a result of subsequent collaboration with great performers such as Milt Jackson, Ray Brown, Charlie Parker, Tony Bennett and Winton Marsalis, Alexander developed and mastered a unique style, which welded Jazz and Blues with the rhythms of his beloved Caribbean. He has returned to the land of his birth many times to work and perform with some of the island's most legendary musicians.

In 2000, the Government of Jamaica honoured him with the title 'Commander of the Order of Distinction' in recognition of his sterling role as a musical ambassador to the world. To date, Monty has produced over seventy CDs and still tours regularly, equally comfortable in clubs and concert halls as he thrills audiences worldwide with his eclectic mastery of jazz piano.

CHAPTER 3

OUT OF MANY

Jamaica has benefited greatly from its diversity of ethnicity and religion, built over the centuries of conquest, slavery, indentured labour, and religious refugeehood. The tolerance and tension that led to that diversity have created a rich ethnic mixture, ideal conditions for the island's remarkable energy for sports, the arts, academic pursuits, diplomacy and other endeavours, inspiring the motto 'Out

Holland America Line's SS Potsdam, the vessel that brought my grandfather to the Americas.

of Many, One People'.[1] Had it not been for religious persecution in Europe and the Middle East, I probably would have been born on the other side of the world and not grown up Jewish in Jamaica, and, of all things, a Lebanese Jew.[2] My grandfather, Shukrella Michael Haddad, was born in 1880 in Chouviefait, Lebanon, Syria. At the time, the Turk Ottoman Empire ruled that part of the world. In his day, once a young man turned eighteen, all male Christians were given four choices: first, convert to Islam; second, join the Turkish Army; third, starve, since all provisions were primarily for the army, and finally, emigrate.

Shukrella's brother and nephew were shot to death by elements of the Ottoman Empire while trying to escape. Ironically, my great-grandfather's brother, Melhem Haddad, was conscripted into the army, impressing authorities enough for him to attain the rank of Pasha or Agha.

In 1901, Shukrella found his way to France, where he boarded the new 2100-passenger *SS Potsdam* (Holland America Line's largest ship) at Boulogne for its maiden voyage.

After nine days at sea, he arrived at Ellis Island, New York, where he lived for a short time with his cousin Mansour. He later moved to Jamaica, where he had many encounters with the law, mostly innocuous in nature. It did not help that he could neither read nor write English.

My grandfather somehow found himself drawn into the first major uptown murder trial in the 1930s (Crown vs. Alexander & Wehby et al) which went on for weeks. The accused murderer had occupied his premises at 115 Princess Street as a tenant tending to his bread-making business at the time of the murder. Shukrella's gun may have been used to commit the crime. Defending the accused was the Rt. Hon. Norman Washington Manley, the first premier of Jamaica.

Shukrella and Edward Rasheed Hanna (father of renowned Eddie Hanna), founder of R. Hanna & Sons Ltd., 'exchanged monies' and conducted some sort of business. My grandfather later started his own enterprise, selling all manner of items, including olive oil. He went into the production of leather shoes, boots and other leather goods, as well as backpacks and hats for schoolchildren. He imported all kinds of leathers, and also established the first Syrian (pita)bread business in Jamaica. On occasion, he would receive barrels of goods from the old country, only to find the containers filled with stones!

From all reports, although he was very kind to others, he was a very stubborn man. One day, he decided to expand his store front past the boundary adjacent to Princess Street, a busy commercial thoroughfare that ran straight to the harbour. The authorities warned him not to do so under threat of having it demolished. The addition was demolished a week later!

The rugged Shukrella survived the 1907 earthquake, two world wars, the Great Depression, typhoid and influenza epidemics, and a massive flood in 1933 when his property was awash with bodies from Kingston's Sandy Gully.

My father was the eldest of Shukrella's sons. He emulated his father's characteristics, and in many ways improved and surpassed them. For example, he helped his siblings financially and bore total responsibility for them when his parents were not at home. B. S. Haddad was exempted from matriculation and was set to go off to the University of London to study medicine. According to family legend, someone told him that he needed to stay in Jamaica to monitor Hanna's business. Few people knew why, until after Eddie Hanna's death in 1978. As they say, the rest is history. My father went to work at Hanna's and became the company's factotum and essentially ran everything at Hanna's. An expert on income tax, he taught himself accounting.

My father retired at age thirty-nine, after using his savings to acquire real estate all over Jamaica. Unlike his brothers and most other people, he was frugal with money and actually built his own house using blocks he made right on the property. Practical to a fault, he was still driving a quarter-century-old car in 1972.

Each January 1, like clockwork, he would sell one piece of real estate, bringing him just enough money to get by for the year. "The price is five thousand pounds," he would tell a potential purchaser at the moment of truth, "not a pound more nor a pound less, tek it or lef' it. De land can't rot, you know!" B. S.'s transactions helped change Jamaican real estate law (including the definition of a 'trader', one who bought real estate and sold it within a thirty-year period). The sale would be taxed on the appreciated value. If no trading (purchase and subsequent sale) occurred during a continuous thirty-year period but a sale was made after that time, the sale would be completely tax free. The idea then would be for older folks or pensioners to keep their 'own' money at a time when it was most needed. My dad was a party to one of the most protracted court cases in Jamaica, a contest lasting over thirty years.

Although everyone knew that B. S. was the man behind Eddie Hanna, he had no job title and shunned publicity. He was certainly not a public figure, but was a tireless conversationalist and would come to control and participate in all of Hanna's real estate dealings, as well as events at Hanna Sons Oval in Vineyard Town, a business-house sports centre he practically built.

Ironically, when he left R. Hanna & Sons Ltd, as the de facto CEO, the ex-commissioner of income tax, Sir Charles Campbell, was brought in to replace my father, but according to a member of Eddie Hanna's family, did not last very long. B. S., with his indefatigable work style and willingness to handle so many aspects of the company's operations, had left shoes too big for Campbell to fill.

My mother's family came to Jamaica thanks to the Morranos, Spanish Jews who had survived a mass extermination of at least 100,000 by Christians during the Spanish Inquisition.[3]

Her family, including her parents, five siblings, grandparents and others, lived in the Jewish Alms House on Duke Street, close to the Shaare Shalom Synagogue at the time.

★ ★ ★

The family values of thrift, toughness in adversity, and a thirst for knowledge were all ingrained in me as a child. Those qualities would come in handy many times in my life. We had a sound academic and extra-curricular education, and were supervised in the latter's practical applications just as thoroughly in the classroom as outside of it. In my case, I had been as curious as a Boy Scout as I had been in the school laboratories. And we all had a healthy respect for discipline. I firmly believe that this rigorous and broad-based training provided us with skills we would employ and the sheer perseverance we've been able to sustain ever since.

Among the things my father taught me were the importance of respect and courtesy, of listening carefully, being determined, and saying nothing unless you mean what you are about to say. He believed in studying the environment, knowing what to eat and what not to eat, and observing safety with implements and weapons like knives, machetes, and guns, as well as basic survival training. He wanted us to depend on no one, be steadfast, and judge no man. B. S. stressed education, education, education; to give thanks daily; to remain calm under all circumstances; to value health before wealth, and family, family, family. He taught us to be disciplined, and to compare ourselves to no one.

B. S. believed that everything had value; nothing was thrown away (some of our toys, like a jeep and tractor I can think of, are still around today, even after my children used them in Jamaica in the 1980s). I, too, am guilty of holding on to early possessions. I still have a tricycle given to me on my second birthday by my godmother, Lorice Hanna.

A stickler for detail who never went to church, my father only attended weddings, as far as I can remember. My mother was the religious one.

END NOTES

1   Race and Class Interaction in Jamaica—and its Impact on the World – *Jamaica Magazine* – Commentary:

In all my years in Jamaica, I never once was asked to identify my "race." So I find it discomfiting to respond to the questions I frequently get here in America—when I have to fill out some government document, for example.

It seems absurd to describe myself as Caucasian or African-American or Hispanic or Pacific Islander… or whatever. All I know about being Caucasian is that there are some mountains in Russia by that name. I have never laid eyes on the vast continent of Africa, don't speak Spanish and couldn't find the Pacific Islands on a map of the world.

The bottom line is that I am a Jamaican – an unhyphenated Jamaican.

Looking back on my Jamaican experience, it seems we are identified more by a class system than by racial labels.

I know, "class system" sounds snobbish or worse. It has an unwholesome connotation, the implication of castes from which there is no escape. But I don't recall the Jamaican class system as being etched in stone. I recall the sons and daughters of domestic servants sometimes becoming wealthy doctors and lawyers, powerful politicians and bureaucrats, venerated members of the clergy, and so on.

The education system, although admittedly inadequate, included scholarship opportunities that could provide a ladder for upward mobility. (Not enough, admittedly. But the opportunities are not as sparse today as they were in my time, and I am confident they will increase in Jamaica's next half-century as an independent nation.)

Jamaica's class system is based on money, of course, but there are other criteria. These include European-based notions of etiquette and decorum, as well as education and the way people dress and speak. But there was something else, something that inherently defines the Jamaican concept of class.

From what my mother taught me, it was "respectability." Respectable people lived by certain standards. They weren't "raw-chaw."

Vulgarity, obscenity, drunkenness, arrogance, rudeness, slovenliness, idleness and "showing off" were considered signs of a "lower-class" upbringing.

Another unspoken expectation of people in "our class" was decency.

Decent people had integrity. Decent people didn't "take advantage." Decent people "did the right thing."

Did all the members of Jamaica's "upper class" behave according to these standards? Of course not. Some abused their positions of privilege.

But, as I remember it, those who betrayed the trust placed in them usually paid the price sooner or later. You were held accountable in the Jamaica where I grew up. As the Bible reminded us, from those to whom much was given much was expected.

I cannot think of another society in which the Bible is so influential. Foreigners might think of Jamaica as some kind of hedonistic lotus land where Rastas in "dreadlocks" constantly play reggae music, dance suggestively and smoke ganja. But to me this is a false image probably created to lure tourists and sell records.

The Jamaica I know is a churchgoing society. The Rastas I know spend more time talking religion than playing music.

And the Rastas I know give and expect "respect."

In my mind "respect" and "decency" distinguish the real Jamaican culture. The "rude boys" and "hos" that abound in hip-hop and rap lyrics are looked down on in Jamaican society, no matter what color they might be.

Are there bigots in Jamaica? Of course. Bigotry is one of the world's most pervasive blights. It's everywhere.

And there is a lingering "shade prejudice" inherited from slavery. Slave owners often had sex with slaves and produced offspring. Sometimes the slave owners would marry the mothers of these children, sometimes not. But, in either case, the slave owners would often protect these children from being sold into slavery by having them declared legally "white." They lived in the Great House with their father and enjoyed privileges denied other children of slaves.

I think it may have been this tradition of privilege that gave lighter-skinned Jamaicans a special status – an advantage that still persists to some extent, although it has faded a lot over the years.

Complicating the picture, expatriate communities have created tiny, isolated cultural pockets outside of the Jamaican mainstream experience. And tourist resorts sometimes pander to prejudices alien to Jamaicans. What I am trying to examine is the indigenous culture that developed in the Jamaican heartland over the centuries.

I cannot claim that Jamaican culture is perfect. We live in an imperfect world, after all.

Undoubtedly Jamaica's class system is unfair. Without question, people born into Jamaica's underclass have to struggle much, much harder to achieve economic and social success than the lucky few who are born to privileged parents. Sadly, many decent, respectable people find themselves mired in poverty and subjected to indignity. And usually, these "sufferers" belong to the predominantly black underclass.

But social injustice is not unique to Jamaica. These words from Grey's "Elegy in a Country Churchyard" come to mind: "Full many a flower is born to blush unseen and waste its fragrance on the desert air." That country churchyard was located not in Jamaica but in England.

Where Jamaicans may be unique is that we are far less obsessed with skin color and ethnic origin than any other multiracial society I can think of. Jamaicans can honestly boast of being (as the national motto proclaims) "out of many, one people."

Consider the horror of Apartheid that existed for so long in South Africa. And consider the United States of America.

For generations, black Americans in many states were forbidden to use white washrooms, drink from white water fountains, shop at white grocery stores, eat in white restaurants and even attend white public schools. Throughout the South, they were physically shunned by the white majority and even required to sit at the back of the bus.

Abominations like the Ku Klux Klan brought injustice and terror to black Americans throughout the South. And this loathsome organization persists to this day, as does an infestation of other groups that preach "white supremacy."

The segregated school system did not end until the mid-1950s when the federal government brought in troops to escort a handful of black children into a white school in Little Rock, Arkansas.

Legally enforced segregation persisted through much of the 1950s, 1960s and 1970s, and it took widespread civil rights demonstrations, marked by bloodshed and martyrdom, to turn public opinion overwhelmingly against this aberration.

Although no longer legally enforced, de facto cultural segregation continues. When I migrated to America I was astonished to find some churches with entirely black congregations and others without a single black face in the sanctuary on a Sunday morning. There are communities in America that are almost totally black. Even some large cities, like Detroit, are basically "segregated" because of "white flight." As black (or Hispanic) Americans move in, white Americans move out.

For reasons that I cannot comprehend, the fear of African contamination was once so great in America that Southern states used to classify as black anyone with "a drop of Negro blood." As I understand it, you had "a drop" of "Negro blood" if you were one-thirty-second black. That made you ethnically African-American if you had a black great-great-great-grandparent.

Don't you wonder how many Americans know whether one of their great-great-great-grandparents was black? Don't you wonder why they would care?

But until the mid-1960s, it was against the law in some states for a white American to marry someone black. So, as I understand it, if your great-great-great-grandmother was black, you would have broken the law to marry a pure-white American.

To anyone who grew up in Jamaica this is preposterous.

My mother's fair-skinned aunt married a black schoolteacher, and after his death, a black dentist. Her daughter became the first female city clerk of Kingston, Jamaica's largest metropolis.

My cousin's daughter married a Chinese man and they have the most beautiful daughter. My cousin is half Jewish. His wife is a former Miss Mahogany (remember when Jamaica had those shade-conscious beauty pageants?). Is my cousin's granddaughter Chinese? Jewish? Black? White?

Who cares?

As far as I am concerned, she is an American-born Jamaican.

In Jamaica, Arabs marry Jews. Descendants of East Indian or Ashanti cane cutters marry descendants of English pirates or Portuguese refugees from the Inquisition or Chinese merchants or Maroon warriors – or whomever they damn well please.

At my parents' house on a Sunday, the parson would often sit at the head of the table and say grace. As I recall now, he was sometimes very dark-skinned. But I don't recall anyone noticing at the time.

Come to think of it, Jamaica's wonderful athletes are overwhelmingly black.

Many of Jamaica's most distinguished sons and daughters—journalists, authors, poets, playwrights and academics—are black or mostly black. The Governor General is black. The Prime Minister is black. The list goes on and on.

At a Jamaican party, you will see blondes dancing unselfconsciously with ebony skinned partners, East Indian maidens with their flowing black hair resting on the shoulders of Syrian or Lebanese youths, ivory-skinned Chinese girls flirting with Jewish boys. Nobody is aware of being at a "multiracial" event. They're just a bunch of Jamaicans getting together to have a good time.

When my extended family gathers, you see every skin, hair and eye color under the sun. And the last thing we think about is what "race" we belong to.

We are Jamaicans, that's all.

As foreigners visit Jamaica and experience the relaxed atmosphere of a colour-blind culture, I expect many of them will return to their own countries with a new appreciation of racial harmony.

And as more and more Jamaicans – often the best educated – migrate to other countries, their refusal to acknowledge such nonsense as "white supremacy" or accept such abuses as ethnic segregation cannot fail to inspire change in their new environments.

Jamaicans simply will not put up with such outlandish and oppressive ideas and practices. We mix, mingle and marry as we like without regard to race or skin color. And our example could be a catalyst for worldwide enlightenment – like the child in the fable who cried, "The Emperor has no clothes on!"

As racial stereotypes and ethnic divisiveness diminish throughout the world – and I am sure they will – some of the credit should go to little Jamaica, whose sons and daughters shone a bright light on the dark depths of ignorance where such evils are bred.

About the Author:

George Graham is a Jamaican-born journalist and author who worked as a reporter and editor in the Caribbean and North America for more than half a century. He lives in Lakeland, Florida. His books include *Hill-an'-Gully Rider, Girlie, Brown Skin Blues* and *Jamaica Remembered*. He also published a book of poems, titled *A Passing Fancy*.

---

[2]   According to Ed Kritzler in *Jewish Pirates of the Caribbean* (2008), the triangular dynamic between Spain, England and the seafaring town of Port Royal created the atmosphere for Jews to thrive in Jamaica, both religiously and otherwise:

In the 1660s, Port Royal, with its wealthy Jewish merchants, ship owners, and synagogue, was known as the 'Treasure House of the Indies' for all the booty brought there. Catering to a transient pirate population with one bar and brothel for every eight persons, the pirate capital acquired a reputation as the world's 'wickedest city'. Within fifteen years, pirate raids from Jamaica on the Spanish Main, organized and financed by the merchants of Port Royal, broke the back of the Spanish Empire. In Henry Morgan, the Jews found their Joshua ... Ironically, the pirate Henry Morgan, who ultimately became Buccaneer Admiral Sir Henry Morgan, received his knighthood from England's Oliver Cromwell and was given the title Knight Commander in Chief of the Island of Jamaica. Welcomed by the English, Jews from all over the New World shed their converso cloaks and emigrated to Jamaica... By 1660, Jamaica had become the Jew's principal haven in the New World.

[3]   Spanish Jews, similar to the Christians in The Turkish Empire, also had four options at the time: a) Flee the country, (some went to Portugal); b) convert and remain Christians; c) convert to Christianity temporarily, and d) accept death. Those who converted to Christianity followed all the practices during the day, but at night, they would move secretly to a dedicated home where they would revert to their Jewish names and practice their rightful religion. These Jews, from which the majority of Jamaican Jewry evolved, were later known as Marranos, meaning, inter alia, 'secret':

"A Synagogue Drawn in the Sand" By Rabbi Dana Kaplan
There are only five sand floor synagogues in the world—four of them in the Caribbean (with one being the Shaare Shalom Synagogue in Kingston, Jamaica). How has the tradition been maintained for hundreds of years?

During the Spanish Inquisition (14th–15th century) synagogues were not permitted to operate, the conversos who were still committed to practicing Judaism had no choice but to meet in private homes. Though these gatherings were an open secret, the Jewish community felt it was better to be as discreet as possible. As such, they put clay and sand on the floor of the prayer rooms to muffle the sounds made by the comings and goings of worshipers, and the prayers themselves. Regarding the midrashic connection, it is said that the sand symbolizes the terrain of the Sinai Desert, through which the Children of Israel wandered for 40 years after the Exodus. Among earlier generations, this may have been understood as emphasizing the idea that, even though they were living in a tropical paradise, they were still in exile.

On a more positive note, there are those who believe that the sand symbolizes God's promise to Abraham to make the Jews as populous as the sands of the sea: "I will bless thee, and in multiplying I will multiply thy seed as the stars of the heaven, and as the sand which is upon the seashore" (Genesis 22:17). This theme recurs throughout the Tanakh, like the verse in Hosea that says, "Yet the number of the children of Israel shall be as the sand of the sea, which cannot be measured nor numbered" (Hosea 2:1).

(Originally published on August 10, 2012 at http://www.haaretz.com/israel-news/a-synagogue-drawn-in-the-sand-1.457357)

★ ★ ★

It is said that some of the first Jews to arrive in Jamaica did so onboard Columbus's vessel that landed at Seville. They lived there before moving to St. Jago de la Vega, modern-day Spanish Town. Interestingly enough, one Isaac A. Haddad was at the helm of the Jewish temple in Kingston, Synagogue Shaare Shalome, first as a lay reader from 1903–1906 and then as the acting spiritual leader from 1906–1910. The responsibility Isaac bore must have been nothing short of overwhelming, as the congregation was probably the largest at the time. He was in charge there during the great earthquake in 1907 and for three years after that. The facial similarities between Isaac and Shukrella, my grandfather, are remarkable.

My grandfather, Shukrella Haddad (*top left*), circa 1900 in his home town, Chouviefait, located in Beyrouth (Beirut), Lebanon, Syria, as it was known at the time when it was controlled by the Turk Ottoman Empire; before leaving for New York in 1901. At *top right* is Isaac Haddad, the spiritual leader of the Kingston Jewish community at the turn of the 20th century. I noticed the startling resemblance between the two men while doing research on my family for the book.

Bottom Right: The remnants of one of the remaining residential structures in Chouviefait, Lebanon, built, circa 1890. It was built by Shukrella's brother, Latfallah. Additions to the home were made in 1962 and 1970 and another in 1980, in order to accommodate three generations of his family. It was abandoned in 1983 during the civil war (1975–1991) but withstood numerous small arms and artillery shells. Latfallah was a building contractor. Both he and his son were killed by soldiers of the Turk Ottoman Empire while trying to escape —*Photo taken by Geoffrey B. Haddad in 2012.*

Top: Shukrella Haddad journeyed to the New World from Boulogne, France in 1901 aboard the Holland America Line's largest ship, the new 2100-passenger *SS Potsdam,* on its maiden voyage. After more than a week at sea, he arrived at Ellis Island in New York, where he lived for a short time with his cousin Mansour. He would later arrive in Kingston to start a new life, even though he was unable to read or write English.

Bottom left: Shukrella was an avid bird hunter and outdoorsman. *Bottom right:* (Taken in 1924) Shukrella and his wife Eliza with children (*left to right*): Edward, Leonie, Elias and B. S. Haddad.—*Photo courtesy of B. S. Haddad*

Top: Norma Haddad (DaCosta) poses with her husband's pride and joy, the 1948 Ford V8, K 5439. She would learn to drive in this vehicle, but B. S. Haddad worried too much about her safety to let her drive on her own. A devoted mother, she was one of Jamaica's top competitors in badminton, a sport in which all her four children excelled as junior and senior players. *Photo courtesy of B. S. Haddad.*

Bottom left: My father, Badia Shukrella Haddad (B. S.), in Portland, Maine circa 1946. He was a strict disciplinarian who doted on his family. He retired from business at age thirty-nine, in particular for the raising and mentoring of his first-born son, the author, Geoffrey Badia Haddad. *Photo courtesy of B. S. Haddad.*

Bottom right: Well into his retirement, B. S. is featured in the *Gleaner, in an article* 'Father of the Birds' in 1999.

Top: B. S. Haddad (*standing left*), a member of the managing committee, and prominent Jamaican businessman Eddie Hanna (*seated right*) pose with Hanna's business house football team in 1939 at Issa's sports clubhouse

Bottom: Hanna Sons Oval, the epicentre of the business-house sports in Kingston. Built in 1940 and sponsored by Eddie Hanna and Sons, the facility was virtually brought into existence by the company's factotum, B. S. Haddad. Outside of his bird shooting activities, which took place seven days a week, in those days, before/after work (or both), B. S. resided here. All this was in keeping with his love for sports and the vision for cohesion of an estimated fifty companies, numerous managers and hundreds of staff. Sports played here included cricket, football (soccer) tennis (men and women) and even dominoes. —*Both photos courtesy of B. S. Haddad*

In this 1939 photograph taken at the Issa Park, twenty-eight-year-old B. S. Haddad, secretary and member of the managing committee (standing at centre) is flanked by Eric and Roy Morin, executives of the Business House League. Seated (left to right) are Mrs. Torrie, wife of the manager of the Bank of Nova Scotia, Mrs. Mary, and Elias Issa, her husband. The Morins and the Issas were prominent business establishments for decades. The Issas continue to be major players in the tourist industry in Jamaica and throughout the Caribbean—*Photo courtesy of B. S. Haddad*

Top: Me at three years old in my Willys Jeep, a toy my children would enjoy as late as the 1980s. *Inset:* My well-preserved tricycle, given to me by my Godmother ; now more than sixty-three years old. I would later become very much like my father—a keeper and hoarder, being appreciative of things and times of historic importance.—*Photo of jeep courtesy of B. S. Haddad*

Bottom: My neighbours and friends called themselves The Windsorites and collaborated to produce several dramatic short films on 8 mm (under the banner 'Windsor Playhouse Presents') such as the western Stranger and Goliath (at right). In those days, they sent the film to New York for developing before editing could begin. I am seen (at left) as the bartender in the movie. —*Photos courtesy of Robin Crawford*

Jamaica, High School, Hope College. — St. Andrew — Jamaica.

Top: Jamaica College in 1930 showing Simms Hall, the centre of school life.—
Photo/postage card courtesy of Dorothy Kew

Bottom: Simms Hall, Jamaica College, in 2012

Top: One of the top junior badminton players in the 1960s, I am shown here with the Jamaica College tennis team. I was the last member of the hikers to be confirmed for what was expected to be my first trip to Blue Mountain Peak. Roger Bates sits astride his Bantam motorcycle. George Hussey, the de facto leader of the expedition, would have his courage and judgement called into question in the jungle

Bottom: Inseparable during their teens, Cecil Ward (left) and Gordon Cooper (centre) were part of the early wave of surfing fanatics operating on the beaches of eastern Kingston and the northeast coast. At right is Donnie Soutar, who dropped out of the hike due to the flu, making way for my participation. His father, W. Donald Soutar, was, in 2013, the lone survivor of the 1939 five from Jamaica College who almost lost their lives in those very mountains. *.Jamaica Surfing Association photo*

CHAPTER 4

PLOTTING THE ASSAULT

Thursday, December 14, 1967 (one day before end of term)

Shortly after finishing a mathematics class in Simms Hall, the school's main building, I overheard a group of final-year boys huddled in discussion, in the way boys that age hatch a plan. Quickly I discovered that they were planning a hike up to Blue Mountain Peak. Obsessed with the bush and anything involving the outdoors, I was immediately intrigued. Having never gone up as far as the Peak, I approached Roger Bates, a science classmate of mine. He was one of the plotters.

"You guys goin' up to the Peak for de holidays?" I asked anxiously.

"Yes G. B.," Roger offered. "Me and George talkin' 'bout some plans for a few days now."

"Listen nuh, Roger," I continued, ready to plead my case. "If you want one more, I comin' too, so tell George I interested, right?"

"Well," Roger said, readying himself to dish the details, "so far who goin' is me, George, Coops and Donnie. Mo, T, Rob and Ozzie might be in too, but I don' see why George should mind—especially you, since you are a bird-bush man. Tell you what, G. B., I goin' talk to George lunchtime an' get back to you."

That satisfied me until it was time to hear more from George. It was just around that time that T (Tony Lancaster), Mo (Morris Epstein), Rob (Robert Epstein) and Ozzie (Steve Solomon) gave up the idea of joining George's party. Apparently, as I later found out, they had a suspicion that George wanted to do a non-traditional hike, so they opted to do one of their own, using the regular and morewell-trodden trail beginning at Mavis Bank.

When these boys heard I was interested in going up, I would have been just as happy to join this group instead. As it turned out, the option was short-lived. The second party cancelled their plans and I was left with no alternative but to try joining George and his group, if they weren't going to cancel theirs as well. But was a proper invitation even going to come my way? I waited and hoped.

Maybe Roger's upbeat attitude had made me too confident that I would be in the party when they set out. Perhaps, in consultation with George, they had decided one more would be too many. Perhaps my late inclusion would upset the practicality of any plans they had made. I left school thinking that I would not get tapped to join the group. Maybe (and I've thought about this) I didn't really want to be chosen to go along. Somehow, full of these uneasy thoughts, I had dinner and the usual interactions with my family, then went to bed and dropped off to sleep.

I said nothing about the plan.

★ ★ ★

I was rather heavy-hearted as we assembled for the traditional end-of-term service in Chapel the next morning, the start of Christmas holidays. We were done with school for 1967 and there had not yet been any word about whether I would be included in the trek.

The boys were just filing out of the building when a voice floated to me above the excited buzz of boys who were all looking forward to the break. But there had been no reason for me to fear the worst.

"Hey G. B.!" came the shout. It was George. "If you want to come up to the Peak wid us, we havin' a meetin' in de empty dorm upstairs Simms Building in 'bout ten minutes. We goin' settle de food situation and talk 'bout what we goin' be up against."

I was thrilled to be present at this grand meeting of minds final-ising the trip that Friday morning. There is nothing that could have been headier as I climbed the stairs in Simms on that last day of term.

Intently, I listened to George, who proposed the path for the trek as he unveiled The Plan.

George claimed that his uncle, Desmond Stanley, had traversed this route a number of times in the past. Prior to this, I had no idea that the intended route was any different from the standard climb to the Peak. Compared to what I'd experienced, it was most unconventional, to say the least:

1. Clydesdale (approx. 3500 ft.)
2. Cinchona (approx. 4750 ft.)
3. Sir Johns Peak (6332 ft.)
4. High Peak (6912 ft.)
5. Main Ridge Gap (approx. 6000 ft.)
6. Mossman's Peak (6703 ft.)
7. Portland Gap (approx. 5250 ft.)
8. Blue Mountain Peak (7402 ft.)

In short, we were to go from Cinchona to the Peak via the Blue Mountain Ridge.

The return trip from the Peak was to take the well-marked and frequently used trail as follows:

7. Portland Gap
9. Whitfield Hall (approx. 4500 ft.);
11. Penlyne Castle (approx. 3500 ft.);
12. Mavis Bank (approx. 2250 ft.), and from there by road to Kingston.

There was no discussion about how to get back home, but I assumed that either Gordon or Roger's father would be there to meet us on the Tuesday or Wednesday at the latest.

Our starting point, Clydesdale, is a hamlet nestled in the foothills of the mountains. It is a coffee plantation irrigated by the pristine cool waters of the nearby river, complete with its own antique waterwheel. Clydesdale has an area for Boy Scouts and other youngsters to enjoy themselves at Chestervale Youth Camp. Prior to 1967 when I had camped there more than once, there had been an open area with more spartan accommodations such as bunk beds and other bare necessities.

Whether there was any remnant of a trail, we had no idea. We were not unduly worried though, because in theory, as long as we stayed on the main ridge running west to east, we should have been able to see the north slopes and coastline of the island at our left, and the south slopes to our right at all times. We knew that the southern slopes were inhabited, farmed and fairly accessible, just as we knew the northern slopes to be treacherously different in their inhospitality and solitude. We were satisfied that we had made a sufficiently foolproof plan.

We did, however, have another way home if it looked as if we might run out of time. George's uncle, Desmond, did not think that we could complete the hike in under a week; the rest of us disagreed. Without much justification for our confidence, we were pretty positive that we could make it there and back in no more than three, maybe four days at the outside.

So far as I could tell, apart from our team, only George's uncle was aware of the complete plan. The list of precautions taken and the fact that we were brazen, invincible boys made it unnecessary to advise anyone else, especially Headmaster Middleton. After all, the boys of the 1939 expedition did not think it prudent to advise their headmaster and scoutmaster, Reginald Murray, even though he had tremendous experience in the jungle they were attempting to conquer.

This alternative would follow the intended route, then divert just before Main Ridge Gap to a trail leading to 10, Farm Hill Works, 11, Penlyne Castle, and back to the safety of 12, Mavis Bank.

It was reassuring that the route still existed on the official topographical survey we took with us, but perhaps it was a bad omen that George's uncle believed we would have to resort to it. We had estimated that if the group moved steadily, we could make Main Ridge Gap and Mossman's Peak by the end of day two or three. Gaining the Peak from there would be easy.

★ ★ ★

At the meeting, George took charge of the details, and so most of the questions were directed at him:

"So George, yu have any pictures of what the hilltops look like?"

"Dis map up to date?

"Who bringing the 'lasses?"*

"When las' yu uncle really went up there, he went by himself? I have fi find a very good reason for my ol' man to allow me on this trip, yu know."

"G. B., maybe you shouldn't give him any details! Don't you and yu ol' man go bird bush often?"**

I nodded.

"So, any problem yu can't handle?"

I shook my head vigorously.

"Who bringing the compass?" someone asked.

"Anybody have an extra sleeping bag?"

"Coops, yu taking yu surfboard?"

Everyone laughed.

"How we getting to Clydesdale? My ol' man not going to drive the Ford there, yu know," I informed them.

"Coops already say his ol' man going tek us up."

It wasn't until the morning of our meeting that I discovered that Donnie had a more intimate connection with our planned adventure than any of us could have imagined. He was the son of W. Donald

---

*   Cutlasses or machetes.

** My father often took me, from a very early age, bird shooting in the lightly wooded areas on the south coast just outside of Kingston. I was attending Campion Hall Prep at the time and we would have to leave town at about noon to catch the afternoon 'flight' (of birds). School was not over until 2:30. He would write excuses to my teacher Father Coleman to leave early, saying that I had to go to see either Dr. Stockhausen, our family doctor, or Dr. Gerald Hollar our dentist so that I could go with him. I suppose him being the only one of his contemporaries and shooting partners who had 'retired' he needed company. I dreaded the day that father Coleman would ask to see a chart from either Drs. Stockhausen or Hollar.

Soutar, who himself had been one of the teenage boys from Jamaica College lost in the Blue Mountains in 1939.

Cecil's participation was still not certain, as he needed to secure time off from work. Cecil, being a full-time employee to a company specializing in photography and only recently employed, was probably reluctant to ask for time off so early in his tenure. After all, jobs were expected to last a lifetime in those days, and staff typically didn't want to rock the boat.

Transportation to our starting point was settled. We would be taken to Clydesdale, close to the Cinchona botanical gardens by Gordon's father. He would let us know the precise time we would be picked up.

Donnie Soutar dropped out due to the flu, and Cecil confirmed that he would definitely make the trip. I did notice that Donnie was not present at our meeting, and it began to dawn on me that George knew or had already decided that Donnie would not be going along. I surmised that I was included, at the very last minute, for this reason. We would be five.

In retrospect, I think we were something of an odd group. Gordon and Cecil were surfing buddies, pioneers in Jamaica's growing but still largely unknown surf scene, concentrated on the shores to the east of Kingston and as far around the north coast as Boston Beach in Portland.

Except for the obvious link between those two, we didn't really know each other well before setting out, and had had little interaction outside of school beforehand. But being confederates from Jamaica College was enough to bind us in the enterprise. Prior to being in Lower Six, Roger, Gordon, and I had been in the same class. George was in the same grade, but in another class. Although Cecil was a 'working man', he was a JC old boy.

Apparently, my love for having a grand time in the salubrious hills was the same as theirs. It was thrilling to think of conquering faint trails and learning some of the secrets of those mysterious heights. We planned to set out with a spirit of invincibility.

"Okay, Coops," said George, "Give me a buzz when you know, and I'll tell the other fellas."

"Mek sure an' leave a message if I'm not there," I replied. "I'll be out late tonight and again early tomorrow morning, so don't leave without me."

I was a full-fledged conspirator now, and inserted myself into the lively brainstorming session where we worked out what we would do 'up there', the breakfast schedule for each day, the weather, and so on. Then, it was time for full disclosure, who had what, who could bring what, who was good at what, what we would do if this or that thing happened.

I guess the whole thing, coming as it did at the end of the school year, was in a way a kind of rite of passage for me, a time to finish growing out of my shell and more into the shape of the man I was to become.

This was also about the time that my father began feeling comfortable about my occasionally taking the bus home. I had planned to take the bus, and since it was the end of the school term, I was grateful that I had no books to carry. Except for the thoughts going through my head, the bus ride was uneventful. Had I been too hasty in deciding to join the group? How was I going to break the news to my father? I couldn't just lie and say that I was going to the Peak via the usual trail; surely, word would eventually get out from someone related to the parties. The trip was going to be unusual and a first for everyone, mainly because none of us had ever been away from home alone for an extended period. It was common for us to spend weekends with friends, but only with parents, a scout master, or some kind of adult presence whenever we were away from home for more than two days.

Once in the house, I somehow became confident about the venture and secretly began putting together a kit for the climb. Since I shared a room with my brother at one end of the house, somewhat isolated from my sisters and parents, I had just the right amount of space for some subterfuge. Nervous about the departure planned for the next day, I was relieved that my father was not at the table for dinner that evening, and I remember wanting to leave the house again as soon as possible to avoid anyone's questions.

Later that evening came the confirmation that Gordon's father wanted us all at the Cooper residence, ready to go by 1:00 p.m.

While I was out, George called my home and spoke with my father, allowing the old man a vague idea of the route we planned to take.

Finally, the team for the hike was cemented for good:

- **Roger Bates** (age seventeen) was an 'A' student and school monitor, destined to be a 'scientist' if he survived his many motorcycle mishaps. He had been to the Peak before.
- **Gordon Cooper** ('Coops', age seventeen) was an avid surfer who represented Jamaica College at hockey. He had a great interest in animals, but also had a number of career aspirations if his many jaunts and camping trips to the Hillshire Hills in his 'convertible' Jeep didn't kill him first.
- I, **G. B.** (age seventeen) was a school monitor, outdoorsman, model airplane enthusiast and avid bird shooter. An all-round sportsman, I also represented JC at tennis, hockey and badminton, in which I was school captain, and had been Under-19 All Jamaica badminton triple champion from 1965, at age fifteen.
- **George Hussey** (age seventeen) was an army cadet and school monitor, who loved reading and performed librarian duties; he had already been to the Peak a number of times.
- Rounding out the five was **Cecil Ward** (age eighteen), known to Gordon as 'Cece' (pronounced "cease")—a camera fanatic, who along with Gordon and Donnie Soutar, was an avid surfer.

★ ★ ★

At home, my father was a man of few words, and not a very good communicator. When he did speak it was with authority; no one ever questioned him. He was loving and thoughtful, but rarely showed any of these traits outwardly. Even so, by the way he doted on us, it was clear that his children came first in his life. Next to us came his home, where the structure and outward appearance was always in tip-top shape.

(I will never forget his last words, as my mother told me on July 14, 2001. In her arms, feeling cold and knowing that the end was near, he asked, "Is the roof leaking? Is the eggshell [light green] paint on the walls peeling off? How about the children? Are any of them in trouble or owe any money?" Then he took his last breath.)

★ ★ ★

I arrived home late on that last evening after school, hoping to avoid my dad, if at all possible. As it happened, my mother opened the door, and I don't recall ever seeing him that night.

Mom mentioned that one of the boys had called and told my dad about a trip that I was going on in the morning and that he had not said a word since. Then, she pointed to the kitchen table.

"There are two haversacks,"[1] she began, "plus a canteen and a plastic water bottle that your father has taken out for you to use. He has already scoured the water containers three times, but you had better check on those haversacks."

She also said that my father was adamant about taking extra water, "as you never know what to expect in the bush."

No one but my father could adequately sanitize anything to his standards. Even when all the glasses, dishes, and cutlery were washed, dried and put back in place, he would seek them out, then proceed to repeat, over and over, the entire process until he was satisfied that they were as good as new.

My dad was like that with his precautions, especially where there was a lesson in preparedness for me to learn. For example, I once had my wallet stolen; it had all of five shillings (about seventy cents US) in it at the time. Although lunch and a mid-morning snack could cost no more than one-and-a-half shillings, my father thereafter topped up the remaining amount to five shillings daily, just in case of an emergency.

Believing that the one-quart (quarter-gallon) World War II-era canteen that he had bought from US Army Surplus would suffice, I had not considered taking along the two-quart (half gallon) bottle. I was not, however, going to get into an argument with my father, especially on a night when we were clearly avoiding each other.

The bigger bottle was not going to be left behind.

A World War II-era backpack, similar to the one I took along.

END NOTES

[1]   My rig, including my haversack, canteen and water bottle (all three having been acquired by my father at the end of WWII from the US army stationed in Jamaica) was selected by my father and proved to be very different from what the other fellows would carry. The plastic water bottle originally held some sort of fruit-flavoured drink and had a loop near the top, making it easy to lash it directly to the pack.

The bag was an improvement on the M-1910, which was later replaced by an upgraded bag developed in 1928. However, the M-1928 backpack did not go into production until 1940. In 1944, the Army began replacing the haversack and its canvas field bag with a combat pack based upon the 1941 U.S. Marine Corps pack and which was very similar to the one I took. The main exception was that mine had no suspenders. Instead, it had a single strap in the centre-top by which it could be carried, by hand, alternately to the two main shoulder straps.

It was made of cotton canvas in Olive Drab Number Seven, a darker shade than what was previously used. It had a waterproof liner, interior divisions, straps for closing the main flap, attaching a blanket roll, and for attaching the cargo pack. The waterproof liner was an ingenious device, allowing clothing to be kept dry, no matter the weather conditions. The shoulder straps proved to be very tight under the armpits and shoulder blades, even at their maximum allowance. When tested later on, this design would prove burdensome and excruciatingly painful. The weight of the haversack combined with the coarseness and narrowness of the straps only exacerbated the situation. In an attempt to ease this pain, I would try to spread out the load by placing a rolled-up vest between the straps and my shoulder.

CHAPTER 5

POINT ZERO - CLYDESDALE

Saturday, December 16, 1967

At age thirteen, I was able to conduct the entire Sabbath morning service, both the Hebrew and English sections. After my Bar Mitzvah I did so frequently, and I've officiated at Bar Mitzvahs, a funeral, and other types of services. By the time I turned sixteen, I was a Sabbath School teacher and would later become a director and trustee for the synagogue.

That December 16 was no different, except that my mind was not at the Shaare Shalom Synagogue that morning as I tried to visualize the trip ahead, factoring all the possible difficulties, asking myself if I was prepared in the way my father would have been.

Although cooler at this time of the year, Kingston was still a hot and dusty city, and as I stood there in my suffocating tweed and tie, I was sweating profusely, as I normally did when conducting a service where the majority of the attendants were by far my seniors. Duty called for worship, but this time I was distracted.

I guess when you're very worried, perhaps gone beyond the point of being afraid, important details get ignored, even forgotten. I honestly do not remember if it was I who told my father about the trip being more than a day's hike, or whether he had heard it from George. I'm pretty sure, however, that I never saw him at all that Saturday morning as I got ready to leave.

I returned home just in time to answer the phone. It was George.

"G. B.? Yu still with us?" he inquired breathlessly. "Try to be at Coop's house by 1:00 p.m. His old man is still set to drive us to Clydesdale. Oh, one more t'ing. Last night when I spoke to your old man I kinda' wise him up a bit about de plans, but of course, not all the details."

That was about ten minutes before midday. Thankfully, all members of my family were 'with the program', except, of course, for my father, who was still not out of bed and in circulation around the house.

"Yu mad or something, George?" I retorted, firing back a couple of cusswords. "Yu better delay Mr. Cooper or else is hell to pay! Anyway, I goin' try my best. I can't get everyt'ing into one haversack. Goin' have to bring two."

"Bring dem and we'll see what can be done," George said confidently. He had some news, too. "Yu know Cecil takin' Donnie's place?" he asked me. Although I already knew, the reminder that Donnie was no longer part of the group only landed somewhere on the edge of my very busy consciousness.

All I got out was, "A'right. See you, George."

I had been contemplating taking along my BB gun, but figured that because it was weighty and would deprive me of a free hand, it would be more of a hindrance than anything else. Also, if it was going to be brought along for 'protection', it could do little harm to a wild boar, one of the dangerous indigenous animals that roam the mountainside. Perhaps subconsciously I was thinking of hunting birds.

I hurried around the house, throwing odds and ends together and spewing a barrage of cuss words in my mind every time somebody got in my way.

"Mummy, de two barbeque chickens ready?"

"I haven't been to Monty's to pick them up yet," she replied. "You seem to think you're the only one who needs attending to in this house. And you better stop the noise before you wake your father up."

That was enough to calm me down, at least for the moment. Then she made me stop lashing out at my brother and sisters.

"Listen nuh, the other children have to have lunch too, so stop pushing them around!"

"Just pass dat transistor radio over here, please," I continued fussing. "Where is the flashlight and the set of new batteries?"

I did have my own camera, a Brownie 127, given to me at age thirteen. Since it could only produce black-and-white pictures, I was most certainly not going to take it along on such an expedition. I pointed to my mother's Kodak Instamatic camera 101, capable of taking twenty shots at a time; I knew was already loaded with colour film.

My mother's Kodak Instamatic 101, the source of many colour photographs illustrating the actual 1967 events.

"Hey! I goin' need dat camera to prove I been up there, you know!" I remarked.

In hindsight, I never bothered to see how many shots were left nor had the foresight to take along an extra roll or two.

At that point I was satisfied that my packing was A-OK, so I made hasty tracks from my own house at 25 Windsor Avenue to number 16. I was a member of a close-knit group of teens who had grown up on that street, and we had made several 8mm movies at our 'studio' located at Number 16, where the house and grounds featured prominently in our movie making. We affectionately referred to it as 'Windsor Playhouse', and it had seen the proud production of movies like *Stranger and Goliath, Hunt the Man Down, Hush Hush, Sweet Charlotte, Colony Spinner, Room 13, The Rebel,* and several others that we never got around to giving a title. We had actually added sound to the ones that gave us the most pride. As a creative, fun-loving group of twelve or so boys and a couple of girls, we had lots of energy and lots of ways to spend it.

One of the girls was Jill, the daughter of a minister whose family occupied the 'manse' opposite 25 Windsor Avenue. She was impressive to anyone who had the chance to meet or engage in conversation with her. She was not only beautiful and smart, but she was one of the better soccer players in our circle, and a tomboy to boot, with a carefree spirit. For whatever reason, she was never featured in any of our productions, and had already migrated to the UK by the time we began to really experiment with more sophisticated

Windsor Playhouse had an 8-millimetre movie camera for shooting elaborately scripted costume dramas.

shooting and editing. Another was Chantal, who played the lady who kept company with the bartender (played by me) in *Stranger and Goliath*. Her boyfriend was Dominic, who lived down the street. He had a part in *Stranger*, but his role in the gang was not very extensive, since he was not a very active sportsman. He and Chantal eventually got married.

The key figures in the merry band were Victor Huson, the stage name of the managing director of Mother's Enterprises Ltd., Victor Carlysle Hudson, 'Huddy' for short. There was also Donovan, Joe (Texas Joey) and Vernon (Booflink), Jennifer Haddad (my sister), Mad Clunes, Ian ('Bombardier'), David G. (Skrag Head), Robin and Roderic Crawford, David Wynter, Mark and Steve Ho Lung, Liz Westhorp, Robin ('Sin Side'), Martin Ford, Pedro Floro, Jackie and John Mackie.

Jeffrey Dujon, who lived next door at Number 27, became involved in our sports arena sometime later. My father was instrumental in setting up his first batting practice facility. It consisted of a tennis ball secured by a piece of string inside a sock. The string from the sock-ball was strung over a beam in the garage shed of the Dujon's, up to about knee height of this small boy. He would practice stroking the ball for hours under the watchful eyes of B. S., his brother, and his father. Shortly after he joined the big league on the lawns of Number 25, there was a problem when he broke one of the Chen's bedroom windows at Number 23. The solution was to set up the stumps on his front lawn at Number 27, and bowl over the hedge from Number 25. That gave us an extra ten yards or so of runway.

Jeff Dujon would become the star wicketkeeper/batsman for the legendary West Indies cricket team of the 1980s, serving as captain near the end of a career in which he scored nearly 10,000 runs.

Cricket and football(soccer) were the mainstays on the empty lot adjacent to the Haddad family home on Windsor Avenue.

My father's house sat on two lots he had bought in 1937. The vacant lot, Number 23½, was where we played our sports. This was to his great satisfaction, because he had intended the space precisely for that purpose.

We used the open space for conventional sports like badminton, football, and cricket. One year, we even put on a boxing match. We had real boxers and coaches prepare for a fight over the course of a year, complete with proper training programmes and espionage into each other's camps. We charged for the event, which featured an experienced referee and ring announcer, all staged at Number 16. And then there were the games we invented, such as marble racing, marble cricket, and even some kind of wasp racing, proving that we could put on tiny events to amuse ourselves just as well.

My parents loved to be with us out on the lot. Dad liked to referee, coach, and champion us as we played; my mother would often supply the 'belly wash' (lemonade), which was a sheer delight to weary teenagers on hot, sweaty days. No doubt they were also keeping an eye on us, relieved that our entire base of operations was located within the world of Windsor Avenue.

★ ★ ★

My father taught my mother to drive in his brand new 1948 Ford V8. This was a major happening, because no one besides his mechanic, Rennie Williams, was allowed to drive the car, which bristled with spare parts in the trunk, more than the vehicle could reasonably need. He also owned two Willys Jeeps he bought from the US Army when they vacated Vernamfield after

At the end of World War II, B. S. Haddad acquired two Willys Jeeps from US Forces stationed in Jamaica.

the end of World War II. The mechanic (who was also the father of Miss Jamaica 1967, Laurel Williams) was the one who drove my parents to their honeymoon at Pine Grove in the Port Royal Mountains. Willie was chief mechanic at Hanna's Garage, which serviced all the vehicles for the Hanna Group of Companies, including R. H. Hanna & Sons Ltd.

Although she had her licence, my mother never drove my father's Ford later on because it had the dreaded mechanical clutch. What if it broke down on the road and Willie was not around to help her out of a jam?

In 1965, my mother bought a blue 1962 Ford Cortina with her own money, liberating her from

Norma Haddad's 1962 Ford Cortina

having B. S. take us everywhere—to school, badminton, tennis, cricket, weddings, synagogue, funerals, movies and parties. This was a blessing, because my father was never on time, something that can prove very embarrassing to teenagers and their plans. The only time I remember my dad being early, despite his setting all ten clocks in the house one hour fast, was for his nephew's wedding. For that event, we arrived at the parking lot at Saints Peter and Paul Roman Catholic Church at 4:30 and found no one else there. He fumed, but my mother told him that she thought that the wedding was at 3:30. It was, in fact scheduled for 5:30.

★ ★ ★

When we were getting ready to go up the mountain, Mummy had already been teaching me to drive, but the ride to the Cooper's house on December 16, 1967 was not going to include a driving lesson. I needed her to get me there without any extra-curriculars, because I was on a mission.

I gulped down as much of my mother's savoury soup as my excitement would allow. She hovered and fussed, then reluctantly drove me up to Coop's house. Before we got in the car, my mother said she was taking me over there since my father was 'not available'. She gave no reason for his unavailability, a fact that was highly unusual, considering how much he fussed about and influenced everything we did. We didn't discuss it further, but I did know that whenever he was concerned or felt apprehensive about something, this was his *modus operandi*. He withdrew his presence and his moral support—visible support, at any rate. I knew he was still in his bedroom and I was grateful for his self-imposed seclusion.

Needless to say, the ride to the Cooper's was a sombre one. Up until this point, I was not sure what George had told my father or what, in turn, my father had said to Mummy about my plans. She seemed nervous, concerned about this 'last-minute trip', as she called it.

"Who are these boys?" she wanted to know. "Besides the Bates fellow, do you know them? How long are you going to be away? Why are you not going along the regular trail? Who's the guide? I don't want to be the one to get in trouble if anything happens to you. You know your father will blame me. Why don't you ask him to drive you there to get some more information?"

In cavalier fashion, I brushed off all my mother's questions and concerns. Truth be told, I really didn't know much of what I was getting myself into, having only been briefly apprised of the plan's broad outlines during the previous afternoon. Apart from my experiences in the bird bush, I had only been as far as the foothills of the Blue Mountains and only on the southern side, when I'd gone on treks up to Cinchona and Catherine's Peak. But those were along more well-defined pathways, the routes taken by casual hikers, tourists, youth clubs and students alike. Regardless, I was already dead set on going, and there was no time left for questions.

Like my mother, I should have had some concerns.

★ ★ ★

Roger was on spot to meet us. He also seemed ready to handle my mother, and once he had given her a satisfactory briefing using some of the details, she bade us all goodbye, cautioned us to be sensible, and wished us a great hike. As she drove away, I took my place with the others on the Coopers's front verandah. The parental issues were dealt with.

To see us that afternoon, we must have looked like a proper British bush expedition. Backpacks cluttered the floor and paraphernalia were littered among the bags, from food and utensils to clothing and toiletries. Realizing that whatever went up the mountain with us would have to be carried on foot, everyone tried to reduce the weight of his load. After some editing, we weighed the packs, removed something, weighed again, replaced something else, and weighed one last time. I got the general idea and removed one of my blankets, expecting my stuff to get lighter through that gesture. George got his pack down to a respectable eighteen pounds; Gordon's, Cecil's, and Roger's averaged twenty pounds, while the combined weight of my two was nineteen.

Hauling two haversacks was going to be a problem.* If I had to carry the second one all the time, I would only have one hand free. I must admit that I was the smallest boy in the group, weighing only a slight 115 pounds, so I was never going to be the best bet for keeping up with the group while carrying a big load. Someone quickly suggested that the other four boys could take turns carrying my second pack. All agreed.

Our entire food supply consisted of six cans of condensed milk, three pounds of rice, one tin of Milo (a type of granulated cocoa), six potatoes, three packs of chicken noodle soup, three cans of corned 'bully' beef, three tins of sausages, three tins of sardines, and one pack of Ryvita biscuits.

My mother would not hear of my going without taking along something that would trump a hiker's ordinary culinary fare, so my haversack was upgraded with some delicacies that included a few slices of ham, two packs of cheese (eight slices each) and two whole barbecued chickens. The chicken would be pure luxury for us; we knew they could remain edible for at least four days of inclement weather at considerable altitude and still be delicious.

I had packed five shirts, two pairs of jeans, one extra pair of shoes, a sweater, a windbreaker and a change of underwear. For just four days in the bush, I thought this would be plenty, in the same way I felt that the weighty half-gallon water bottle had to be overkill as well. I thoughtfully took along glucose tablets for those moments when my energy might wane. My bag also had chewing gum, peppermint, and barley sweets at the ready.

Other sundries included a toothbrush and toothpaste, the military-style insulated canteen, a twenty-foot length of copper wire, a transistor radio, and Mom's Kodak 101 Instamatic camera. For first aid, I had a pint of white rum, some Tiger Balm (an Asian concoction of menthol,

---

* The weight of the load we started out with was considerably less than that carried by the 1939 group. They went with rather more luxurious items such as store-bought hammocks. The individual weight of their packs was closer to forty pounds.

camphor, cajuput, and clove oils) and a bottle of Radian-B. The latter two items were liniment rubs, popular for soothing a range of ills from muscle stiffness to actual sprains. An additional plastic bottle (which once held an Avon shampoo product) containing eight ounces of Jamaican white overproof rum was taken along to unclog or purify anything.

'Whites', as the rum is affectionately called by farmer and socialite alike, has a pure alcohol content of sixty-three percent. It is quite effective for basic disinfection or congestion, and therefore widely considered a panacea for most ailments. It can be the cane farmer's standard cocktail for lunch, undiluted and on the rocks. Notwithstanding its ability to wreak havoc on livers and kidneys, the farmer will swear by white rum's other function, the easing of the burden of life and work, and by its secondary function, the swift destruction of any and all germs. At least that's what local 'rum-heads' were fond of saying when they explained their love for the legendary spirit.

Among us we carried three compasses (including one military-approved model), a topographic map from the Survey Department encased in plastic for protection against the elements, two cutlasses (machetes), medical supplies, an alcohol thermometer, a basic mercury thermometer and a mercury maximum/minimum thermometer (capable of registering the high and low temperatures for the day and which was reset daily), plus Roger's small Primus stove and his Kodak box camera. Cecil also brought along a white 'waterproof' tarpaulin, which we decided could be rigged into a tent.

We packed our belongings successfully into the trunk of Mr. Cooper's Humber Sceptre and piled in. As we drove from Coop's house in upper Barbican, we saw that most of the boarders at JC had already left for home, and the tumult of boys' school life was dying down for the holidays. We also noticed that the playing fields were empty, but our eyes were glazed over with the joy of being out of the house and on vacation. Familiar sights made no impression.

A pressurized burner Primus stove, similar to the one Roger had.

It was while we were all in the car that I confirmed in my own mind that George had decided it was okay to include me in the party well before he advised me.

Surely it was before Mr. Cooper agreed to take us all to Clydesdale, because his oversized sedan would have had a tough enough time fitting five grown boys and their luggage, plus the driver. Where would I have been if Donnie had been included? Home perhaps.

After a stop for some last-minute supplies like a few sodas, bun, cheese and the like, we were on our way. Packed into the car and fresh out of school, we made a high-spirited picture as we strummed imaginary guitars and beat make-believe drums to the hits we heard playing on the radio. At the time, we were pretty stuck on the Beatles' album *Sergeant Pepper's Lonely Hearts Club Band* as we left sunny old Kingston behind:

> *What would you do if I sang out of tune,*
> *Would you stand up and walk out on me?*
> *Lend me your ears and I'll sing you a song*
> *And I'll try not to sing out of key.*
> *Oh, I get by with a little help from my friends . . .*

As we passed the turn-off for Gordon Town and Mavis Bank, Mr. Cooper asked, "You fellows sure you don't want to go up along the usual route here? You could be up and back in a day or two, you know."

We were sure we didn't want that option. That was for novices who didn't have our compasses, food, bush experience and extra water. We were going to blaze a new trail to the Peak!

We made Irish Town* before long and descended into a valley, just as fog did. We noted nearby Bellencita, the country retirement home of Jamaica's first prime minister, Sir Alexander Bustamante. It became his permanent residence on March 31, 1967.

---

* I spent many a Saturday afternoon there on a property owned by the father of one of my friends. He had constructed a 'cabin' from corrugated aluminium sheathing there for weekend jaunts to get away from the hustle and bustle of Kingston. The area was heavily wooded with tall standing bamboo grass (trees, similar to those at Bamboo in St. Elizabeth) and we would hike and sometimes build all kinds of frameworks with the fallen bamboo limbs. He also always brought along his ham radio claiming that the reception was much better at this elevation!

Next, we approached Newcastle, the old army hill station established to avoid the heavy loss of life among British soldiers to pestilence on the humid plains of Kingston. The spot also offered a deadly vantage point for action in the defence of the island. It is nestled high in the hills along the way, about as far as school kids generally went up into the mountains. Nearby Catherine's Peak is popular with hikers and routinely used for training exercises by the military. As we passed through Hardware Gap, the fog thickened and the cool mountain breeze brought us all welcome refreshment.

Mr. Cooper was ready with another interjection, something well meaning, but probably probing as well, just to see if we would change our minds:

"Last stop for food. How about it?"

There was a unanimous 'no' to that, too. We were in a hurry; no more stops.

It was just about 3:30 p.m. Behind Newcastle and down a muddy road, which was in fact a shortcut up to Clydesdale, we passed a Jeep packed with fir trees on its way to the old mill house. Mr. Cooper recognized the driver and beckoned him to stop.

"Benjie, how you do?"

Mr. Cooper gestured in the direction of a rather elderly and weather-beaten man who appeared to be in charge of things in the area. He was in fact the area's forest ranger.

"Oh, well t'ank yu, sah!" the man shouted back.

It seemed like a chance meeting, and the encounter put us in even higher spirits. Cecil had wanted Mr. Cooper to procure six young fir trees from whoever had the authority to provide them. This was the very man, and running into him did nothing to dissuade us from going up in the way we had planned.

"One of these young fellows want half dozen of the young firs. You t'ink you can raise six from the nursery for him?"

"Oh yes, sah! Sure t'ing."

Benje and Mr. Cooper chatted for a little while about fir trees, the kind that is traditionally brought into the Jamaican home every year during Christmas season. Benje was pleasantly accommodating at every point:

"Yes, sah, yes, sah, Okay, sah," the forestry man fawned.

When Mr. Cooper asked him what the trail would be like for our group, and suggested that he go look for us if we didn't return by Wednesday, Benje remained untroubled and good humoured: "Alright, sah!"

Gordon's father laughed. We drove off. No sooner had we gone 200 yards along a bumpy and potholed road when the car jolted to a halt. There was no mechanical problem. The ride was over.

"Well, fellows," Cooper told us, "this is as far as you go by car."

We got out from our cramped positions, stretching our limbs among us and filling our lungs with the fresh mountain air. There was a sense of relief, after having been packed like sardines into Mr. Cooper's Humber, to lurch and jiggle up a hill that was all bumps and potholes. The vehicle had done well up the incline and through the occasional mud puddles with its payload of five boys, one adult, six haversacks, a few sleeping bags, and all that miscellaneous camping paraphernalia.

I stretched with a mock groan, all the time with an eye up ahead. It was time to tackle the mountain.

The five of us posed for a couple of photographs, which Mr. Cooper was happy to take. The pictures captured us happy and confident, ready for anything. We quickly said the obligatory "thanks" and "see you soon" to Coop's father, then watched the retreating Humber make its way back down to the city.

Everything felt good as we shared a wordless look among us.

Yes, this is it, our glances said. *We're really going to do this.*

CHAPTER 6

THE EXPEDITION BEGINS

We unceremoniously took a few more pictures using one of the cameras, mine or somebody else's. At 4:00 p.m. the weather was fair, with a moderate temperature of 68°F (20°C) and the faintest hint of rain. But we were undaunted, and so we set off.

I remember being curious about the conversation George had with my father the night before. One of the other boys brought it up. George was quite sure my father had said to him more than once that this was going to be 'a trip we would never forget'. It was vaguely unsettling to hear that. Was my father referring to the jungle beauty that we would encounter on our trail? Or did he somehow have an inkling that we were asking for trouble by taking an outlaw path up the mountain?

We tossed his words between us in speculation, but it became point-less and slowed us down. Just then, we heard a faint sound, just before the mountain quiet was broken by the present and unmistakable roar of a diesel engine as it made its way up the grade. When it cleared the bend, we saw that it was a big dump truck, empty save for the few workmen aboard with their digging implements. The driver, a consider-ate fellow, nodded yes to our signs for a lift. We were aboard in no time and headed upward.

It was a short bumpy ride as the truck was manoeuvred expertly along the narrow, rutted dirt road cut into the hillside. The vehicle ground to a stop just as a workman asked, "Is Cinchona yu goin'? Is up dat way," he directed, pointing to the left-hand side of the fork in the road.

The five of us thanked the truck driver for the five-minute ride and hopped out. Once again, we were on our way by foot, eating sweets and chewing gum as we went. Soon we reached an open spot that offered an unobstructed view of Kingston and its environs. But even that spectacular view was challenged by the beauty of the flower garden that lay just north of the open spot. There were flowers that seemed to be of every bright and subtle colour, special pinks and reds and things that defied the crayon box entirely. Almost in the middle of this garden was a large Y-shaped tree with two well-feathered peadoves perched on either side as if they were on a postcard. They seemed too pretty to shoot, a rather useless thought, since we had taken no firearms or slingshots along.

The botanical gardens at Cinchona are on a mist-swirled bluff about a mile above sea level. They overlook the valleys of the Clyde, Green and Yallahs rivers, offering a great view of the Blue Mountain ridge and its main Peaks. Founded in 1868 as a coffee plantation, the camp-friendly area was also for many years used for the propagation of exotic orchids, Assam tea and strawberry plants. The name 'Cinchona', however, came from colonials' plans for the cinchon tree, prized for the quinine it produced for fighting the dreaded 19th- and early 20th-century scourge, malaria. The project failed, but along the way Cinchona evolved into a botanical and bird-watching haven, fragrant with a stunning array of semi-tropical blooms and trees, such as rubber and oak, juniper and eucalyptus, cypress and cedar, mulberry and camphor, with pines towering well over a hundred feet. From this serene spot, we began the second leg of our hike.

Our first noteworthy obstacle appeared shortly afterwards. Dead ahead was the result of a landslide that had started twenty feet above us on the right-hand side of the road. The debris had clattered down the slope, spanned the road and had come to a precipitous stop on the left bank. There was only one way past the new obstacle and that was to go straight over it. Roger went first by making footholds with his cutlass, then tying himself to a tree by rope. We followed him over using the free end of the secured rope.

Leaving Cinchona behind, we started looking out for the trail to Sir Johns Peak. Quite easily, we were soon on it. Almost immediately the dirt track became a mere footpath, lightly overgrown with bush and spotted with ferns.

About 5:50 p.m., George, the army cadet, decided we needed to put a halt to the day's march.

"We betta' make camp here for tonight," he advised, "it gets dark up here pretty quick."

By sunset, with our expedition truly underway, we decided on a spot for Camp Site 1. A huge rock, roughly thirty feet wide and twenty feet high, protected us from the whistling north-east winds.

The ground was covered with a layer of soft pine needles graciously provided by the surrounding trees. We gathered all the kindling we could carry and used it to build a nice fire. It warmed us well once we had taken precautions not to set our surroundings alight. We enjoyed our Milo, and while sharing one of the barbecued chickens for dinner, Roger was quite insistent that he get the 'parson's nose', the chicken's rump. We obliged him.

By the time we had finished dinner, the temperature had dropped to 62°F (17°C), but felt a lot colder, due to the windchill factor from the continuous prevailing northeast winds.

I turned on my transistor radio and we listened to music for a short time. Cecil's 'waterproof tent', really a large tarpaulin, was hung up overhead in case of rain. Gordon and Cecil had sleeping bags; Roger and I were in our blankets that had been sewn up like bags, and George, the most experienced hiker of the group, seemed satisfied with only a blanket. In order to keep the moisture out, I also made use of a huge plastic bag into which I inserted myself. I had got it from the neighbourhood dry cleaners, which was owned by the family of a friend, and whose suggestion it was to take one along. It would be large enough to cover most of my body, I figured, from the bottom of my feet to just under my armpits. More important, the plastic did double duty as protection for my blanket, which I carried on top of my pack.

There was a good deal of laughing and joking while we made our crude preparations for bed. As soon as everyone snuggled up contentedly in his own corner under the tarp, we dropped off into our first night's sleep.

I awoke to the glow of an overhead moon. Its silvery light filtered through the tall firs that lined the path and encircled us.

"Roger, what time it is?" I asked, feeling it was some late, magical hour.

"Mrmpf!" Roger snorted, annoyed to be roused for something so mundane. "Cho man, G. B., is only 9:30!"

Next, there appeared to be some sort of altercation involving Coops, but with who? He awoke suddenly, thinking that he had heard a wild hog in the camp. Grabbing his flashlight, he shone it along the path in both directions and within the area. There was no hog, but the grunting continued. After listening carefully it dawned on him that it was Cecil snoring. He laughed and went back to sleep.

Soon after that, the rustling of the plastic bag under my feet had awakened the camp. Except for me, the group seemed to have no problem nodding off again. All told, I only managed to get about four hours' sleep. But everyone else seemed to have rested well enough through the night. The next morning found us fit and ready to go.

CHAPTER 7

TACKLING SIR JOHNS AND HIGH PEAKS

Sunday, December 17, 1967 (Day 2)

By 6:00 a.m., we had brilliant sunshine, and after a chilly night, the group wasted no time being up and about in its warmth. The fire had died out overnight, but we rekindled it for making hot morning beverages. Now we had two heat sources, and they warmed and loosened up our bodies quite nicely.

Breakfast was ready at 6:30. Each of us quickly polished off a cup of hot Milo, plus one sausage with cheese and ham on Ryvita biscuits. Delicious.

The morning's plan called for a climb to Sir Johns Peak, at 6332 feet. We hit the trail by 7:00 a.m. and moved at medium pace, with everyone in high spirits. The temperature had already risen to 68°F (20°C) and the weather was looking like it would hold fair. It wasn't long before we came upon a panoramic view of the ridge we intended to conquer, looming just behind Cinchona. We were now passing through St. Helen's Gap.

A valley about two miles wide as the crow flies lay between our location and Sir Johns.

"We can't go across the valley?" Cecil asked of nobody in particular.

"No," George replied, "we'll have to go around this ridge we're on now, on to Sir Johns Peak and from there along the main ridge."

Cecil was brimful of enthusiasm and made bold predictions about reaching Sir Johns that day, High Peak the next and then, pointing to

Main Ridge Gap, "up there the day after that". He concluded confidently that we would not make Blue Mountain Peak before Thursday, a full day later than planned.

We weren't ready to have any doubt cast over our ability to stick to schedule. Besides, Cecil was not at any of our meetings and therefore could not have been very familiar with the detailed plans. He relied heavily on Gordon's knowledge of them, and so we dismissed his prediction.

It was just about here that we saw numerous strawberry plants scattered over the hillside. They weren't in fruit at the time, but we were happy to think we might find fruit-bearing patches as we went on. That never happened, and we subsequently learned that strawberries were long in coming. We discovered when we consulted our map, ironically, that the area bore the name 'Strawberry Hill'.

Down in the valley to our right, we could hear the sound of moving water and the faint strains of a barking dog. George, who was in front, spotted the animal later, a small brown and white mongrel. The dog must have realized we weren't going to feed it and, apparently irritated by our singing, soon ran away. We passed a patch of large cedar trees which would have provided us a cool shaded area to rest, but we didn't stop. For another two hours, we pressed on, eventually stopping at a steep incline a few hundred feet from the Peak we had targeted for the day.

Most of us wanted a breather at that point, but Cecil and I wanted to go on ahead. We pushed out from the pack, arriving on the North side of Sir Johns Peak (elevation: 6332 ft.) at 9:55 a.m. The others arrived about ten minutes later.

Cecil climbed the highest tree in the area, trying to assess the lay of the land between us and the north coast. He was able to make out the shoreline, but reported that the view to the South was shrouded in dense fog. It was at this point that the real test would begin, so we all took a brief rest before tackling the ascent.

The next target would be High Peak, rising to 6912 feet or roughly 600 feet above where we were. It seemed at least two miles away, and any track we had followed up to that point had evaporated. We checked our bearings and accepted 122 degrees as the key to our forward heading. In fifteen minutes, we were ready to move again.

★ ★ ★

Eight miles east of Kingston, in balmy weather on the South shore beaches of Cable Hut and Brooks Pen, the usual Sunday groups were going through their routine. Included among them were the Haddads, Crawfords, Dempsters and DaCostas, as well as relatives and friends of those families. Some of the conversation that weekend, naturally, turned to our trip to the mountains. The chatter began good-naturedly between Robin Crawford, the boyhood friend I had trusted with our true hiking plan and Dennyse Dempster, my girlfriend who lived in a house on Fairway Avenue, close to where I lived. Since her parents were long-time friends of the Crawfords at Number 16, she was a common thread among the kids on Windsor Avenue. The only one who had a surfboard, she was not involved in our sports or moviemaking, but was a brilliant girl who was very serious about schoolwork. She went to St. Andrew High, as did my sisters, and so when she rode in my dad's Ford to Girl Guides meetings, it was usually with me in the car's front seat.

"So Dennyse," Robin began teasingly, pointing in the general direction, "Geoff and some JC fellas gone to the Peak. Look see if yu can see dem, seven thousand foot up there."

"Yah, they left yesterday," Dennyse replied, unfazed. "Geoff, Gordon Cooper, Roger Bates and two other fellows. They'll back Wednesday."

She knew. She just wasn't letting on how concerned she may have been.

"Geoff came to see me before he left," Robin started in again. "Those guys goin' try cut a new trail to the Peak, y'know. G. B. explained the route, but he didn't want me to tell his father the details. The folks believe it's just a little deviation they takin' from the regular road up to the top. Just thought I'd let you know."

"He never said anything like that to me!" Dennyse cried, nonplussed now.

"Yu know how positive and upbeat Geoff is, man. He was ready for it, but when he said if we don't see them Wednesday that we should 'call out the army'; that sounded kinda ominous."

"What?"

"He was just jokin', but yu know, it cold and wet up there, especially at this time of year—an' dem not following no trail. Maybe he was just covering his bases! But all the same, don' worry yu head. Yu know Geoff find himself in trouble already in bird bush and come out alright. He's a survivor. Come, let's try out yu new surfboard."

"Hey you guys!" Roderic Crawford chimed in, "yu order de fry fish and bammy from Miss Puncy yet? Get mi an extra helping of pepper, onion, vinegar and a freezin' cold Pepsi! Goin' do some belly board surfing around the reef there. Save some of the food for me !"[1]

Rod headed off to enjoy some surfing at Copacabana, the adjoining beach with waves in the vicinity of three to five feet.

Had I not been in the mountains that weekend, I most certainly would have been at the beach, but my environment at that moment was so extreme and different compared to the seaside that I may as well have been in different countries.

Weather-wise, what had started out as a promising day had deteriorated. The mountaintops had become fogged over, the sky was covered with many small billowing clouds, and near the horizon was a dull grey wall of air, saturated with rain. Our plan was to follow the top of the ridge as closely as possible, staying on its Kingston (south) side as long as doing so was practical.

In his diary, Roger describes the trek we had completed so far:

> Up to this point we had been walking through a damp mossy sort of forest interspersed with fern patches and hanging with curtains of bamboo grass. Damp and a bit cold we moved on.

Upon leaving Sir Johns, the terrain and vegetation changed drastically. Gordon describes it in the summer 1968 edition of the Jamaica College magazine.[2] Then we stepped into the bush. The vegetation consisted of thick prickly tree ferns about ten feet, small gnarled and twisted trees covered in mosses and lichens and wild pines all in a dense mass. The ground was soft and muddy and covered with rotten trees and leaves. Movement was slow; we squeezed between trees, crawled on our hands and knees, and became entangled in vines. We had to cut our way and soon we came to the almost impenetrable bamboo grass. This is a dense mesh of thin interwoven joints looking exactly like miniature bamboo. It grows between the trees in huge clumps, too green to cut and too strong to break through by force, so we either detoured or took the arduous process of cutting through. Even after cutting, it constantly became entangled around our haversacks or ankles, slowing us to a snail's pace

The first two fellows in line would cut a path (if you can call it that) through thick vegetation so the rest of us could walk through. It was a troublesome business. Every time a cutlass was swung at the grass, it seemed to spring right back up in our path, as if by spontaneous regeneration. In truth, we were temporarily knocking grass over as much as we were cutting it down. We were trying to make progress while chopping at strands, which would be as close as half an inch away from our bodies.

"Hey Cecil!" Roger laughed, "Sooner or later, you gwine castrate yuself if you don' watch out!"

It actually wasn't much of a laughing matter. Cecil almost lost an ear. I came close to losing my left thumb, but managed to emerge from the thicket with only a puncture wound I estimated to be about an eighth of an inch deep. I cleaned the incision and Roger, the official medicine man, was immediately on hand with some Savlon antiseptic and bandages.

We were all relieved to move on. Amazingly, there was the trace of a track, which had managed to retain its impression over the years, but it turned out to be of little use. Every few feet, it disappeared for a few hundred more, so we gave up on the ghost trail and went back to using our compasses. To make sure that we stayed on course, the man who was cutting would say '122' (meaning 122 degrees) every five feet. That essentially meant 'we're in business' or 'straight ahead'.

Our next obstacle was a maze of tree roots very similar to the kind of mangrove roots found in swamps. These were not as parlous as the bamboo grass, but posed a challenge nonetheless. We had to crawl under and over the moss-covered tentacles set at random angles, unless they were rotten enough for us to break through to go straight ahead. The entire area was waterlogged, so its undergrowth was scanty.

After we overcame these roots, the going was relatively smooth. We passed rapidly by trees and patchy scrub until the warning shout came from the man up front. More bamboo grass! Collective sighs and groaning followed. This time, the vegetation was interlaced with impenetrable elephant grass. Lucky for us, it spread over only a distance of about twenty to thirty feet, and within ten minutes, we were clear of it. But now we had slowed to an almost funereal pace.

Fighting through the grass and mangrove roots had taken its toll on our energy. Moreover, the exertion was stimulating our appetites. We stopped to rest and refuel at 2:00 p.m. and enjoyed Ryvita biscuits with cheese in the clean and refreshing mountain air.

At 2:15 p.m. we pushed on and penetrated into more bamboo grass. When we were a few hundred feet from High Peak, Roger shouted, "Ferns! Dis is the thing Donnie's old man was telling us 'bout, yu know."

Indeed, Donnie (via Gordon) had warned us about these ferns. He had said his father had encountered them and remembered their ferocity. They were gigantic—about seven to eight feet in height and so tightly interlocked that they could withstand the body weight of any one of us. They extended along the top of the ridge length-wise, not breadth-wise as the bamboo grass had done. The plants' stalks were covered with 'puss-claw macca', sharp prickles shaped like a cat's claw, so that when we cut at them, the skin on our hands was ripped. George attempted to cut through them, but in vain. What he did manage to do after some fifteen minutes of hacking away was to clear a tunnel about five to six feet long, just wide enough for him to climb through.

Tree ferns proved to be the bane of our existence in the mountains.

While he was occupied with that job, Cecil and I decided not to get cut up and were very fortunate to come upon an egress by detouring wide to the left. By late afternoon, after passing through another patch of bamboo grass, we made our second destination. We were at High Peak, nearly 7,000 feet above everyone else we knew.

There was barely enough time before nightfall to clear a patch approximately eight feet by six feet, space enough for us to bed down. We had just finished a hard day's walk of more than ten hours, and after a little corned beef and a half-cup of Milo each for dinner, we were soundly asleep on the ground by 7:00 p.m. I made a notation referring to this spot as Camp Site 2.

It began raining an hour later. We were partly covered by trees, but that didn't improve things any. As it rained, a fog had blanketed the ridge and formed condensation on the tree leaves. To make matters worse, there was a northeast wind howling at us. The result of this apparent collusion between the forces of nature was that we were exposed to steady streams of water. In no time at all, we had become thoroughly drenched.

The five of us sat positioned back-to-back in an attempt to expose as little surface area of our bodies as possible to the rain and to minimize heat loss as best we could. We also tried our best to refrain from urinating, an outdoors trick that we knew would help maintain our body heat.

Cecil and Gordon had already covered themselves with Cecil's tarp, but it wasn't long before Gordon threw it off in disgust.

"This t'ing not waterproof!" he barked.

"Wha de rass", George complained eloquently in his Jamaican best.

"Wha' happen," Cecil mocked George, "patoo spit 'pon yu?"

"Ah so," (meaning "obviously") he replied sourly.

Poor George was none too impressed by the drenching and was low on humour. The tarp was in fact waterlogged, and it was too heavy for us to carry. Cecil was disappointed in its uselessness. Being practical, he decided to leave it behind, even though it looked as if the weather had no intention of cooperating with us.

At that point, I had developed gas pains and wasn't breathing properly. Immediately, I became scared of triggering an asthma attack identical to the one I had

'Patoo' is Jamaica coinage for the owl.

had at age thirteen in bird bush. The atmosphere was just as humid now as it had been then, but I didn't want to scare the group by bringing that up. Furthermore, I was embarrassed at the thought of jeopardising the hike with any notion of frailty. As I sat there quietly hoping the discomfort would go away, my mind went back:

It would happen after I had exerted myself playing some sport on the open lot. Even after I had been attended to by our Edinburgh-educated, thoroughly Jamaican family doctor, I still knelt on the floor beside my bed for what felt like hours before the attack would finally subside.

Some years later, my own father, without medical training but with acute observational pragmatism, suggested his own hypothesis for my condition to Dr. Sleem. As soon as I arrived home from school, I would go out to my backyard concrete ponds and feed the fish with dry oats held close to my face. Could it be the combination of inhaling the oat dust and physical activity on an empty stomach that my bronchial tubes could not tolerate? Dr. Sleem could not say, but my father fed the fish for the month that followed. I never had another asthma attack. My father was satisfied that his guess had been right, and upon my return from McMaster University in 1970, I found he had taken a sledgehammer to the fish ponds I had so carefully built; with that, he put an end to the fish I had tended for so many years.

In the present, the discomfort in my chest had not gone away. In fact, it had worsened and I had begun to wheeze. I had to be sensible.

"Roger, yu have the stove nearby?"

"Ya, right here," Roger answered, "why?"

"Boy, I feel the asthma coming on. Yu may have to boil up some water for me."

Roger attempted to make me a cup of hot Milo. It was unsweetened, so it didn't taste the least bit as it should have, but it served its purpose. The sharp pains that were causing me so much discomfort very soon subsided. I was feeling fine in a matter of minutes, but I was still wet and a bit miserable, as were all of us, from the downpour.

That night, raindrops crashing onto the hot glass broke Cecil's lantern, but he carried it around for another two days because it held kerosene for Roger's Primus stove. Anyway, he said that that was the reason. Perhaps he was also a bit disconsolate after having had to discard his 'tent', and was loath to get rid of anything else.

Strange things can happen to a bunch of young teenagers newly bonded and in unfamiliar territory, but one cannot explain the reasons why stories were now being told about robberies and burglaries, the theme *du jour*.

Before retiring for the night, we took inventory of our water supply. It was not encouraging, and the intermittent rainfall was not reliable enough to warrant our building some kind of contraption to replenish it. The day had claimed a lot of our energy, so we had to be thankful at least for the fatigue that allowed steady sleep for the rest of the night.

END NOTES

1   Fried fish and bammy has long been a tradition of beach-going Jamaicans. Their day at the beach is just not the same without it. Many go only for the food, which is tantalizingly delicious. Fresh fish are brought right in from the sea, seasoned to perfection and cooked over coals in the open air. The final product is served piping hot, covered with sliced onions, pimento seeds (allspice) and locally grown Scotch Bonnet peppers, all pre-soaked in vinegar. Bammy is a product of the cassava root, dried and pounded into a thick circular shape, and later cut triangularly and fried. The tasty alternative is fried fish and 'festival', a sweetish dough rolled into something resembling an elongated egg roll. Miss Puncy would have been one of the operators of the several beachside canteens that colourfully dot the seashore. So at these two canteens, Brooks Pen and Cable Hut, no Miss Puncy meant no fried fish, no bammies, no bullas and no ice cold Pepsis.

2   As Gordon Cooper would later put it (in the article "Thoughts and Feelings", *Jamaica College Magazine*, 1968):
    When we were in the mountains we 'thought' under two kinds of circumstances. We thought when we came to some obstacle and had to think of a different route, and we thought in the night while waiting for sleep to come. You came to the obstacles in the day while you pulled and pushed and climbed through the bush. When you saw that you could continue no longer in that direction you wanted to die, all that energy wasted, you felt weak and helpless and you could not believe that this was really happening to you. You who just last weekend had set out on a crossing of the Blue Mountain Ridge, you who before the weekend had lived happily at home with your family, doing the things the other guys did. Was this really you sitting on a rock feeling the pain run up your spine, sitting here in the damp and cold, your back against a moss-covered tree, staring blankly down the mountain side at the moss on tree trunks and vines and vines below. You just could not believe it.
    It seemed as if this whole thing was just a game, but a very real game in which the Liberator and J. J. Fate sat up on the clouds playing chess, and you knew that when J. J. Fate won his game (he was not such a good chess player) your fate would be sealed. But for every game J. J. Fate lost you got a chance to move on for another day, and you had to get out before J. J. Fate's day came.
    It had been so many days now in the bush. How much longer would it be? Why should it be you? Please help me, G-d. You prayed that by the end of each day you would be safe and the ordeal would be over. But each day came and it was the same, no sign of hope at all. You wondered how much longer you could last. You felt weak and you knew now that soon the day would come when one of you could not go on, then what? It was impossible to carry any one in here, absolutely impossible. Then probably the others would stay with you and sit there hoping you

would hurry up and die, or they might leave you to die alone. But soon death would overtake each of you, the weakness then the death until there was one left and he would have to die alone. But each of you would have to sit there and watch yourself fade away, waste away to nothing, and you knew it would take a long time.

Nobody could follow you this far, and you felt sorry for anyone who might try, though you hoped that somebody would find you. Your only real hope was to be spotted from the air. But you dared to look up at the dense canopy of trees overhead. The trees grew too close together and they were tall, slim and hardly had any branches at the top. The branches which could support you were too large at the base and you were too weak to even try to climb. So your only hope was a clearing somewhere, an open space in which you could be spotted from above. It would have to be on a ridge, a very high ridge and on the side from which the planes would come. A fire would help but the wood was still wet and the rain still came.

But the disbelief became reality and you stopped dreaming of home and of your parents and the Christmas spirit and the gaiety, the lights, the warmth, the dryness, and pulled yourself up and struck out again. But as the day wore on and you got weaker and more disheartened you wished for the night and the sleep and the warmth of each other's bodies and the false sense of security that came with the night.

As the days passed you slept longer, moved out later and camped earlier. With the evening you decided to make camp, build a lean-to after cutting wood with the dull machete, spread the by now-torn-up raincoats as best you could to make the roof watertight and the sleeping bags on the ground, then after a drink of water and a squeeze of toothpaste, you settled in like a bunch of pup pies, all huddled up for warmth.

With the night you were happy, you felt the strength creep back into your bones and you felt warm and dry, except for the side of you that was not covered and was cold because of the growling wind, and you hoped that the rain would not fall that night and that you would sleep well and dream happier times. The darkness seemed to shut out the alien world of mountain faces, cold, wetness, trees, rivers and waterfalls. But the hunger never left you and your stomach growled for food.

And you thought about your parents, how they lay in their beds thinking about you and if you were dead or alive, lying there helpless, clueless as to your position as you yourself, and how they could do nothing, and neither could you, you could not phone and say: "Dad, Mom, I'm OK. A little hungry, cold, wet, and sad maybe, but on the whole I'm alright, so, see you soon."

You were sorry that they had to go through this, and you felt determined to get out so you could make it up to them. But you laid there hoping, wishing, thinking and dreaming. You thought of what you had been through already, hell, you could take a couple more days of it, you were a man, you could take it if you would get out, but you were not so sure so you prayed, prayed hard like you never prayed before. Then you lay there thinking, waiting, for sleep to overtake you but it would not come. You only slept for short periods then you woke up cramped and cold, but you could not turn over because you did not want to disturb the others, so you kept still, waiting for the day.

CHAPTER 8

HEADING FOR MAIN RIDGE GAP

Monday, December 18, 1967 (Day 3)

We awoke by 6:30 a.m., still shivering from the cold northeastern air that had blown in gusts through the night. We had our maximum/ minimum thermometer, capable of displaying temperature reasonably accurately at both ends of the scale, but for the entire trip we would underestimate the cold. We relied on this and our other simple instruments for measuring temperature but they were incapable of measuring the windchill factor; whenever the wind barrelled in from the north of the ridge, it produced effective wind temperatures below freezing.

We had by now got somewhat accustomed, if not fully acclimatized, to the relentless cold. When the stove was going at night, we couldn't really feel when our hands had got too hot. If we had thought to be aware of it, the singeing of the hair on the backs of our hands would have been a reliable indicator. A tin of bully beef and some sausages were warmed on the Primus and divided among us. The lion's share of the meaty links went to George, who did not care for corned beef at all.

We took a sip of water from our respective canteens and water bottles, and by 7:30 a.m. we continued on our way again. Just like tourists who are shocked to find that Jamaica can be occasionally chilly, we saw that overnight temperatures had fallen to a low of 52°F (11°C) but had climbed back up to a mild 64°F (18°C) by the time we set off. We had veered a bit off course and the lead man's bearing was now '160'. Our immediate destination: Main Ridge Gap.

★ ★ ★

Quite easily, we managed to cut through the remainder of bamboo grass we encountered, much more so than we had anticipated. It was more or less a downhill trail for the early part of the journey until about midday, when things started to get tough.

All along, it appeared that we were following the remnants of an old trail, which when it disappeared from the ground could, on rare occasions, we assumed to continue by observing a corresponding clear opening through the trees above. But there was no time to get comfortable, since we now encountered another patch of bamboo grass. This time, at a height of about six feet, it stood level with us or taller, and grew out from among the shale and rocks scattered about. We were surprised to discover that the grass had configured itself around the stones and sometimes grew even underneath the surface. The vegetation had fused itself onto the stones and we were fortunate to make passage without sustaining any twisted ankles or worse.

Having cleared this latest obstacle, our progress was confined to a path of scattered ferns and loose patches of the troublesome bamboo grass. After that, the ridge turned roughly north and tapered off to a hillock. Reaching the top, we came upon what we thought was the first sign of habitation among the elephant grass that covered the brow of the small hill. But the two bottles and the rusted tin we found buried in the claylike soil lay there without any suggestion as to who had used them.

We were delighted and amazed, though, at the sight of the coast of our island home. The fog had cleared and the view the general direction of Hope Bay, Buff Bay, Annotto Bay and Port Antonio was simply beautiful, allowing us a precious few moments of pure joy. The three 'cameramen' brought their cameras out and tried to capture the clearly defined coastline in the sunlight. The sky was filled with very light clouds, and a magnificent rainbow now spanned the ridge we had left behind. Almost as if in celebration, we brought out some chocolate and shared it. But these idyllic moments don't last long at high altitude, and very shortly thereafter the fog returned, along with a fresh northeastern gale in full force. The ridge ahead disappeared from sight and visibility promptly fell to thirty feet.

We passed on down the hill into the valley, where any view on both sides of us was now obscured. Now we began a fairly steep climb. Hardly twenty or thirty yards up ahead, there came a familiar yelp of frustration from the point man. It was George's turn, and he had come upon a patch of ferns that extended up the slope as far as we could see.

I was exhausted. I had already done my share, chopping for two hours straight. I preferred to do it that way rather than in instalments, so I could have one long tour of duty then rest, instead of several short stints. Cecil joined me in a sort of hopeless gazing while the others, who saw no fruitful alternative, tried to help George make a way for us through the foliage. The thought suddenly struck me that we had met something similar to this before. I consulted Cecil and we came out with it simultaneously:

Meet a patch of ferns seven feet tall? Detour and avoid.

I volunteered to look around. Moving to my left, I operated as close to the fern bed as I could. George wanted to know what I was doing, so I shouted back to say that I needed five minutes more. That was all I needed. With a new burst of energy, I scooted to the top of the slope and looked down in the direction of the track to Blue Mountain Peak from Mavis Bank on the south side of the ridge.

"Come on, you lazy fellows!" I shouted.

That was enough encouragement for George. I yelled up a request for somebody to bring my second haversack. George started out with it, but returned a few cuss words and refused to bring the bag any farther. I went back for it, then resumed my position in the lead. Fog encircled us now. In fact, it blanketed the entire surrounding area, and as we travelled downhill, it gave us the impression that we had entered a gap in the mountain range. It was definitely a gap, caused by the foliage of three small hills. Covered by elephant grass, the position afforded us a view of Farm Hill Works and most of the ridge on which the regular trail to Blue Mountain Peak lay. Farther to the south, we could see all of Kingston Harbour and the New Kingston area, particularly the outstanding feature down there, the British American Insurance building.

Cecil and I scouted ahead but we didn't go too far because the weather did not bode well. The grim and foggy conditions, replete with wind gusts, were expected to return at any time and we were afraid to lose our way back, our sense of surroundings, and thus our relative position. We got back to the group with good news, though. It appeared that Main Ridge Gap was some 300 yards ahead and easily accessible to us. This was cause for rejoicing, but also not without much strife between George, Gordon, and Roger who were tasked with sharing the burden of my second pack. If Main Ridge Gap was so close by, it meant we had done three-quarters of our journey—and this was only Monday evening.

"The sooner we can make it to Mavis Bank the better," Gordon mumbled.

"I want to be home for Christmas."

"If we can find that path tomorrow, we should be able to reach Mavis Bank by Tuesday evening," I volunteered.

We still had to go to Mossman's Peak, Portland Gap, then up to Blue Mountain Peak before heading down the fourteen-and-a-half mile trek to Mavis Bank.

"Well, I'm in no hurry," George declared, untroubled and still within reach of his confidence. "I want to sleep one night on the warm banks of the Yallahs River. When you guys get home, just tell the ol' lady I'll be home on Wednesday."

Roger and Cecil decided that they would follow Gordon and me, provided we could cover good ground from there onwards.

The next day would be the decider.

We halted there for the night (Camp Site 3). Dinner was a few sausages, a tin of bully beef, and a swig of water from our canteens to wash it down. By now, the water was almost gone. I was already on to my half-gallon plastic water bottle as my canteen had been sipped dry a while back. By now, all the other canteens were empty or close to dry. For the foreseeable future, this would have to serve as the group's only water supply. I remember being grudgingly glad that my dad had insisted on the extra bottle.

We prepared to bed down among the clumps of grass.

"Well, tonight we won't be bothered by the northeast wind," George remarked. He figured on using the tall grass for shelter and as a source of good bedding material.

He was wrong. This was elephant grass, which bore a stark resemblance to guinea grass, except that the cutlass was unable to cut a patch that would allow us to lie down comfortably. Instead, we had to resort to curling our bodies around the roots of the plants as best as possible. From the air, we would have resembled a number of giant, multi-headed snakes, contorted about the stalks of vegetation.

While Roger and I were still contemplating where we might get the most comfortable rest, Cecil, Gordon, and George decided on their positions for the night. As I looked up at a fat rain-bearing cloud, I wasn't so sure. I joined George and, using our handkerchiefs as strainers, strained some water which we collected from the wild pines around. Roger got the Primus stove going. We boiled the filtrate for ten minutes or so, hoping it would serve our needs.

Since we were on a ridge, the sun didn't set until after 6.00 p.m. This gave us ample time to arrange our niches for the night. By 6:30, we were all tucked in. I turned on my trusty transistor radio, but got no clear reception from either of the two radio stations: Radio Jamaica & Rediffusion (RJR) and Jamaica Broadcasting Corporation (JBC).

The moon rose and filtered its glow through the light fog that moved quickly over our world. It was fairly commonplace not to have completely dark nights along the ridges. Tonight was no exception. At that height, it was a nature display that struck me as wondrously routine. By 7:00 p.m., a ring of well-saturated rain clouds had encircled the moon, producing a magnificent colour spectrum. The whole thing reminded me of the aurora borealis and its mystical colouring. We were all bedded down in raincoats. Serenaded by the melodious song of the wind, we sank into a deep sleep.

About an hour later, our rest was rudely shattered by an ice-cold shower of rain. Since I had cocooned my lower half in plastic, I was comparatively warm but for the spots of condensation that dotted the inside. Our non-waterproof headwear, consisting of baseball caps and floppy bucket hats, only helped a bit to prevent the rain from pelting us directly. And then there was Roger's hat, which was made of a light plastic material with a small hole an inch or two from the rim. He wore it at a slight tilt and skilfully manoeuvred the hole to be in line with his mouth. By doing so, he was able to feed himself a periodic dribble of water whenever he wanted.

The dampness of everything certainly made for a miserable night, but the water was not the worst part of it. I awoke at about 10:00 p.m. And, glancing upwards, thought that I was looking at creatures strolling on the surface of the moon. Was I becoming delirious? I was stunned for the moment, thinking how strange a thing my grogginess and the mountain air had conjured up.

It was we who were alien to the area. What I then saw was that the sheaves of elephant grass covering us were infested with giant wasps. The insects apparently lived in the roots of the grass, and like nocturnal burrowers (such as crabs), left their lodgings for drier accommodation during rainfall. As the wind intensified and the sheaves swayed more purposefully to it, so did the flight of the swarm of giant nervous-looking insects.

The moonlight seemed to enhance their activity and we were not at a loss for cuss words when at last they attacked—first Gordon (wrist) and Cecil (a finger and shoulder)—but we could not and did not move. We just figured that it was too late, and we were too exhausted to fight back and enrage them even more. How the rest of us avoided getting stung was simply a matter of good fortune.

We and the giant wasps survived the night.

CHAPTER 9

DESCENDING INTO THE ABYSS

Tuesday, December 19, 1967 (Day 4)

We awoke with the sun and were surprised not to see the big wasps anywhere. All of us were a bit grumpy, but grateful to have survived another night without any serious problems. Apparently, and thankfully, the insects had returned to the roots of the elephant grass. Cecil awoke with a waterlogged and aching ear. After draining his ear, he got a bit of relief once I poured a capful of my white rum into it.

The ridge looked clear, and in the distance we could discern Main Ridge Gap. Unfortunately, despite our assessment the previous afternoon, between ourselves and the gap lay 300 yards of hopelessly intermeshed foliage comprising shrubs, ferns, and some trees.

Our conversation on the situation went ahead in good democratic fashion, but we knew beforehand that we couldn't achieve our next target destination with the dwindling food and an almost depleted water supply. It was massively disappointing and sobering, but we knew better than to chance unnecessary vulnerability in this sort of terrain.

The deliberations focused on what we would do differently. The new plan required that we would no longer take the ridge to Mossman's Peak, Portland Gap, and then onward to Blue Mountain Peak. We would, if we could, find our 'alternate route' (as the map indicated) by hitting a trail beginning up ahead at Main Ridge Gap instead.

From there, we would descend the ridge on the south side and follow the tributary of the Green River to its junction with the Yallahs

River via Farm Hill Works and Penlyne Castle. We could then pick up the trail to Mavis Bank. We actually didn't have an option at this point, having arrived at a spot on the map close to the Gap where a trail was indicated. Try as we might, we were certain that we would not find a trail or track, with nothing to follow. To make matters worse, the environs were now completely fogged over and we could just barely make out the tree shapes around us. Our good fortune, such as it was, had begun to run out.

I felt that there was a collective sense of 'obstacles and crossroads' among the boys, but no one voiced it definitively. We had been ahead of schedule, but something felt different now. Our interactions had a different tone. The substance of our talk lacked much of its former togetherness. None of us was sure of himself anymore.

We continued to fumble around the perimeter of the gap and thought ourselves extremely fortunate to find what we thought was the track to Farm Hill Works. Instead, it turned out to be the beginning of a little river course. This served to raise our hopes quite a bit. Its waterway was quite dry, but we were sure that shortly it would lead to life, to drinking water, to a proper trail. We passed by a hog-wallow, but saw no sign of animals.

The last of our water was gone.

The largely unspoken anxiety to find water made us quicken the pace. We stopped only now and then to suck on any damp thing we came across, be it moss-covered stones, rain-saturated tree ferns, or wild pines. Sometimes we paused briefly but only out of necessity after each attempt to extract water or to spit out insects and prickly contaminants. With the persistent fog all around and no proper sunlight to show the way, we could not tell in which direction the ridge lay.

Furthermore, we were so preoccupied with the need to find water that we accepted the rather baseless conviction that we were on track to reach the Yallahs River. We needed, therefore, only to stay on course. As a consequence, we did not use our compass. Not that the device would have helped us any because we no longer had a reference point from which to take a reading and correctly determine a target.

The 'trail' wound maddeningly in 'S' bends, seemingly in circles. According to one of the boys who had been to the Peak before, it reminded him of a very similar feature encountered on the ascent along the regular trail, known as Jacob's Ladder; north one minute, east, west, then south and north again, constantly traversing steep terrain, trending downwards overall, but ascending and descending all the time.

At 11:15 a.m., we were thrilled to finally hear the sound of running water. Joy turned to horror when we realized that the river, which seemed so close, was separated from us by the ledge of a dry fifty-foot waterfall—dry, just like what we had encountered at the head of the river, but much more formidable.

George went down first, and we lowered the haversacks to him by rope. Gordon and I stayed put, waiting for a response from Roger and Cecil. They had climbed up the sheer adjacent cliff on the left side of the riverbed in an attempt to reach the water source. The trouble was that as soon as water appeared, it did so as a thin film of water on the surface of a miniature waterfall before disappearing underground.

In minutes, a shout of joy ripped through the silence.

"Pass me the rope! This t'ing really taste good!" Roger shouted after downing a canteen full of water. He was beside himself with glee, and was soon putting a refill to his head and drinking deeply. Without further bidding, we gentled down my big plastic container and watched, mesmerized, as the rope brought it back up again, brimming with the clear, life-saving stuff. The bottle made several more trips.

Before setting out, we rested in the spot for about twenty minutes feeling mightily relieved. We remained aware, though, as we got going, that neither food nor water would satisfy us as long as we couldn't get our bearings for a clear way home.

About 1:00 p.m. we got to the head of the river after some tough going along its rocky bed. In fact, it had been flowing underground all along, but it was only here that we got a good idea of its size. Whenever we could, we waded along in the water, which was only one or two feet deep at the start. Before long, when we came across something insurmountable like a waterfall or some other obstacle, we left the river and climbed up onto the lower ridge, whether it was on our left or right.

Whichever ridge we chose, we always found the going harder than it had been in the river. After trading difficult for more difficult on three occasions, we'd had enough, and returned to the river to make our way from a point where it looked like it might level out. Very soon after we did so, we came upon another waterfall. Luckily, there was a reasonable way to move past it.

Across the ridge we just descended, the bank was much gentler. The water was now about three feet deep, so we set out to cross it and follow that bank. Roger, Cecil, and Gordon inched their way along successfully, taking the precarious route along the waterfall's ledge, a truly treacherous surface. Although three of us were safely over, what we were doing at this point had an obvious inherent danger. The waterfall, twenty feet high and just as wide, had a rock ledge that had been smoothed by water over the ages and was very slippery underfoot.

George followed suit, but was handicapped by his British leather-soled combat boots, the kind with steel studs in the soles. Armed with the cutlass in his right hand and the map, rope, and compass in his left, he got himself onto the ledge. With his hands occupied, he struggled for balance a few times, always in danger of losing all his tools. Then, very soon after he started out on the surface, he slipped. Mercifully, George had the presence of mind to let go of the cutlass. He steadied himself, just enough to grab on to the edge of a protruding rock.

By that time, I had manoeuvred into position to help him to safe footing. A clear sense of tension lingered strongly until we were both safely over. Once we were all together on the other side, the relief of the group was palpable. But we were also coming to grips with the loss of one of our two machetes, knowing that trying to find it in the turbulent foam below would not be worth the risk. Nobody bothered trying. We were still five, but the team was now down to one chopping implement and without a file.*

The valley now began to darken and George called a halt to our current progress, suggesting that we give up on following the river and

---

* Unlike ourselves, the 1939 group had no cutlasses, but did have an axe and a file.

cross up on to the ridge to our left. It was horrendously steep on its eastern side. We pressed on anyway, trying to get around to the south side so as to avoid another night of northeasterly winds. With the south slope of the ridge no more than thirty degrees off vertical, what we saw made it almost foolhardy to climb.

The massive trees were now spread out randomly at about six-foot intervals. Moving uphill from one to another was only accomplished by bending over almost parallel to the ground. For support, we used our hands to dig divots into the soil for support. Seldom, however, was there much to grab onto. At times, two steps uphill resulted in a fall back down one. A much-needed rest was taken at every second tree, and there were numerous occasions where the only way forward was to crawl on our stomachs and dig in with hands and feet before pulling ourselves along the surface of the ground. Fingernails sometimes broke and the skin of our fingertips appeared to have been stripped by rough sandpaper (as was someone's chin). In addition, the pain from the blisters between thumb and forefinger caused by our constant chopping with the cutlass became even worse.

"Head for the top!" George commanded half-heartedly, "there's still some sunlight up there!"

I followed, presuming that someone else was carrying my second haversack. Hope was beginning to drain from me. Ten minutes had passed. There was no shout from the man up front, and no welcome news was forthcoming.

Finally, we heard, "We haven't reached the top yet!"

It was then that George and I both stopped at the root of an enormous, broad-rooted tree. We shouted to the others to return and guided them down to us with flashlight signals. The tree root was three feet wide, shaped very irregularly and similar to that of a cotton tree. It had other smaller trees and vines all around, like a handy wild coat rack for securing our haversacks. We boiled* an entire pot of chicken noodle soup, then devoured it in short order

The flashlight had to be used sparingly to enable us to change our clothing. To bed down, everyone except Gordon aligned himself with the steep slope of the ridge, feet resting against the small trees and vines around it so as to resist rolling or sliding downhill. That was all the space available for this particular sleeping arrangement. It would have been enough, too, had Gordon not squeezed himself between the tree and our feet. Although it would just spit rain over the hours that followed, that night at Camp Site 4 proved to be one of our most uncomfortable.

★ ★ ★

On Windsor Avenue, folks began to miss having me around. Although the festivities had been over for more than a year, we might have still been discussing some of the highlights of the August 1966 Commonwealth Games, where I had been an official with all the attendant privileges. I managed to get free passes to many of the events, most of the times enough to be able to share them with my comrades. Sometimes when we didn't have the right credentials, we would just 'beat the gate' by using one of the unofficial tunnels.

Windsor Avenue was only a short run away from the National Stadium via the dreaded Bundy Lane and what is now Arthur Wint Drive, the main approach to the sporting complex. I didn't fear the area, however, as my father, a people's man, was well liked over there. I guess he was loved but also feared. At some point, he may have begun walking around at night with his twelve-gauge shotgun, flashlight, and dog while doing his rounds; he'd check windows, and pipes for leaks and so on, once he had designated himself the neighbourhood watchman. Everyone on Windsor, Old Hope Road, and Bundy Lane knew

---

* Water and many other liquids boil at a relatively lower temperature at these elevations due to the reduced air pressure. Coupled with this and the constant cold weather, the resulting product was a drink that was only a little more than lukewarm.

that Mr. H was armed; they slept without a worry. During the daytime, with all that time on his hands, he would often hold court for hours in one of the neighbourhood's Chinese grocery stores or pet stores, engaging the congregated locals in discussions about the topics of the day.

Writing nearly fifty years later, my trusted friend, Robin Crawford, remembers how he felt on that fourth day after we had set out:

> I remember your nervous energy on the morning that you left. I remember thinking how lucky you were at having the opportunity to embark on such an exciting-sounding adventure. However, I don't recall being jealous or envious. If anything, I remember a feeling of emptiness and, looking back, I may have been a tad melancholy at the thought of not having my good friend around at the start of the crucial Christmas 'holidays'.

> I was on the side of the road just outside my gate at #16 late Tuesday afternoon—the date [the fourth day after leaving] you had said you had planned to return—when I flagged down Mr. Haddad, who was driving home.

> We all had assumed that he had gone to collect you, but were very disappointed to learn that you had not yet shown up. I was very troubled to also learn that none of the other parents received any word from the group. Mr. Haddad however, was not particularly perturbed as he was an avid bird-hunter and therefore was somewhat of a bush man himself. He might even have been a bit upbeat with the confidence that you would be home 'at any minute'. Perhaps he was hiding his real feelings! We all had heard of the many trips he made both by mule and by foot to the foothills of the Blue Mountains to hunt ringtails.

> On another note, I vividly remember thinking at that time about the cages in his back yard in which he kept and bred white wings, peadoves, and barble doves. He

had some baldpates, one of which survived twenty-three years, a feat unheard of in the wild.

A number of these were ones which he wounded in the bush but had a chance of living, so he nurtured them back to health. He was sympathetic in many ways.

We all agreed that later that evening or the next day—after all, it was supposed to be a 3–4 day hike at a maximum—the travellers would suddenly materialize around the bend at the upper end of Windsor Avenue and beguile us with tall tales of their adventure.

But that was not to be the case.

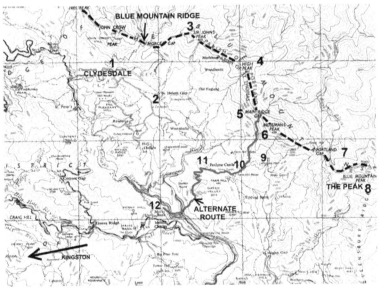

Top: Jamaica College sixth formers huddle to examine the book's manuscript in Simms Hall, sitting in the same location in 2013 where the 1967 Blue Mountain plans were hatched — Photo taken by Geoffrey B. Haddad

Bottom: The route planned by the Blue Mountain five in 1967, showing key numbered targets 1–8. As a failsafe, the boys planned an alternate route, 9–12, if conditions made it necessary

Top: An aerial view of the route planned by the boys, showing elevations — Photo courtesy of Jack Tyndale-Biscoe

Bottom: Saturday, December 16, 1967:, The five hikers unload their packs at the first staging area at Clydesdale. At left is Mr. Cooper's Humber Sceptre, the last vestige of civilization. It is the last time that all the boys appear in the same photograph on their trip. *Left to right:* Gordon Cooper, George Hussey, Roger Bates, me , and Cecil Ward — Photo taken by Mr. Charles Cooper

Top: Panoramic view of the Blue Mountain Ridge looking north towards (left to right): John Crow Peak, Morces Gap and Sir Johns Peak. Photo taken Sunday, December 17, 1967 from St. Helen's Gap.

Bottom left: Cecil takes up his position in tree at St. Johns. *Bottom right:* with the blade coming perilously close to his ear, Cecil hacks through the fern and tree thicket high up in the jungle terrain.

I (in cap) make my way with George (behind) and Cecil through the dense mountain forest. Note the water bottle strapped to my backpack; I only brought it along at the insistence of my father.

Top: I, on the left, take a break in the bush en route to Main Ridge Gap with (from left) Cecil (who was out cold), George, and Gordon.

Centre: The boys settle in, surrounded by elephant grass, Left to right: Me, Cecil, Gordon, and George (checking map).

Bottom: George gets a fire started, while I (holding up a pot at right) petition the others for breakfast. Cecil (back to camera) looks on wearing Roger's plastic hat. *Photos courtesy of Roger Bates.*

Top: Taken during one of the few brief breaks in the weather; I'm standing in my raincoat, at Main Ridge Gap, with Jamaica's north coast in the distance.

Centre left: Dressed in raincoats, we assess the situation with the north coast in the distance.

Centre right: Cecil writes in his diary at Main Ridge Gap.

Bottom: Looking southeast towards the trail from Mavis Bank to Blue Mountain Peak and the island's south coast.

Top: Cloud formation on the south side of the Blue Mountains. Note cottage at Blue Mountain Peak at lower left.

Bottom: These waterfalls (which can be as high as 1000 feet) and landslides are typical of the terrain on the north (Portland) side of Jamaica's Blue Mountains. *Photos courtesy of J. S. Tyndale-Biscoe.*

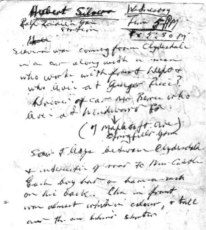

Top left: B. S. Haddad's detailed notes chronicle his understanding of the boys' plans and actions in the mountains, from Desmond Stanley. Right: B. S. Haddad's appeal to the Police at Mavis Bank.

Bottom left: A report that the five boys - "one almost white in colour" - had been seen between Clydesdale and the intersection of the road to Newcastle - a place we never visited or stopped.

Bottom right: This aquamarine pool at Reich Falls in Portland is very similar to the one we found on the Speculation River. When we reached it, we thought it strange that such clear blue water, so high above sea level and on such a fast-flowing river, could exist.

CHAPTER 10

DEEP IN THE MOUNTAIN JUNGLE

Wednesday, December 20, 1967 (Day 5)

Our grumbling bellies awoke us. It was not until now, when it was time to plan for a meal, that we realized that someone had forgotten to bring along my second backpack. It had been left a good distance behind in our haste to get uphill on the previous night. Right away, an argument broke out over how stupid the person was to have left such a valuable item behind. After all, it contained our potatoes and the water bottle with the majority of our remaining water supply. Even more problematic was the question of who was going to go get it.

The boisterous argument resolved one thing unanimously: Gordon would go, not because he drew the short straw or anything so democratic, but because he caused the commotion during the night that resulted in none of us getting a good night's sleep. We waited anxiously for him to get back. After much cussing, Gordon reappeared, exhausted as the day before, but with the second haversack and water bottle in hand.

Roger's Primus had only a little kerosene left, and we didn't want to exhaust it. Instead of making a beverage, we opted for two spoonfuls of Milo, some condensed milk, and a mouthful each of water. The sweet taste was a welcome alternative to more noodle soup, and the sugar put us in rather a good mood. We broke camp shortly before eight o'clock.

I changed my shoes before moving out. The ones I had set out in were now threadbare, to say the least. Soles smooth as a baby's bottom, they had the toes on the right foot 'beggin' bread' as we would say when toes burst out of shoes, exposed. It wasn't like I hadn't anticipated their demise. After having spent so much time tramping around in the hills or on rough concrete badminton courts, I knew how much life my rubber-soled shoes had in them. They were hardy, to be sure. Manufactured by the Bata Shoe Company and known locally as 'buggas' or 'crepes' (sneakers), they were perfect for school activities and jaunts around town, but were no match for what I'd put them through over those past several days.

I had always kept two pairs. Breaking in a new one took some time, and it was never practical to wear fresh ones on the court, especially during a hotly contested match. A certain amount of slippage or 'give' between the shoe and court was required so as to reduce the possibility of seriously injuring my ankles. I wore them alternately until one cried out for replacement. To reduce friction between my feet and the sole of the shoe, I used a trick taught to me by my father, who had also taught me skills for the mountain hike itself. Soak the socks in soapy water, he would say, and allow them to dry like that. The result was less friction between sock and foot, less chance of blisters and reduced pressure on the footwear, thus extending its lifetime. It actually worked and was now most useful, particularly when going downhill.

A pair of Bata sneakers in those days would set you back thirty shillings, the equivalent of four American dollars at the time. They were by no means cheap, but a worthwhile investment, especially for the mileage I could expect to get. The fact that I had a back-up pair with me wasn't as well thought out as it might seem, though, because this time, I had started out wearing my better pair. Now that the newer Batas had expired, I had to turn to their replacements, which were already three-quarters worn. I remember hearing that distributors La Parisienne, which I believe was part of the Hanna Empire, once sold 400 pairs of Clarks shoes in five days to stores in the city. Clarks, the popular desert boots, and Wallabees were all the rage in Kingston at the time, and I would have given anything at that moment for a pair.

We completed the rest of the walk up to the top of the ridge in good time. The fog had cleared momentarily and a view of the range of the hills ahead was picture-postcard clear. From there, we hoped to see cultivation, habitation, any sign of human life.

"You recognise any of those hills, Roger?" I asked.

"Difficult to say, G. B., but that dip at the end of the range may be Hagley Gap," he replied, pointing to what he believed was the trail leading from Main Ridge Gap to Mavis Bank, the alternate route we had planned.

We followed the top of the ridge for five minutes or so with the dull cacophony of our pots banging defiantly against the peace of running water.

The general mood turned to excitement.

"Ah find a track!" Gordon shouted at the top of his voice.

"Yu lie!" Roger returned.

"Hey Gordon, lemme see dat t'ing," I demanded, ready to lay eyes on a saving trail.

"This probably is the trail to Mavis Bank," George mused.

"Bwoy, I supposed to be home today," I heard myself interject, cutting to the heart of my concerns. "If ah don't reach, panic will reign."

After following the path for an hour or so, it just disappeared. The only thing to do now was to backtrack.

"Well, that's an hour wasted," George said, disheartened.

Our spirits lightened in anticipation of regaining our bearings. The pace quickened. We were also descending marginally as we continued. At times, the path seemed to vanish, but just as before, it would reappear underfoot in a matter of a few feet. Only about two feet wide, it was a virtual highway to us compared to what we had been seeing. We thought a bird hunter might have made it, but couldn't be sure.

I was now walking the point. Apparently, from the mutterings behind me, I was always going too fast when it was my turn. About a half mile down the track, my progress stopped when I saw some fresh bird feathers and two empty twelve-gauge shotgun cartridges. I waited for the others to catch up. We were not in no-man's territory, then, we thought. A little farther along, we saw more empty cartridges and a few rusted tins. I picked up a few cartridges, rolling them back and forth in the palm of my hand for closer inspection. From their condition, they looked like they had been fired no more than a few weeks before. We just couldn't make a connection between the rusted cartridges and fresh feathers. Perhaps a bird had succumbed naturally and had its feathers scattered by scavengers.

Bulla is a hard, round gingery sweet bread that is another favourite of Jamaicans, who enjoy it with pear (avocado) or cheese. Like the world-famous Jamaican patty, the treat is enjoyed year round.

Closely related to the lychee and longan, the ackee is a fruit brought from West Africa to Jamaica to feed slaves, and is one of the components of Jamaica's national dish, ackee and salt fish. The ackee tree bears reddish pods which house three or more yellow, black-seeded arilli which are extricated when the pod ripens and opens naturally. The ackee is cooked with seasoned codfish and though eaten most often as a breakfast dish, it is enjoyed by Jamaicans anytime and anywhere. A note of warning: Ackee must be allowed to ripen fully naturally, then picked and prepared properly. If not, the fruit's toxins can suppress the body's ability to release appropriate supplies of glucose, which then plunges the blood sugar level, potentially leading to fatal levels of hypoglycemia. In Jamaica over the years, several deaths have resulted from ackee poisoning, which is commonly referred to a 'vomiting sickness'.

As we pressed on, I was still up front when we came upon faint traces of footprints. They couldn't have been more than three or four days old by my reckoning. Spirits were buoyed again.

"All I want when we get to Mavis Bank is one dozen bulla an' two col' Pepsi," Cecil said.

Someone seconded that motion. Then we dreamed up a catalogue of food orders for the lucky shopkeeper at Mavis Bank.

Roger knew of a little shop not far from there that sold hard-dough bread and salt fish. At the mention of this mouth-watering delicacy (although it is anything but that) we fantasized greedily, leading to talk of our other favourite dishes: sweet-and-sour duck, shrimp fried rice, ackee and salt fish, and the like. It wasn't the smartest thing to do when we were so far removed from more luxurious fare, but we were quite hungry. Fantasizing about food only made it worse.

The trail led us up and down two ridges until it finally disappeared at a point of flowing water we took to be the junction of the headwaters of the Green River. We did not discuss our assumption in any great detail, but we knew that that river flowed southwards to Mavis Bank where it joined the Yallahs River. The two bodies are key to the regional water supply, serving not only that area but the nation's capital as well. Their waters were diverted to Kingston via a nineteen-mile pipeline to the city's main reservoir at Mona, adjacent to Jamaica's campus of the University of the West Indies.

We crossed the river, a mere two feet deep, and on the other side paused to devour, rather than savour, our last barbecued chicken. Despite our privation and other difficulties, we weren't surprised when Roger again insisted on having the 'parson's nose'. I asked George whether we had any peppermints left, but the mints, the chewing gum, the little barley sweets, and the glucose tablets were gone, apparently disposed of at a tremendous rate.

When the meal was fairly well digested, we resumed our accustomed tack of following the river. As we had now become used to doing, we had to leave it whenever the course threw up some impossible waterfall in our way. Afterwards, it would always mean a significant expenditure of time and effort to get ourselves back onto the ridge.

We were plagued by wasps, as well as the cockroaches that had begun to infest our bags, but it was up for speculation as to whether the vermin in our bags had already nestled there before we left home. When mosquitoes started to harass us, however, the other kinds of bugs were a small nuisance by comparison. And mosquitoes were up there in abundance, renewing their efforts at drying out our blood supply. Their numbers were aided by infinite numbers of water puddles that collected into rock beds for their wholesale regeneration. It was nothing personal, but just like the wasps had, they buzzed and stung as if they quite resented our intrusion into their world.

Darkness overtook us on a fairly gentle slope. We took immediate advantage by felling a few small trees and erecting a frame for our first lean-to. It was about two feet high by six feet wide by six feet long. We roofed it with broad leaves, which also proved useful for covering the ground. For added protection against the inevitable rain, we put our raincoats on the roof, thinking that they should be enough.

This was Wednesday. We were all supposed to be home already.

★ ★ ★

It had been a long and hard day's tramp, and we were tired and hungry. Next, our attention turned to feeding ourselves, and as we sat down to enjoy the pound of boiled rice that beckoned from the stove, I was the only one who mentioned our deadline or the little matter of worried parents down in Kingston. At the time, the others didn't appear the least bit concerned.

It seemed like so long since we set out, from the time when I'd last seen my trusted friend, Robin Crawford. I told him that our hiking plans were unconventional and asked him to keep them secret, especially from my father. Why worry him needlessly? "Call out the army," I remembered saying to him, however jokingly, "if I'm not back by Wednesday, December 20." Just like that. Now, I was hoping and praying that Robin would remember the half-joke and take it seriously. I had said it in such a glib manner, and now Wednesday had not found us safely home. Nobody had broached the subject as yet, but it was beginning to seem quite likely that we were in very real need of having somebody sent out to find us. I hoped now that my friend's intuition about trouble would spur him to do something.

My parting words to Robin gnawed at me. What had been flippant to my mind turned out to be deadly to his. Two recollections, nearly fifty years later, give voice to events as they occurred. First, Robin Crawford's:

> Tuesday evening dragged into Wednesday morning (December 20) and soon there was a frenzy of telephone calls between the concerned parents and the authorities. Surely one of the group would have had the sense to call. Still, I was fairly confident that everything was fine. After all, surely Geoff had purposely given some slack in the timing when he confided in me, saying, "If I am not back by Wednesday, call out the army." I was now holding an important piece of information that would

need to be shared no later than Thursday (tomorrow) morning.

By this time, rumours of sightings were beginning to crop up but none seemed to pan out. The seasonal cool Christmas breezes were beginning to sweep the plains of St. Andrew, reminding everyone of the relative temperatures that prevailed on the mountain. There were also forecasts of rain to worry about. Could supplies have been depleted? The late-night radio bulletins served to intensify the anxiety and amplify the concerns being felt by everyone.

It was that time of year. Parties were being held and there was no Geoff. I remember one at the Ho Lung's at 23 Windsor where his speciality, Chinese food, was being served. I could see the pleasure in his face as he gobbled down his favourite items. His girlfriend at the time began to call, particularly in respect of the 'secret' I had divulged to her at Cable Hut Beach on Sunday the 17th. She was also missing the parties and was to miss those to come.

The nights especially brought about a sense of trepidation for the plight of the teens that were now confirmed missing in the Blue Mountains. I lay in bed, listening to news on my transistor radio, thinking about the hikers and trying to block out my worst fears. We congregated daily at #25 for the latest updates. Later on I shared with Norma the fateful words that haunted me, but I was of the opinion that already the police and military were in full search-and-rescue mode. With my hand-me-down 8mm movie camera always close at hand, I daydreamed about being the first to spot Geoff and the others, filming them as they coolly walked down the road with big smiles on their faces.

And this from Carlysle Hudson:

> My recollection of the event, as we all move towards
> slight Alzheimer's, was that we (the Windsor Avenue
> group) were all really concerned, worried, panicked,
> and totally shocked about Geoff's disappearance days in
> the mountains from a hiking trip. We prayed collectively
> and individually for his/their safe return. We all had
> positive thoughts throughout the episode.
>
> We all gathered daily for several hours at Geoffrey's
> home at Windsor Avenue after listening to the news
> on the radio and other press of the missing boys to try
> and come up with a plan of how we could find them
> and also to try and console the entire Haddad family,
> who were distraught because of his disappearance. But
> those plans were to no avail on days one and two, which
> made it even more worrisome.

★ ★ ★

I turned on the transistor radio, but there was no music, or news
forthcoming, nothing more than a steady stream of static. The isolation
was complete and depressing. Our sense of alienation deepened.

Later that night, Gordon and Cecil beckoned me aside. We were
out of earshot of the other two fellows when they told me what they
were feeling.

"G. B.," Gordon confided, "we t'ink we in trouble. We shoulda been
home today and the parents must be worried. We behin' schedule,
almost out of food and water, and everybody starting to feel weak. No
way we goin' make it to the Peak. We know you a bush man. Me and
Cece wan' turn back while we still have a chance to get out. We wan'
turn back an' head for home. What you t'ink?"

My instinct was to be inclusive and maintain the strength of our
numbers. "De way I see it is if we going turn back is all five a we
turning back. We have to be united. I'm not interested in that, but you

guys can talk to Roger and George if you like; after all, George is the 'leader'. This was his and his uncle's idea."

Furthermore, the whole time we moved around, we had not thought to use the cutlass to make notches on the trees as we passed them. How could we have forgotten to mark the way? Hansel and Gretel remembered; so did Theseus in the Minotaur's labyrinth. You're supposed to leave marks behind that will show the way back. We were in this pickle partly because we did not plan to return the same way we came.

When we were supposed to smash through the roots in our way, we had traversed the lighter ones, deceiving ourselves that our direction would turn out to be the same. This was a huge mistake. To keep on our calculated course, we needed to have broken through the roots that made the going difficult. By choosing the path of least resistance, we had veered off course. We were never going to return past the wasps, the camp on the slope, the shotgun cartridges or the giant shelter rocks. There was no going home that way. After all, we had set out determined to make the Peak via a lesser known, perhaps entirely nonexistent path. Nightmares do come true.

No more was said as we returned to camp, and somehow, the group dynamic had changed. Fear began to creep in. Those of us who had talked about the way forward now disagreed on what to do, and there was an uneasy feeling of betrayal emerging, a sense that we had not all hashed it out together. Gordon and Cecil became more vocal, echoing each other with their grave concerns.

"Why should we continue at this point? We're not in charge of what we're doing anymore. We need the help of God to get out of here," and so on.

It began to appear that they might make their own decision to separate from the rest of us and turn back together. I was scared too, but tried hard to remain calm. Undoubtedly, we would not conquer the Peak as originally planned, but I knew we couldn't retrace our steps either, since we had left no trail. It would be virtually impossible for anyone to find any trace of us, never mind the tarpaulin. Additionally, after the first few days, with little or no food left, there was not much waste left behind, whether the commercial or human kind, and so that would not have provided any clues for rescuers either. After all, we generated almost no trash and would never have 'done our business' close to our campsites or trail.

All rivers run to the sea, right? That was a mantra that also had to be our way out. But which river? At which coast and at which town would we arrive? Not that any of that mattered. Any town would lead us home.

There was a paradigm shift in my thinking, probably in the minds of the other guys as well. Defeat no longer rested in not doing the hike we had planned. We were past that. Defeat would rest in not getting out alive. I would have to rely on all the training I had as a Cub Scout, Boy Scout, and bird hunter. It was going to take everything I had.

We were now at Camp 5. As we sat around feeling pretty low in our predicament, George provided some comic relief. A small whistling frog was caught in the beam of his flashlight.

"Come ya mek me eat yu, froggie," he mugged.

For some reason, perhaps starvation for levity, we found the remark very funny and for a while, we had fun imitating him. We might have stayed up late to enjoy the distraction some more, but we were tired to the bone and had to make preparations for sleep. The two sleeping bags we had, however, were rain-soaked. Ignoring their condition, we spread them on the ground just as they were and shared our blankets.

Roger, who had been left outside while he was packing his Primus stove, could not fit under the lean-to. When he finally joined us, the situation had reversed itself momentarily. Cold wind and rain were conspiring to force me more and more towards the right-hand side of the structure. I could bear the rain falling directly on me, but I was being made most uncomfortable by the overflow of water that was collecting in small pools on the roof. By inching away from the annoying drops, I created a space at the foot of the lean-to; Roger took it.

A Jamaican whistling frog.

We noted thankfully that the mosquitoes seemed to have gone in search of a drier location. Not surprisingly, a good night's rest wasn't in the cards that night. I might have dozed for ten minutes or so before I was awakened by the overflow of water from my own ear. I emptied it and used a plastic bag and towel-pillow to prevent any recurrence.

We were now a full day late in getting back to Kingston, and thoroughly lost, a fact that we were now beginning to accept. Hopefully, someone down there would as well.

★ ★ ★

The planned mountain trail had by now become public knowledge. Our lateness was not lost on my father, who sprang into action by going to meet with personnel from the Jamaica Defence Force. He also telephoned George's house and demanded to know what his family was doing to find us. It wasn't his first call. Mrs. Hussey's response usually ran something like this:

"What will George think of me? He won't even think that I trust him. You're going to spoil their fun by having a search party find them!"

This kind of wishy-washiness in a life-or-death matter would only have served to make my father absolutely berserk.

On that Wednesday night, when we were beginning to really imagine the level of our parents' concern, Mrs. Hussey was down in Kingston saying that Desmond Stanley, her brother, had gone up to Whitfield Hall to collect us. He did not think, she said, that we would have got out before then. My father let it go at that for the moment, and asked Mrs. Hussey to have Stanley contact him as soon as he got back.

As my dad must have feared, Roger's father returned from Mavis Bank, having gone there from earlier in the day, saying that he had found no trace whatsoever of us. Stanley's call that night communicated the same thing, but he at least promised he would return to the area the next day to try again.

My father was a meticulous man, even in ordinary non-crisis situations. He was a careful listener, an almost non-stop talker, and quite relentless in pursuit of what he thought was right, reasonable or even promising. He had always kept copious notes, and now that he was retired and found himself in this extraordinary circumstance, he fell back upon what had always served him well. Immediately after speaking with Stanley, he penned these notes:

> Route planned by Mr. Desmond Stanley, Phone 41388,
> as follows: Cinchona, Morces Gap,* Mossman's Peak
> via Ridge to Portland Gap to Blue Mountain...If time
> is running out, they might return via Green River, or
> Farm Hill Works from Main Ridge Gap.

And this one, after a conversation with a man at the service station where he had stopped to refuel the big Ford:

> Hubert Silvera said that between 5:00 and 5:30 p.m. he
> was coming from Clydesdale in a car along with a man
> who works with the Forestry Department and who
> lives at Ginger River. The driver of the car, Mr. Berris,
> who lives at Windward Road (7 Mapletoft Avenue,
> Springfield Gardens) saw five boys between Clydesdale
> and intersection of a road to Newcastle. Each boy had a
> haversack on his back. One in front was almost white in
> colour and tall and the one behind, shorter.

My parents' house now served as the unofficial search and rescue operations centre. Once our expected return had passed the deadline, hundreds of telephone calls from concerned relatives, friends, and business associates began pouring in. Both radio stations had someone liaise with my home base through my sister Jennifer, who had for a while been writing down the names of everyone who called and asked to be notified of developments. It was neatly documented in her handwriting.

An urgent meeting was convened at the Haddad residence. Present were Ernest DeSouza and Phillip Langford. Both were family friends, scoutmasters, as well as ham radio operators. Langford had additional experience as a telecommunications and computer technology professional in both the UK and Jamaica. Two officers of the Air Wing Division of the JDF were also on hand.

---

* We had swapped our approach to Sir Johns for a more direct route, eliminating the need to pass through Morces Gap.

"According to Cooper," my father surmised, "he dropped the boys off on Saturday at Clydesdale around 3:00 p.m. They planned to hike to Cinchona and sleep there that night. According to Stanley, they were then to stay on top of the Blue Mountain Ridge and follow it all the way up to the Peak. He says that they should have been back today at the latest!"

Inevitably, B. S. Haddad's focus and emotions would turn to his thoughts of me.

"Well, my son is up there," he said firmly, "so damn Stanley and his plans, that bush—you have any idea what Portland jungle looks like, man? I've been in the area, in the foothills many times. I've always done the trail by mule, but never on foot through the bush! There's enough prickle, grass, and vines in that jungle to wrap them up. There's also ferrel* grass to contend with, you know. Hell knows how tall the trees are wherever they are and no sunlight. They can disappear in there, Phillip! What do you think?"

"OK, here is the topography for the area," Phillip offered as he unrolled a map. "In that kind of terrain, I doubt a soldier worth his salt could even cover two to three miles in a day," he said. On the chart, he used his compass to scribe two-mile incremental concentric circles from Sir Johns Peak.

"Take a look at this."

My father was distraught but logical. "My God, you can bet that they must be on the north side of the ridge," he reasoned, "and only enough food for four days. They must be almost dead. Have you been looking at the weather and the temperatures for that area? Below fifty degrees and rain, real Portland rain, for hours a day!"

The men were doing their best to divine what moves we might be making up there, thinking of how we would use our experience to minimize risk. "The best we can hope for," Phillip said grimly, "is that they've realized they're in over their heads. They're sensible boys; let's hope that they stay on the ridge and wait for help. May God stop them

---

*   A tubular fern known as ferule or bracken, commonly referred to as ferrel, in Jamaica.

from going down one of those gorges into Portland. This is day five. So let's look at the circle here using a ten-mile radius, and here, they could be anywhere in this shaded area."

"Damn it, man! This is serious stuff. My son is up there; I'm not waiting here any longer!"

B. S. Haddad was a man of care and control, but his fuse was lit, and an explosion could not be far off. As good as his word, he made contact with Commissioner of Police Gordon Langdon, as well as Army Lieutenant Colonel Rudolph Green and Brigadier General David Smith. He arranged to meet with the officers. Soon after that, he made the short trip south on Old Hope Road to South Camp Road and into the military's headquarters at Up Park Camp.

Undercooked and overconfident, our simple and daring plan was now a national problem. Within a short time of my father's initiative, two national uniformed forces were developing emergency plans, with five lost schoolboys as the objective. The soldiers and police would be able to draw on their experience and training in search and rescue, some of it in those very mountains.

CHAPTER 11

WANDERING AIMLESSLY

Thursday, December 21, 1967 (Day 6)

Back in Kingston, Roderic Crawford recalls, nearly fifty years later, that B. S. appeared cautiously optimistic.

> B. S. appeared positive while theorizing what we might have been up to. I believe that Norma [my mother] panicked much earlier in the game, but B. S. lost it near the end. This is somewhat anecdotal as it may have been intimated to me from Huddy while describing B. S.'s sudden burst of emotion while in the midst of talking up a storm.

Almost as confirmation of Roderic's supposition, B. S. dispatched the following note to the police at Mavis Bank:

> Send message to Whitfield Hall House (Mr. Allgrove) telling the boys to ask Mr. Allgrove to send a runner to postal agency to advise Kingston that they are safe. Police to tell them to come to the station at Mavis Bank and await transportation back home.

★ ★ ★

Thursday arrived with sunshine and clear skies that lifted our spirits. We hadn't seen such a cheery morning since Friday last, the day before we left Kingston, and it made us imagine a normal day in the city, with all its noises, smells, characters and, of course, the sight of the Christmas poinsettia, growing a brighter red every day we were gone.

We headed for the top of the ridge on which we had just spent the night. The sound of whistling frogs was replaced by the shrieking of solitaires, a small, insect-eating kind of thrush, just one of the many species of birds found at these elevations. After we got to the top, we chose to slide most of the way down via a dried-up tributary full of loose shale and small stones. More disappointment descended when the section of the 'river' we had so desperately anticipated turned out to be another waterfall. We would have to climb yet another ridge to get around it.

As if to dampen our spirits even more, the beautiful sky had darkened considerably, threatening rain that wasn't long in coming. We donned raincoats, refreshed by ducking our heads underwater, re-filled our canteens and big bottle, then got back to the task, holding our course to the top of the ridge to our right.

The earth was very loose in places, making the going quite precarious. Ever so often, the occasional small rock was dislodged and sent plunging while we carefully picked our way across rotten tree roots. The effort was backbreaking. Aside from the risky business of using a machete to dig hand divots and footholds into the hillside, the going was steep and threatened to pitch us over backwards, sometimes throwing one of us into a seemingly unstoppable slide down the hillside.

Tired, hungry, annoyed, and questioning our life choices, we managed to maintain a sense of 'just getting the thing done', which was by now a fairly joyless exercise. Having gained the top, we immediately descended some twenty feet on the other side and came upon another tree with gnarled, widely spread roots. These always signalled that they were places to take a breather. We took five minutes there but we were already more than despondent and quite upset at having not yet arrived at the sand banks of the Yallahs River. But what point was there in dwelling on it? We couldn't afford to be sabotaged by a paralyzing loss of hope.

The five of us moved wordlessly down the hillside at a speed comparable to a steamroller going uphill. I was ahead by some thirty feet;

Roger followed, about thirty feet above to my left. As a preventive rule, we did not normally descend any dangerous slope, especially one containing loose shale and rocks while moving in single file. We knew for certain that dislodging a sizeable stone and sending it hurtling down to the man in front could cause serious injury or worse.

I would be the one to test the rule.

"Watch out, G. B.!" Roger screamed to raise an alarm, breaking the stillness. When I heard the shout, I was clutching the roots of saplings not yet substantial enough to bear my weight. Spinning around, I saw that I was in the direct path of a sizeable boulder, twenty to twenty-five pounds in weight, thumping along as it hurtled at me. I had only a nauseating split second to appreciate the immediate danger before I let go of my petty support and cocooned my head between bent knees, body curled as low as I could get. I gambled and waited.

The seconds that followed seemed protracted and unreal. Then came the echoes of the rock splintering violently as it settled. Unfortunately, it had done human damage before it came to rest far below me.

"Coops, G. B. get lick, catch his haversack!" Roger yelled. There was also a bit of a landslide, which brought Roger scrambling to my rescue, sliding towards me on his behind. The next thing I knew, he was right there.

"You alright, G. B.?" he inquired, standing over me, frantic.

"How is everything down there? George shouted from farther back.

At first, I had no breath for an answer, leading Roger to ask the question over and over. When I finally could respond, it was to put voice to my shock and pain. I yelled in agony. George, Gordon, and Cecil, still some fifty feet above and behind me, heard my cries. They didn't show up on the spot as quickly, hindered perhaps by their care not to set off another landslide. Maybe they were afraid of what they would see. Roger yelled up a caution to Gordon, who thought that I was dead, telling him to tread carefully and to bring my haversack.

The rock had made contact with my backside just about my waist and hipbone, turning me violently around some 90 degrees to the left.

"Fine, thank heavens!" Roger finally yelled back. What he meant was that I was certainly neither dead nor seriously injured.

When the moment passed, I saw I was again clinging to some tiny tree, with no memory of how or when my arm stretched to grab onto it. I lay there still groaning, but holding on for dear life. I felt dazed, with my thoughts coming hard and fast, fuelled by the fear that this was the start of the end. *I won't be able to walk,* I thought. *If I can't continue, what will the fellows now have to contend with? Am I maimed?* We had no stretcher and no means of assembling a makeshift one. And even if we did, it would have been impossible to carry me through this kind of terrain and forest. Would they have to leave me and return with help later on? If they did leave, how and when would they find me again? Thankfully, none of these horrible things unfolded. I sustained a nasty bruise, but my hip and legs felt more normal soon, and I was able to continue.

We were all taken aback by how close we could have been to sudden tragedy. The others supported and commiserated with me until the shock, both physical and mental, subsided. A huge black-and-blue welt was beginning to develop, spreading halfway across my waist and hip. It was a bit frightening to look at, so I averted my eyes as they applied the Radian-B ointment. I just lay there, yielding to the soothing sensation that was coming from helpful hands. The salve worked well, so when I finally felt ready to move, we pushed on down towards the river.

We reached the water without any more close calls, but discovered that the river was flowing north!

This was not consistent with what we remembered from consulting our map. The consensus was that the Yallahs River should not be flowing in that direction at all, except for one point just above Mavis Bank—and even there, it would have been meandering in a north-northeasterly direction. Out came the map once more.

"I feel that we are in the Swift River valley," I said.

"But how could we be? Where did we go wrong?" Roger replied, defending the former alternative, believing that we could really be on the Yallahs River.

"Forgot it for the moment," George interjected, "let's try to cook something."

But we couldn't have been mistaken! No, had we been at the right spot, the river would have been bordered by wide sandy banks. We were someplace else, in some other river gorge, and there was little doubt that we were now in serious trouble. For us all to admit that, however, would have been an admission that we were now in an even bigger pickle than before. That would have been too much of a scare to grapple with just then. Map-reading notwithstanding, we chose to believe that we had to be on the Yallahs River; on the south side of the Blue Mountain Ridge.

Because we had frequently changed direction due to the contour of the land, with no reference point behind or up ahead, our compasses were no longer of any practical use. Later on, we would learn that the magnetic content of the rock and soil in certain areas of the Blue Mountain Ridge are so concentrated that they can cause an offset of up to thirty degrees with the most accurate of compasses. We understood that this was established by the British contingent at 'Calypso Hop', the traditional army exchange between the British military and members of the Jamaica Defence Force. Additionally, we often took compass readings with our cutlass in close proximity to our compass, sometimes even holding both cutlass and compass in the same hand. This of course provided us with less than accurate readings. Looking back now, I believe that that fact was unearthed much later into our journey when compasses really did not matter.

From that point, we crossed several tributaries of the river.* Mosquitoes harassed us ceaselessly, and our difficulties worsened as we tackled steeper inclines, narrower gorges, and faster flowing bodies of water. As if nature were mocking us in our depressed state, nightfall came earlier than expected, as can happen at higher elevations with this type of topography. The headwaters of the Swift River originate one mile below Blue Mountain Peak and meets the Speculation River approximately one mile north east of Mossman's Peak and a quarter mile north of Robinsons Flat at an elevation of 3000 feet.

---

* The river we were traversing all along was the Speculation and not the Swift. It is the largest 'tributary' to the Swift River and originates at Main Ridge Gap. This was later explained to me by mountaineer extraordinaire John Allgrove (a.k.a. Mountain Goat), whose family still owns the hostel at Whitfield Hall, and who continues to practice civil engineering.

Unknowingly at the time, the last river crossing we had made was that of the Swift River.

As the light faded away, we called council to decide on a site to bed down for the night. Before long, we agreed on a spot on the gorge's riverbank, which had a huge boulder to provide shelter from the direct cold air draught of the river. We built our second lean-to on the leeward side of the huge rock, and we were grateful for whatever comfort it could provide as we bedded down for the night. My pains from the day's earlier trauma were making themselves felt again as I sat down on a smaller rock just to the left of the sheltering boulder and away from the others.

Cecil had rustled up some firewood and was trying his best to get and keep a fire going. He used the better portion of our toilet paper supply and the only lighters we had left, but gave up after he got nothing more than smouldering material where a fire should have been.

"Light up the Primus, Roger," Cecil said finally. Roger dug into his haversack and brought out the little stove. He poured some methylated spirits around the burner and ignited it. Using the small pump on the side, he injected a spray of kerosene, attempting to catch a flame. No dice. We badly needed a warm cooked meal, but like the firewood, the darned Primus would not burn properly either.

"De kerosene finish," Roger said morosely.

It was a depressing scenario. We managed to just barely warm a half-pound of rice from the three pounds we brought, in the pot that had yielded cooked provisions the night before. We now had a good supply of water, so we were able to swallow the raw rice in the hope that the grains would swell in our bellies, creating a sensation of fullness. While searching his pack, Roger dug out a few cockroaches, but threw them away, horrified that Cecil appeared to have culinary designs on them.

"Wha' happen to de potatoes, G. B.?" George asked, his maddening hunger palpable.

I was drained of all energy. Without a word, I tossed him three of the half-dozen potatoes I still had and turned in for the night

Although shivering uncontrollably and with teeth chattering, fatigue knocked me out quickly and I awoke around midnight to the sound of heated voices and the unmistakable screech of a pot being scraped.

"Where is my share of the potatoes?" I asked, fully intending an accusing tone.

There were none for me. There was, however, a rash of feeble excuses: the potatoes weren't cooked; I probably wouldn't have been interested in uncooked potatoes; they didn't want to disturb me.

All told, the food wasn't much to speak of, but it amounted to the same thing; the potatoes had been eaten and it made no sense to argue over something irretrievable. For my part, I refused to divulge the secret of my three remaining spuds. They would sustain energy when we were in the most dire need. I sincerely believed that that hour was fast approaching.

Since I was now awake, I sipped from my canteen, had another spoonful of raw rice and a slice of raw potato that had somehow escaped the other boys. I felt a bit more relaxed for having slept, but my mind wandered to thoughts of home. The thought that a search was likely to be launched for us at any moment, if it hadn't been already, should have been reassuring. It wasn't.

Before going back to lie down, I checked Cecil's thermometer. The glass-encased crude alcohol read 43°F (6° C). Sleep would not come. Lying in pain and utter despair now, my thoughts drifted back to some of my happiest days in the bird bush with my father.

★ ★ ★

I was just nine years old when I got my first gun. It was a very powerful Daisy air rifle, and although it only fired BB pellets, it was dangerous at close range. At my father's request, my uncle had brought it down from New York. Firstly, my father taught me safety. "Always treat a gun as loaded," he would say, "and never point it at anything unless you're going to pull the trigger." The gun, which had a magazine capacity of fifty pellets was pump operated. At just nine, I was not able to crank the mechanism required to load a pellet into the chamber; he had to do it for me.

My first target practice was in our garage, the space designated as 'the range'. The distance to the target, which comprised the bottom of a condensed milk can, was twenty feet. Dad took the first few shots from a standing position and proclaimed that the sights were out of sync. After a few adjustments, he was pretty satisfied that the gun was now properly 'sighted in'. Then it was my turn. Noticing my struggle to keep the firearm horizontal, my father thought it best that I resort to the prone position, using my left hand, propped up by my elbow, to stabilize the barrel. The trigger mechanism was so stiff that I had to exert quite a bit of pressure to pull it. I managed to fire, jerking the rifle upwards. The sensation frightened and excited me. My mind raced toward the day I'd be able to truly go hunting for the first time, with all the power and independence that that would bring.

The BB pellet hit the wall above the can and zinged past my ear, striking his well cared-for car smack in the grille. For what seemed like a long time, B. S. froze and went deathly silent. Things were like that when I felt he would erupt into yelling or worse. Not surprisingly, he halted the exercise there and then, but he wasn't upset. There was no explosion of rage; he just figured that my first shot was as good a point as any to quit for the day. He did get angry years later when the government imposed a license fee that would have applied to my rifle, so rather than submit to the tax, he would smash and bury it.

My next attempt at target practice saw both of us wearing glasses, not the proper type, but at least they gave us a sense of security for the next time a wayward BB went hunting for an eye. Even with instruction and practice, it was weeks before I could hit the can consistently. Once I could, it was time for the real excitement outdoors.

On the first outing with my dad, he allowed me to head off into the bush with one of his bird-boys to track small sparrows, doves, and the like. He had always cautioned us that safety was paramount.

B. S. took up a position in his 'stand', awaiting the passing of flocks of various types of birds such as white wings and palomas. I would have to return to the stand each time I pulled the trigger for him to crank the gun again. After a short while, this became impractical.

On our next outing, he taught Trammy, my bird-boy who had been trained by Dad in handling all sorts of techniques, including tracking and retracing our steps, to crank my gun. He had specific instructions to always stay behind me when I was about to take aim. He was also never to crank the gun until I was absolutely ready to shoot.

A few years later, it was not unusual for Trammy and I to drift as far away as half-mile into the Warieka Hills area just east of Kingston. I vividly remember us stalking a white wing, which had perched atop a cactus a few hundred feet away, busily eating its prickly pear fruit. The excitement and tension grew as we got within a hundred feet of the patch of cacti. I had never had such an opportunity because I had only hunted smaller birds before. Would I be able to hit the target? Was the gun powerful enough to make a kill? Would we be able to find the bird among the dead and fallen cacti?

We did not notice the dried limbs of cassia and other bushes laced with prickles. I took the shot from about seventy feet and the bird fell behind the cactus. It had been shot through the neck, a stroke of luck. Overcome with excitement and accomplishment, instead of letting the more experienced Trammy retrieve the bird alone, I followed in tow. Suddenly, I felt a sharp pain in the vicinity of my right eyelid. I thought for sure that a prickle had ripped into my eye, and stopped dead in my tracks. The pain was excruciating, but I was not prepared for, nor did I understand, the severity of the problem at that instant.

A few minutes later, I surmised and later confirmed that in pushing my way through the thicket, I had disturbed a nest of wasps and that one of them had attacked me with a vengeance. I howled in pain as poor Trammy, bird in hand, ran back towards me. He was frightened as hell. After all, he was responsible for my health and well-being and fully accountable to my dad.

My eye was closing fast. After searching my haversack for some article of relief, I poured a bit of water onto the affected area and drank the rest of my canteen more out of distraction than anything else. The pain became unbearable as we sat down to assess our situation.

It was now about 9:00 a.m. and we were already a half-hour late for our rendezvous in the parking lot with my father and his group of bird-boys. Unbeknownst to us, we were now about two miles away. Furthermore, we were at least a half-mile away from any semblance of a trail, which we had been marking by placing a notch on trees as we passed by. We studied the hills around us, heading this way and that for some time.

I was famished because I had not eaten my usual boiled egg, hard-dough bread, and Milo before we left home. This was unusual. Also, my water supply was finished.

I trusted Trammy however, as he was a resident of the area. His father and friend, respectively, Bunga and Chi Chi Bus, two authentic Rastafarians, lived in a cave near their cultivations in the bush.

"Don' worry Missa Geoffrey, we goin' manage, I will fin' de way out," he assured me.

Apart from being a first-class bird hunter, Trammy knew me to a 't'. He must have also known that I was worried and hungry, but most importantly, afraid of how my father would react.

Quickly gathering leaves from three types of bush, he crushed them together. He said it was a remedy; I happened to need one desperately.

"A dis we use inna de country," he said reassuringly. I never argued with that kind of information. Neither of us knew that the first thing to have done was to try and remove the stinger. The pain was so intense that I started to cry at first; then I simply bawled uncontrollably. After applying the leaf mixture, gently rubbing it on and around my eyelid, Trammy noticed a small group of ping wing (pineapple-looking shrubs) and immediately cut a stem that carried numerous fruit resembling yellow dates. He quickly gathered some dry branches, pulled out a box of matches he had handy, and lit up a small ganja spliff. In a matter of minutes, he had a roaring fire going. The juice from the succulent berries was sweet, and its meat, which contained numerous small seeds (similar to those found in grapes), tasted delicious. Much care was taken not to let my skin come in contact with the outer part of the berry as an extreme irritation could result.

We pushed on, and after fifteen minutes without any recogniz-able landmark in sight, including the trees we had marked, we began shouting. I did not realize that we were heading slightly uphill until about 10:15, when we stumbled upon a patch of ganja.

Trammy's tone was triumphant. "Ah tell yu no fi worry Missa Geoff. Ah the ol' man yard this."

We were now at the lodgings of his father and father's planting partner. We had found our way out.

Bunga and Chi Chi Bus were in their fields. Once we made contact, they tried to convince me to drink some of their tea made from cerassee (or bitter melon, bearing orange pods with tasty, red gelatin-covered seeds), and to have a few puffs of a giant spliff they were sharing. The spliff was so big that when either one took a draw, an immense flame and cloud of smoke went up, causing me to choke. My novice's discomfort made them laugh.

"A wha' wrong wid yu, Missa Geoff," one of them asked with mock admonition. "Yu nuh like de collie weed? It good fi yu once in a while, yu nuh."

After much convincing, I drank some of the cerassee tea, as I had heard our household helper back home mention it from time to time. The conversation took my mind off the now increasing pain, but my right eye was completely closed. The left one had begun to follow suit.

It was time to follow the well-trodden path towards the parking lot, the usual meeting place after the shoot. Twenty-five minutes later we were on our way, with me holding onto a piece of rope with the other end held by Trammy. He was going to make sure that I did not fall into one of the numerous ravines along the way.

I don't remember the details of what happened when we rejoined the group, or perhaps I choose not to, but I'm sure we missed our usual stop at Mrs. Jones' shop at Seven Miles for our cold Pepsi and bulla cakes slathered with butter. I guess it hadn't been a victorious enough day.

★ ★ ★

But, here I was now, lost in the most inhospitable environment of the Blue Mountains, with tree formations resembling those of a jungle forest I had only seen before in the movies, and facing the most formidable challenge of my life. Was I going to get out alive? For the second time in my life, I was genuinely scared. I lapsed into a slumber, my thoughts continuing into a dream, in which Bunga and Chi Chi Bus had just rescued me from the hills in which I hunted, and we were at Mrs. Jones'.

"Two cold Pepsis, some bun and cheese for me, and a bulla with butter for my son," my father was saying to Mrs. Jones.

I was about to grab on to the cold bottle, but it wasn't there. Instead, my head was wet and ice-cold, soggy with water. I awoke from the dream.

Disappointed, I couldn't get back to sleep.

Top left: Using George's compass bearings, the group created a rosette (in their minds) similar to the one shown on the left, hoping they would find the spot on their map that best fit the parameters of the rosette; then, in unison with George, they agreed on an approximate location.

Top right: Big mountain at bearing 30° ahead. — Photo taken by Geoffrey B. Haddad

Bottom: Composite showing a modern-day ganja camp high up in the Blue Mountains. *Left to right:* Ganja hanging adjacent to the drying house; a cocoa plant between two adults and the daily catch of birds; some young succulent sugar cane. With adequate water and the provisions grown around the camp, the 'farmers' can survive there for weeks at a time.

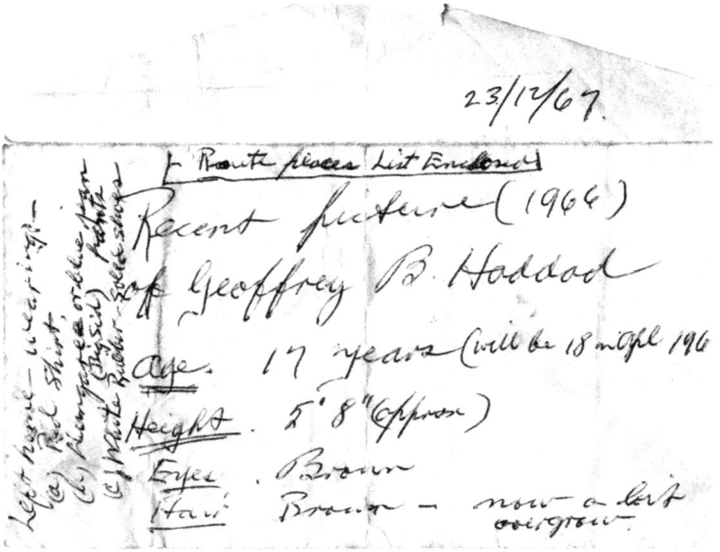

Handwritten note at top:

23/12/67

[Route places List Enclosed]

Recent picture (1966)
of Geoffrey B. Haddad

Age. 17 years (will be 18 in Apl 196[8])

Height. 5' 8" (approx.)

Eyes. Brown

Hair. Brown — now a bit overgrown.

(vertical marginal notes, left side):
Left home wearing:-
(a) Red Shirt.
(b) Khaki pants or blue jeans
(c) White rubber soled shoes.

Five boys missing on hike to Blue Mtn. Peak

A combined search operation by helicopters of the Air Wing of the Jamaican Defence Force and units of the Police Mobile Reserve was started yesterday for five boys missing on a hike to Blue Mountain Peak.

The hike started on Saturday last.

It is believed that the boys are all from the Corporate Area and that their ages are between 16 and 17.

The Military and Police authorities were told that the five — Gordon Cooper, George Hussey, Rodger Bates, Cecil Ward and Geoffrey Haddad began the hike at Clydesdale in the region of Chestervale and were done at Penlyne Castle on the other side of the mountain on Wednesday.

The police said last night the search would continue.

Search for missing 5 intensifies

HELICOPTERS OF the Airwing of the Jamaica Defence Force and units of the Police Mobile Reserve are continuing their search for five boys missing on a hike to the Blue Mountain Peak, who up to Press time had not been located.

A spokesman for the Police Mobile Reserve told the STAR that more men from the Mobile Reserve will be going up to Blue Mountain this afternoon to intensify the search.

SECOND TIME

It is the second time that five boys have been reported missing on the peak in 20 years ago. In 1951, a group of boys from Jamaica College including the College's former Headmaster — and recent General Manager of JBC Mr. Harvey Ranger, were reported missing and a search launched.

The Military and police near[ly] hike which started on Saturday last are: Gordon Cooper, missing on the peak after a George Hussey, Rodger Bates.

Cecil Ward and Geoffrey Haddad.

THE WEATHER

AFTERNOON: Mainly fair and sunny.
NIGHT: Fine.

Bench, Bar exchange greetings

Star Police Reporter

CHRISTMAS GREETINGS were exchanged between Bench and Bar in the Sutton Street Courts yesterday. In the No. 1 Court Mr. Howard Hamilton, of Counsel spoke on behalf of the Bar, he wished all the Officers of the Court the best of health way the Festive season and wished that the harmony that existed between the Bench and the Bar would continue in the coming years.

His Honour Mr. H. Rowan Campbell replied on behalf of the Bench. Mrs. Shirley Playfair, Clerk of the Courts associated herself with the reply.

In Court No. 2 Mr. Hamilton also spoke on behalf of the Bar, His Honour Mr. I. I. Robotham spoke on behalf of the Bench. Mr. I. B. Wolfe, Clerk of the Courts spoke on behalf of the Court staff. Sgt. R. Stewart, Sub...

Officer in charge of the Courts spoke on behalf of the policemen.

But Christmas will not be happy for 34 prisoners who appeared before the Courts including two young girls who are now in custody and will be appearing before the Courts until Wednesday next. Some of them have been remanded and others though offered bail are still in jail.

Top: On the fronts of several such envelopes, B. S. Haddad wrote down the physical characteristics of his missing son and distributed them to aid the massive search effort.

Bottom: The first news headlines announcing the group's predicament, at left, the *Daily Gleaner*; at right, the afternoon tabloid the *Star.*

The Sunday Gleaner

KINGSTON, JAMAICA, DECEMBER 24, 1967

1968 Kelvinator MODELS NOW AT 88 KING ST. Homelectrix

NEW FROST-FREE Kelvinator MODELS AT Homelectrix

The guns fall silent for a brief 'peace on earth'

● Army, Police comb Blue Mountain area

AIR, LAND SEARCH FOR MISSING BOYS

90-minute helicopter hunt planned this morning

Hikers last seen at Clydesdale on Wednesday

ARMY AND POLICE patrols combed the Blue Mountain range yesterday in a search for the five Jamaica College schoolboys who left last Saturday on a hike across the peak—and have not yet returned home.

J.C. boys again!

Air, land search

(Continued from PAGE 1)

hovering low in an effort t
locate them.

A team of foot soldiers was al
sent out to search the are
following the trail which it wa
said that the boys were to hav
followed and to find out,
possible, where they may hav
deviated from the trail.

According to earlier reports, th
boys were to have reached Per
lyne Castle, a well-known poi
on the Blue Mountain Pea
climb, on Wednesday last. The
had obviously not done so.

A report last night that they ha
reached Buff Bay, on the Por
land side of the mountain, wa
not confirmed.

Mr. Charles Cooper, father of or
of the missing boys, said la
night that he took the boys t
Clydesdale, near Chestervale, i
St. Thomas, at about 3.30 p.n
last Saturday, December 1
They took with them food, com
passes, cutlasses, sleeping ba
and methylated spirits.

Mr. Cooper said when the boy
left it was estimated that the
would have completed the tri
by Wednesday last and returne
to Kingston. He said it had bee
figured that they would hav
arrived at Mavis Bank that da
and would have returned t
the city by land transportatio
from that point.

Another source said that, al
though the boys thought the
could have completed th
journey by Wednesday, it ha
not seemed likely that the
would have been able to hav
done it by yesterday (Satur
day), having regard to th
round-about route that the
had planned.

Record spending by Christmas shoppers

Home razed

P.M. Christmas message:

'So as to spread joy...give as much as possible'

The heart was not buried

Christmas tree afire

Greetings sent P.M.

The message

● Flashback

On TV and Radio

By Christmas Eve, with time running out for their survival, the plight of the five was Jamaica's biggest news story, even eclipsing a temporary holiday ceasefire during the Vietnam War. *Inset*: the story continued on page two of the newspaper.

9:30AM 24/1/67

Brown received message + Babs phoned me at JDF, HQ.

"Brown took phone message — Boys have been found — Mrs Baxter."

I asked Barbara to phone Norma for Mrs Baxter number which was not listed in Directory, to confirm + ring me back. Babs phoned me back afterwards: — Billy Du Mont + Mr Biscoe found the boys in Portland and that a JDF helicopter was standing by.

Top: After days of anguish, the good news begins with the note written by B. S. Haddad, announcing: "Billy Du Mont and Mr. Biscoe found the boys in Portland." He had mistakenly referred to the co-pilot/spotter as Billy instead of David du Mont.

Bottom: Tyndale-Biscoe's Delta Yankee circles against a dark, cloud-filled sky, awaiting the arrival of the helicopter soon after he reported that the boys had been located. *Photo courtesy of Roger Bates*

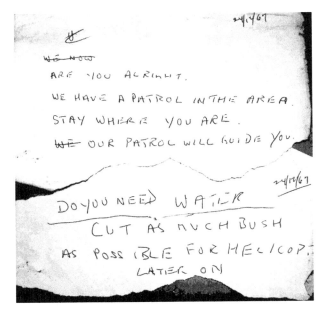

Top: left: The rescue begins at the army helicopter JDF-H1 descends into the opening. Capt. John Dent wrote two notes: one inquiring about the boys' condition, and the other giving instructions. Note the craft's basket stretchers fitted for the initial contact with the boys in the event that an emergency evacuation was necessary. *Top right:* Capt. Bunny Stern descends into the opening with Capt. John Dent lowering supplies to the stranded boys.

Bottom: The army's notes written by Capt. Dent and dropped from JDF–H1 to the boys tell them to remain in place and prepare the area for a helicopter extraction.

Top: This photograph shows the group's final position on the mountain ridge (arrow). The planned route along the Blue Mountain Ridge was as follows: 1. Clydesdale, 2. Cinchona, 3. Sir Johns Peak, 4. High Peak, 5. Main Ridge Gap, 6. Mossman's Peak, 7. Portland Gap and 9. Blue Mountain Peak.

Bottom: Down to their final stand, the five schoolboys are trapped on a ridge of the Blue Mountains, above the Swift River Valley in terrain as inaccessible as anywhere in the world—perhaps where man has never trodden. From here, there is nowhere to go without a rescue from above. Taken with a very low pass of Tyndale-Biscoe's aircraft, this photo shows Gordon and Cecil at the bottom centre in a tree. *Photos courtesy of J. S. Tyndale-Biscoe, taken December 24, 1967.*

From his plane, Tyndale-Biscoe captured the army helicopter (top) moving away from the boys positions in the tree (circle) and fern patch (right). Jack Tyndale-Biscoe would later write on the back of the photo: "Bunny Stern reconnoitring the area. The tree circled was where two of the boys were. The true immensity of the area searched can be appreciated in some small degree by comparing the size of the helicopter with the visible forest in this close-up. Later, Army Sgt. Keith Hall, having been flown in from Up Park Camp, climbed down a rope from the helicopter and cleared an area to enable Capt. Stern to hover the helicopter while the boys climbed aboard two at a time." *Photo courtesy of J. S. Tyndale-Biscoe, taken December 24, 1967.*

Top: Having dismounted to assist with the extraction, Sergeant Hall holds onto one of the skids of the chopper piloted by Captain Bunny Stern. (Note limbs/branches cut from tree and very steep slope on the ridge the boys occupied.) *Photo courtesy of J. S. Tyndale-Biscoe (taken by Gordon Cooper).*

Bottom: Exhausted and in pain from my injuries, I, still wearing my sweater, leave the last lean-to built on the mountain. *Photo taken by Roger Bates*

Sergeant Hall steadies JDF-H1 from the ground, allowing me to climb aboard. Crouched in the foreground awaiting extraction, beneath the tree and to the right of the chopper is Cecil Ward . Roger Bates, the first off the mountain, is already on board. The dramatic rescue image is captured from a tree by Gordon Cooper. At this moment, with two helicopters deployed for the rescue, with only two available seats each—and given that Gordon and Cecil were glued together—it was not clear how or when George would escape. *Photo taken by Gordon Cooper*

A view from JDF-H1, after flying for five minutes away from the pickup point—still showing very dense forest and the fast flowing 'Swift' below. *Photo by Geoffrey B. Haddad.*

Top: The Swift River Delta in 2013. The rescue helicopter JDF-H1 made its first stop here after leaving the ridge. Because of my hasty exit from the craft, there was nearly a tragedy involving all on board. *Photo by Geoffrey B. Haddad*

Bottom: T. P. Bates (left) reunites with his son, Roger (centre) at Ken Jones Aerodrome. I am at right. *Photo taken by Freddy Ramson*

Top: I (in the same shirt which I wore at the beginning of the hike)am greeted by my mother, Norma Haddad, along with family and friends at the Jamaica Defence Force HQ, December 24, 1967

After surviving a state of high anxiety for several days, Norma *(Centre right)* and B. S. Haddad *(Bottom)* fully accept that their son has been delivered to them alive. To Mr. Haddad's right (in sunglasses) is Danny DaCosta, my uncle.

Top; Left to right: Roger Bates, Freda Haddad, Debra DaCosta (my cousin), Norma Haddad, me, Richard Roberts (who drove Mrs. Haddad to JDF-HQ) and Robin Crawford.

Bottom; Left to right, front: Iris DaCosta (my grandmother), Norma Haddad (my mother), David DaCosta, David Gregg, and Carlysle Hudson (two of the 'Windsorites'). In the centre, I give a first-hand account of the nearly disastrous hike to Consie Walters of JBC-TV. Paying close attention, on either side of Mr. Walters, are Richard Roberts and Dennis Crawford.

Top: JBC-TV Consie Walters interviews the boys at the JDF-HQ.

Bottom: One last time, the five hikers pose with the JDF rescue craft.

Top: Airways Charters 180 Cessna Skywagon 6Y-JDY (Delta Yankee) flown by Jackie Tyndale-Biscoe at the JDF, December 24, 1967. A dependable workhorse, this highly manoeuvrable craft made first contact with the boys trapped on the mountain. *Photo courtesy of The Gleaner Company Ltd.*

Bottom: Airways Charters Beechcraft Debonair 6Y-JFC (Foxtrot Charlie) flown by Ian Jacobs (inset, circa 1966) during the December 1967 search. *Photos courtesy of J.S. Tyndale- Biscoe and Ian Jacobs.*

JDF Air Wing, December 24, 1967: With the hikers already safely on the tarmac, JDF H1 and H2 arrive with their equipment. In the foreground is Robin Crawford, armed with his 8mm movie camera. He was the person entrusted to keep my detailed hiking plans a secret from my father. On December 20th, when there was no good news of the lost hikers, he delivered the famous last words, "If I'm not back by Wednesday" to B. S. Haddad, setting in motion the high-level, island-wide searches that followed.

CHAPTER 12

A COASTLINE APPEARS

Friday, December 22, 1967 (Day 7)

We were not weather experts; we hoped we could have conjured up a nice, fair day, but our magic proved weak. Friday came in dull and grey, with a gloom that tainted the air as we moved about. By now, we were two days late getting back to Kingston, and we couldn't hide our anxiety.

As the sun broke through, the very real likelihood that we may never get home was oppressive. We broke camp, officially number 6, at 8:30 a.m.

The difficulty of movement in the morning along a Jamaican river in the steep mountainside, even for the strong and spirited, is not to be underestimated. Pounding rapids produce saturated cold air drifts; drops of water from the low-hanging wild pine branches are ice cold; mosquitoes are savage. Tall trees dominate the landscape with their foliage so tightly intermeshed as to form an almost solid canopy overhead. The undergrowth at times gave way to loose shale, creating treacherous landslides. It was a miserable business.

We could only see a fraction of the sky at any given time and always with relative darkness around us. We had descended a deep gorge and were now following along the largest, fastest flowing river we had come upon so far. We had cleaned up half the remaining uncooked rice, secured our packs, and might have had more hopeful hearts, but the food didn't help with that. We just didn't know what to expect. In truth, we didn't expect much, and with that mindset, we just mechanically plodded on.

The five of us arrived at a strangely familiar spot. It was strange to see a clear pool of blue water at such a high elevation and on such a fast-flowing river. As we stood staring at it, I had fantasies about finding fish that were waiting on us to catch them. How would we snare them? Was this the water we saw as a mirage yesterday?

The water appeared to be anywhere from six to ten feet deep at its centre and lay between our position and a dangerous looking waterfall. Had we not been so depressed and in the throes of an intense longing for home, we wouldn't have thought twice about plunging into its lovely inviting waters.

The splash I heard told me that one of the boys had gone in. It was Roger, and I could tell from the flailing form that his plunge was unplanned. He had gone careening down into the water after the shrub he was holding onto gave way. It provided something to laugh at as he emerged resembling a drowned rat, pride wounded, backpack still in place. Still, it was not so much a happy moment as it was one of emotional relief. Roger pulled himself together and we got going again.

As had become the usual thing, we had to climb the ridge on our right to bypass this 'falling', as the rural people call a waterfall. The last two nights, we had been bedding down with the mutual understanding that the next day we were getting home. Today, that didn't feel real anymore. It began to appear as if we might not get out at all.

We knew that the two-day delayed return to Kingston would be more than sufficient concern for our parents—at least I was certain it would be a four-alarm situation at my house. Surely somebody would be coming, but it was still our responsibility to keep ourselves alive.

In general, things were not looking good. Our food supply was dangerously low, and we were down to a half pound of rice, three potatoes and a single pack of chicken noodle soup. As if the butt of some cruel joke, we had wasted an entire day going around in a complete circle. We truly did not know where we were, and though we hoped against hope to reach Mavis Bank that day, not one of us was convinced that that would happen.

★ ★ ★

As I had hoped, a massive air and land search was indeed under-way. Unfortunately, the mission initially only concentrated itself around some rumoured sightings of us, since our planned route was at first not known, and our actual route was a mystery even to us. This misled the searchers and wasted valuable moments in a race against time. We had seen no one—worse yet, nobody had seen us since Mr. Cooper had left us at Clydesdale at 4:00 p.m. on December 16.

Incredibly, the first of these rumours had been established by Benjamin ('Benjie') Gordon who claimed to have seen us at Clydesdale on Wednesday, December 20. Gordon had been so helpful at the start of our trip, yet strangely he was the one who would later start the dangerous rumour that we'd been recently spotted. Who could be more trustworthy than a forest ranger? Shouldn't he also have known how deadly that sort of wilful misinformation could be? It was massively disappointing to discover that Gordon had done this, but no doubt it was more so for the ones who were searching for us in those anxious days.

Acting on what Gordon reported, a platoon of fifty soldiers had been brought to the area to follow up on his advice that "dem boys probably gone back into the woods again". Even worse, a shopkeeper in the vicinity lent credence to this by claiming that he had sold us food and cold drinks from his shop. He said he recognized us from photographs shown to him.

The soldiers searched the direct trail to Sir Johns Peak. Armed primarily with machetes and drinking water, two-way radios, and with no heavy machinery or tools to support their work, they also hacked their way to it along a rough alternative route through Morces Gap. We never took that route.

At Sir Johns, two schools of thought emerged: first; that we had simply vanished into the jungle, and second, that Benjamin Gordon's version of events was correct, the fantasy in which we had come back out of the woods on Wednesday. They turned back.

The searchers also followed another rumour, originating from the well-known rest stop at Penlyne Castle. This time, it was being said that we had slept there that Wednesday night in full view of a watchman. A backup patrol was sent to comb the Mavis Bank area again. Other rumours included sightings of us at Newcastle on the south side of the mountains and at the quaint town of Buff Bay on the north east coast. Sadly, neither place was along any way we had been. The army and police had responded to several of these false clues and would continue to do so during the crisis.

★ ★ ★

It is important to point out that Jamaica's rural folk are far and away a generous and kind-hearted lot.

I do not believe they meant us any harm in misleading the searchers. It's more likely they thought that with the involvement of military personnel, we would be found in adequate time. But it is a reality that a group of lads from such a different socio-economic stratum from their own, lost in mountain territory, would have inspired a good deal of excitement. The chance to play a central role in the proceedings might well have been too tempting. This sort of thing would not have been too different from when country people claimed they had seen one of the island's folk legends, such as a roaming coffin with three 'john crows' sitting atop it.

We struggled uphill with rather distressed breathing, in what felt like an interminable effort to gain the top of this ridge. We no longer held back on talking about being lost, because we needed to share the hope of being found. Just as

A rural 'shop' in the Jamaican countryside is a curious affair, but a hub of stability for the district nevertheless. It could be a one-room addition to a home, but more often is a freestanding, rather ramshackle structure along the roadside. It is sometimes manned by a child of the shopkeeper gone to get staples like cornmeal, white flour, salted codfish, canned mackerel, cooking oil, kerosene, cigarettes, beer and white rum. It is also a social centre at nights, made lively by men's voices, the jangling and slapping of dominoes and lively music spilling from some old radio or a high-powered sound system.

On occasion, the shop hosts a 'nine- night' to see a community member ushered into the hereafter. The tradition is the Jamaican version of an Irish wake, in which the male relatives and close friends prepare the burial plot. There is the best food(e.g. curried goat and rice), liquor (white rum and Red Stripe Beer) and music to accompany the works.

It goes on for several days and is a great community get together.

important, we needed to anticipate the spirit and actions that the searchers might need from us. I again suggested that we put all our efforts into starting a bush fire large enough to be seen from the air. Inevitably, we began turning on each other, rebuking Cecil for not having thought to pour a good reserve of kerosene oil from his dead lantern into the Primus stove, or letting George bear the brunt of blame for planning the hike in the first place. The stove issue was, of course, something that could have been handled easily during a brief stop. It just provided another reason to argue. And we needn't have saddled George with this very tough burden, because he already felt responsible and guilty, causing his conscience to gnaw at him:

"G. B.," he pleaded, "I promised your old man that if we had to hack through any heavy bush, we wouldn't do it. We would turn back. That was six days ago, yu know!"

George was an independent sort of boy. He was steadfast, if not downright stubborn, proud of his leadership abilities, and quite capable of taking unilateral decisions. He had a youthful arrogance that did not admit failure readily, and because he was less talkative than the rest of us, it was often left up to our knowledge of him to figure out how he was feeling. Now he allowed me to see how much he was tormented by the thought that the expedition was a failure. Worst yet, he seemed to be grappling with the reality that he had reneged on his promise to my father.

I couldn't bring myself to make his agony worse. I told him it made no sense to worry about that now. We

The 'john crow' is Jamaica's carrion bird, a variety of turkey vulture whose significance to the island's culture and whose role in local folklore is deeply entrenched. The bird features in song, in anecdote, proverb, legend, omen and in the language of the streets. In none of these cases is it celebrated as anything other than portending or referring to evil. The darkness it represents runs the gamut from moral paucity to physical destruction. How the name 'john crow' came about has not been established with any certainty, but there are stories. A popular one is that the crow's face resembled that of the Reverend John Crow, an Irish clergyman who preached a rather unfavourable sermon in the seaside town of Port Royal in the latter part of the 19th century. The bird was supposedly given the priest's name in derision.

abandoned it there and then. I believe he appreciated my support at that moment because he seemed somewhat comforted.

We continued to move steadily towards the apex of the ridge. Every now and again, someone would ask, "We gettin' close to the top?" but there was no answer for the most part. Eventually, the five of us got there, shortly before midday. Naturally, we were desperate for any signal to suggest that our ordeal was nearing an end. But there was none, and strangely enough, we had become almost inured to disappointment. This was probably a merciful emotional defence on our part, since having any concrete expectations shattered at that point might have been too devastating. Now, having seen that there was no habitation here either, we stopped to rest and consider our situation as rationally and as calmly as we could.

The problem, Gordon reasoned, was that there wasn't any trail left behind us from Sir Johns Peak, much less at Main Ridge Gap. They weren't going to be able to track us. "They gwine have to see us from the air," he surrendered.

"I said that already," I interjected with more than a little frustration. Gordon spoke again, but this time, not to any of us.

"Lord, why should we all, five decent boys, suffer like this? It's possible for us to die!"

His words were more resentful than prayerful, but there we were, all tired and afraid. In support of our team-mate, we answered him with subdued yeses and nods of the head, acutely aware that we were in grave danger. None of us dared stand in the way of spontaneous appeals for divine intervention. There were several times when we did not really believe that salvation would ever come.

From that point, the only real impetus we had for continuing was knowing that we could not just stop there. From this ridge, we could see the point at which it intersected with the one we had just come down, and we could see yet another tributary. It was not another tributary but the Speculation River again, the river we had been following all along! The situation dictated that we either go down the river or turn back and go over the ridge. No one wanted to do the latter. We never wanted to leave or lose sight of the river again.

Starting off along the ridge's fairly even slope, we moved passionlessly until we came to an abrupt halt, finding ourselves about five hundred feet above the water and perhaps no more than a few hundred on a horizontal plane from it. The configuration was an almost vertical drop, camouflaged by the foliage that had become so familiar but also very adversarial to us.

We prepared to go down—something that, in retrospect, we shouldn't even have attempted. I went first, and within no time at all, I was in trouble again. I had crawled down, feet first on stomach and buttocks alternately, clinging to the precipice by way of shrubs and unreliable-looking vines. I hadn't felt a secure descent since we began, but I suppose I wanted to give it a good go before declaring it impossible. I started through the crook of a small tree that took off horizontally from the cliff, then straightened towards a little opening that obviously admitted sunlight on occasion.

Suddenly, my feet slipped and I instantly realized that my arms wouldn't support me without them. Incredibly, my haversack caught my weight and I hung there, with all four limbs dangling in the air. It might have been a laughable sight in a cartoon, but this was no joke, and I had to collect my senses while I was suspended there. I didn't panic, probably because it happened so fast and the bag had caught me right away. Relaxed concentration set in. There was no option but to ask my boulder-bruised torso to stretch, using delicate but firm finger placement while I kept a sharp eye on how the tree was responding to the movement of my body. It worked, giving me enough stability to reach the solid part of the tree.

Roger was the only one who had seen what happened. A serious, intense countenance betrayed his anxiety. He must have been doubly relieved to see that I was going to be safe. At least he had not inadvertently been the cause of this scare.

I had had enough of this.

"George, you guys, don't bother coming down any further. We can' make it down here!"

Nobody questioned the assertion. They must have had their own doubts, and my face probably said it best. We would have to cross the valley to our right. It was another hour before we were back at the top of the ridge and at the valley end. This was now our problem: we had to navigate another dry tributary, some thirty yards wide filled with shale and loose rocks. These things are not easy to negotiate. Any dislodged rock would increase in speed and size as it tumbled, gathering both clay and shale from underneath. Five seconds would pass, then ten, twenty, thirty, sixty. We never knew when the mass hit the water.

We assured one another that we would do our best to tread very carefully. But not even this settled our nerves, so we took the ultra-precautionary decision to cross one at a time. Again, I walked the point, followed in turn by Roger, Cecil, Gordon, and then George. As each man made it over, he watched the next one cross. Once over, it took close to half an hour to do a gradual incline of shale. Having gained a new ridge, fresh hope of encountering someone other than ourselves sprang up within us.

★ ★ ★

The previous day, we had started to shout for help whenever it seemed possible that we could be within earshot of a climber or mountain dweller. We took up the hollering again.

"Can anyone hear?" we wailed. "Can anyone hear us?! Hello there! Hello! Helllloooo!"

No shout came back. This wasn't surprising, for our tired voices could not have been travelling any great distance, coming from parched and sore throats.

We staggered exhaustedly along the ridge, without any new attempt to shout or even speak. It made sense to conserve our energy, but I doubt we were thinking as constructively as that. We did things or failed to do them as fatigue dictated.

Then, something rustled in a nearby bush. It brought a startled cry from me; Roger was immediately optimistic. "What's that? What's that!?" he asked excitedly.

"It's probably somebody who's heard us!" He yelled in the direction of the unseen entity. "We might be rescued now, guys. Hello! Hello? Anybody, oy!"

Rescue wasn't going to come from the source of the noise. We all froze as we made out the shape of a small wild hog, which peered suspiciously at us from the edge of the bush.

"Pass mi de cutlass, Roger," Cecil whispered, his eyes fixed on the animal. "Roast pig fi dinner tonight."

Fresh wild boar for dinner would have been wonderful indeed, but this animal has its name for a reason. We weren't quick enough at passing the machete, let alone getting to our quarry before it escaped. The little hog shot off down the hillside with Cecil cursing and trying to stone the animal as it went. Hungry and angry, he conjured up an appetizing picture of what we could have had.

"Bwoy, mi coulda really do wid some jerk pork* right now and a Red Stripe beer fi wash it down."

We all felt the same way, but this kind of dreaming helped us not one whit and so we didn't join in with Cecil. We just took the loss.

We came across a tree bearing red berries, looking very similar to ones we had seen on smaller shrubs the previous day. We didn't chance eating them then and so we didn't now. The fruit were small, resembling the edible bilberry we knew (similar in shape to a blueberry but smaller), but we just could not be sure that they weren't poisonous. When we

---

* Cecil was longing for smoked 'jerk' meat. It really was 'rebel' food which has found its way into the national culinary heart from the pages of history. The Maroon people inherited the method of preserving cooked meat from their African ancestors. This they did even as they heroically mounted and sustained resistance to English occupation from the hills of Jamaica for several generations. There they hunted and killed the wild boar, seasoned it with herbs and finally wrapped it in banana leaves before placing it in a pit. The meat was placed on and between hot stones kept that way from slow-burning pimento wood. They learned how to season the smoked meat from the indigenous Taino people. The result is entirely delicious, as seen in the worldwide renown of jerk seasoning today. The standard seasoning comprises pimento, hot pepper, scallion, onion, thyme, black pepper, cinnamon, nutmeg and salt, but each jerk chef will add some often-undisclosed ingredient to his personal style of marinating the meat to be jerked. The meat is best cooked over slow-burning green wood, which, depending on the variety, adds a particular flavour to the end result.

saw a small sparrow making no attempt to peck at them, we felt we had made the right decision, hard though they had been to resist.

It occurred suddenly to my weary brain that I hadn't seen any flocks of ring-tail (or band-tailed) pigeons.

I was the only hunter in the group, and knew it was not unusual for them to appear at this elevation. I assumed they didn't like the inclement weather or had found no food nearby. They are such pretty and distinctively marked birds. Indigenous to the warmer parts of the Americas, they are known more commonly throughout the region as band-tailed pigeons precisely for the beautiful black band that adorns their tail feathers. I found myself wishing they would come by if and when we made our signal fire. They love to assemble around fires that produce lots of smoke, perhaps for the warmth. I did not realize then that in addition to a craving for food, I was also in desperate need of lovely things, pleasant thoughts, memories of fun and better, safer times.

It made my situation bearable to absent myself mentally from the fellows and from the discomfort in my feet, which had been jammed and stressed from the steep going in light sneakers. I retreated into memories, feeling wobbly and painfully slow, moving forward like a programmed robot, yet without much sense of direction.

The ring-tailed pigeon, a species of bird in the Columbidae family, is endemic to Jamaica. Natural habitats are subtropical or tropical, moist lowland forests and subtropical or tropical moist mountain forests. The common example, the columba caribae, is found mostly in the Blue and John Crow Mountain range and the Cockpit Country. Hunting and habitat destruction have reduced its numbers considerably and the species is now listed as threatened.

I was not yet physically depleted. There was still some energy and alertness left. While in the company of avid bird-hunters, mostly older than I was, I felt their motivation to scheme and manoeuvre against the birds. Most of the hunters went by muleback into the foothills of the northern Blue Mountains, others on foot, still others using a combination of both. Treks would last anywhere up to eleven hours and the men often stayed in a good spot for an entire weekend if the birds were plentiful.

Unlike traditional bird shooters, these hunters relied on information from the men who eked out a livelihood above 3,000 feet in the mountains. Hidden from view by towering trees and in a secluded cool climate, ganja farmers tended the most potent and sought-after weed. Camps were established around their cultivations, typically where the land bearing them was burnt to remove its light undergrowth.

The weed was chosen and tended assiduously to produce its best buds, harvested in the proper season, and kept in drying huts in the mountains before being transported for profitable redistribution to a dealer in charge of the area. It was a dangerous and risky business, but thoroughly exciting territory through which to lead a youngster.

I remembered being told how convivial these men were; they were not at all gangster-like. They were helpful, smiling, always ready to strip and offer thick stalks of sugar cane, a warming cup of herbal tea, or country chocolate made with coconut milk. What I wouldn't have given now for one of these men of the hills to appear from nowhere and lead us out.

At one time in the island's history there existed more than thirty illegal landing strips. One of the most ingeniously constructed was found at an elevation of about 3,000 feet and cut into the side of a huge mountain, thereby visually protecting it on three sides. There were no roads wide enough to allow the equipment necessary to build this 'airstrip', only a number of footpaths broad enough for mules to traverse. It was later discovered that these 'entrepreneurial' engineers had arranged for the complete dismantling of a bulldozer and its subsequent reassembly there on site in the mountains. *A prime example of the will making a way,* I thought.

★ ★ ★

George's voice broke the reverie and returned me to reality.

"What's the time?" he asked.

"Ten past four," Roger volunteered.

"Okay, let's keep going till half past, then we'll find somewhere to sleep." George replied.

We all heard the exchange and concurred. Our pace was still very slow. Then, out of the blue, a fern patch materialized just ahead. It was the dreaded ferrel grass my father had always warned me about. The patch was surrounded in an almost perfect circle by densely spaced and very tall trees. These plants were three to four feet high and difficult to walk through. Roger went a ways in, left us wondering for a while, then emerged after climbing the lower limbs of a huge tree about fifty feet from one edge of the patch. He returned very upbeat, reporting that he had seen the horizon and that he had a marvellous but only partial view of the north coast. Roger was certain that he saw a road in the distance and had also spotted a shiny object that he thought was a zinc-roofed house. We became animated and followed the direction he had taken through the patch so we could see for ourselves. I never got to see because my injuries prevented me from climbing the tree. It was a sinking feeling to see that the road seemed several miles away, quite impossible to get to from where we stood.

It was 4:20 p.m. Without a doubt, we were on one of a series of ridges in a very deep ravine on the north side of the Blue Mountain Ridge.

I spotted a suitable place for us to spend the night, a clearing just west of the ferns. We collected some ginger lilies, and using the ferns supported by a vine at the head, the fellows erected a new lean-to, our third. I sat watching, overseeing its construction. Still in great agony from the bruise, I had to move gingerly and so couldn't participate physically in that project. My feet were sore and hurt constantly, and the pain was especially more pronounced when getting them into or out of my shoes. The skin looked colourless, with my toes poking through my socks. As a reward for using them to dig into the hillside, my sore and roughened fingertips were bloody, as were all my exposed body parts, which suffered from bites or self-inflicted wounds made by my scratching, and from regular contact with prickles and sharp rocks.

It was fairly tedious, but the four boys worked quickly with nightfall fast approaching. Though there was no sign of rain, our shredded, battered raincoats were placed on the roof as the final touch. Cecil had a mind to try lighting a fire and backtracked to where he remembered seeing a piece of rotten tree trunk. He hauled it back to camp. After all the trouble of rescuing the timber, it would not, unfortunately, catch fire. It was a horrible time to discover that some indigenous woods would not ignite, no matter what.

Later on, Cecil scavenged the surrounding hillsides in search of different types of woods. About ninety minutes later, he emerged from the forest clutching a stack of wood in his arms, tight to the chest. We lambasted him, poor fellow, for bringing what appeared to be waterlogged woods back to the camp. But he was not deterred. Although rain was not in the forecast, he neatly arranged the woods in a tepee-style framework right in the middle of the lean-to, hoping that some of the water would seep out overnight.

The order of events before we actually lay our heads down was the 'putting away' of some of the remainder of the raw rice and throwing whatever we would sleep on onto the ground. As a treat before bed, Gordon offered some of his toothpaste for dessert. It was much appreciated and an alternative to a few more available grains of uncooked rice. We were gratified that it cleansed and freshened our mouths considerably, as they had all become fetid havens for bacteria. The beams of our flashlights had been reduced to dull glows, but I was fortunate to still have a set of new batteries on hand, so I set about changing mine.

Prior to this, at just about dusk, George had left the camp and made his way to the middle of the fern patch, with Roger's diary in hand. When he returned, he had taken some compass bearings, but for reasons known only to him, he did not divulge the readings. Perhaps it was just too dark or he wanted to sleep on 'his findings', I thought later on.

George was sure that there was a settlement ahead. He had once again climbed the tree. According to him, the road that we had dismissed earlier as a figment of our imagination was, in fact, there. It had to be; after all, he said he had seen the downhill movement of vehicular headlights along it. Serenely, we received this news under the lean-to. By now, we were sure that George Hussey was not leading the expedition. Moreover, it was increasingly clear, as our crisis of supplies and shelter worsened, that he was not going to get us out. He became withdrawn and said nothing else. There was no suggested plan of attack, no powwows or further conversations. Everyone said a prayer.

We were now gone for a whole week. Relatives and friends were absolutely frantic. My father had been trying to rally everyone's spirits and instil co-operative action among the other parents. Up at 5:00 every morning following restive nights, he eventually refused to stay at the Windsor Avenue house altogether. He became a fixture at the headquarters of the Jamaica Defence Force, getting information updates as they happened and helping in any way he could.

Meanwhile, we marked Camp 7 on the map.

CHAPTER 13

TRAPPED

Saturday, December 23, 1967 (Day 8)

We made the front page of Jamaica's *Daily Gleaner* of December 23. This edition of the newspaper would have made its way up and down Windsor Avenue:

> Five Boys Missing on Hike to Blue Mountain Peak
>
> A combined search operation by helicopter of the Air Wing of the Jamaican Defence Force and units of the Police Mobile Reserve was started yesterday for five boys missing on a hike to Blue Mountain Peak.
>
> The hike started on Saturday last. It is believed that the boys are all from the corporate area and that their ages are between 16 and 17.
>
> The military and police authorities were told that the five—Gordon Cooper, George Hussey, Roger Bates, Cecil Ward and Geoffrey Haddad —began a hike at Clydesdale in the region of Chestervale and were down at Penlyne Castle on the other side of the mountain on Wednesday. The police said that the search would continue.

News that we had been at Penlyne Castle was of course erroneous, another rumour. We had never been there.

It was about this time that my father wrote a note on a number of envelopes and dispatched them to gas stations in the corporate area, including Papine (a little village up the road from JC and the point at which the JOS number 6 and 7 buses originate), and also as far as St. Thomas. He also got them to a number of surveyors and their 'agents'.*

One such note was dispatched as far as the police station at Mavis Bank. Enclosed in each envelope was a picture of me from 1966 with the words:

> left home wearing – (a) red shirt, (b) dungaree or blue Jeans pants, (c) white rubber soled shoes. Route list enclosed and d) hair slightly over-grown.

At around eight o'clock, we were awakened by the unmistakable rotors of a helicopter. Immediately, we sprang into action. There seemed to be some amount of method to what we did, even though we were disorganized. Desperate to be seen, we began with noise, lots of it, followed by manic cries for help. Cecil scrambled in record time to the top of the huge fifty-foot tree. Gordon, hot on his heels, hoisted the red-and-yellow sleeping bag up to him and Cecil spread it out as best he could across the tree's uppermost centre of the fern patch, with our necks craned skyward, waving a yellow blanket. We saw the helicopter a few seconds later, coming along the ridge from the southeast. Our emotions soared.

As it started to head towards the northeast, we screamed across the valley and put every possible bit of energy into the most elaborate movements we could make with our arms, attempting to send as many different SOS signals as we could remember. But the few signs we knew

---

* An agent was a person used by a surveyor to look for business. Country folks, for the most part, hardly ever held a proper title to their property, and depended on a simple deed or a will. The boundaries to these properties were features such as a bend in a parochial road, a particular tree, wooden fence line, etc. A family dispute, a feud with a neighbour or a death often provoked the need for a surveyor.

were not practical. Firstly, we were too far below to be seen and secondly, the noise of the rotors made it impossible for our screams to be heard. Nevertheless, we were desperate boys in a desperate situation and so we were not rational. We tried everything.

Even though it was broad daylight, we even defied common sense and wasted whatever battery resources we had left by trying to make flashlight signals. We couldn't tell if we were seen, and just as we had got accustomed to seeing it, the helicopter circled around Mossman's Peak, headed southeast along the ridge and over onto the south side, out of sight.

Then there was a new sound. It hit our ears like a car-sized bee—a plane? A plane. We were now hearing the engine of a light aircraft that came quickly into and out of our view. The plane disappeared for a while and returned. Each time it traversed along or crossed over the ridge, it gave us the feeling that it was concentrating on the south side of the Blue Mountain Ridge at some 8000 feet. We were on the north side, at about 4000 feet. If there was ever going to be an opportune moment for successful signalling, it would be within a very small window. This was the first bit of evidence and reassurance that the search for us had begun in earnest. Whenever the plane made one of its infrequent appearances on our side of the ridge, we expended all we had to signal it. We did not succeed. After about thirty minutes, the droning began to die away. One aircraft, then two, were looking for us. They had to be looking for us. Now the helicopter and the plane had disappeared altogether.

At this point, it was about 9:00 a.m. Our emotions had just run the gamut from frenzied highs to depressing lows. We felt terribly let down and our sense of desperation was growing.

It was agreed that the best thing to do was to spend the day right there since we were in the most conspicuous clearing around. There were no others that we could see, nor had we encountered any up to that point. Shortly after 9:00 a.m., it was certain that the aerial search had been abandoned, most likely due to the fog and dense clouds that had by now rolled in from the north to encircle the ridges.

The collective opinion was that if we were not found during the course of the day, we would try to reach the river by going along the ridge to our right and then moving in a general northerly direction. By the time we came to this agreement, the mosquitoes had begun to feast on us again. I didn't have much strength left to fight them. Additionally, we had neither the vigour nor the determination to even attempt a descent down that ridge, but nobody said a word.

We agreed to keep a keen ear out so that if we heard anything sounding like a plane we could jump into positions right away. As if oblivious to their predicament, the surfers, Cecil and Gordon, would perch as high as they could in the tree, shirtless, of course, to absorb as much sunshine as possible. Their clothes were being dried out in the fern patch, but even with more skin showing, they didn't appear to be bothered either by the mosquitoes or the sauna-like heat and humidity.

George and Roger would go back to the fern patch with the yellow blanket spread out over the plants. I was in persistent pain, likely aggravated by the suspension incident. The injury to my back was not helped by the frantic waving, but I could not persuade any of them to take me seriously. I went with either party, and on one occasion, sat at the foot of the tree with wet clothes, blankets and other sleeping bags, making an attempt to rid them of whatever needless thing was stored in them, before laying them out on top of the ferns.

If I joined George and Roger, the area was more a den of cruelty than a mere fern patch. The dampness harboured thousands of hungry mosquitoes that tormented us incessantly. They sucked at the raw flesh in areas exposed by wounds. We only needed wipe a hand across our faces or other exposed areas to have them blackened by eviscerated pests mixed with streaks of blood. Whose blood did not matter.

When they came close to the inner ear, the menacing vibration of the insects' wings was amplified, sounding more like a flight of high-strung bees. Somehow, our skins had become accustomed to every pinch. That we could bear. It was the sound of the tiny bastards that was driving us to insanity (or whatever it is that comes just before that).

When we were out in the open, the sun was as relentless as the mosquitoes. The intense light made it clear that our bodies were all covered in tiny cuts and bruises, which in turn were covered with mosquitoes and small flies. Preoccupied as we were with the insects and the rough environment, there was no chance for our skin to heal, so the scratches became small wounds. We had little energy left to feel their pain.

Our supplies were at their lowest, and there was no means of replenishing them. Only one canteen of water was left to share for the group, and the only form of fire was Gordon's cigarette lighter. Trapped as we all were, we constantly glanced around at each other, perhaps unconsciously taking an inventory of sanity among peers who had previously never truly known the others very well. George, by this point, seemed more withdrawn and continued to say very little. His hair was more dishevelled than the rest of ours and he had the beginnings of a beard. As I thought that, I could see him, in his tree, methodically grabbing at a branch, then putting his hand to his mouth. He kept doing that in a repetitive, mechanical way until I noticed that he was feeding himself with ants from the tree, plucking them out and eating them as fast as he could.

The wood that Cecil had brought back into camp was taken out into the sun to dry in an attempt to make fire with it later. When he felt ready to try his luck, he returned to camp with it, taking along some of the dried ferns as kindling. We heard nothing from him for a good half-hour. He still had his wits about him as he took the firewood into the camp for fear of setting the fern patch alight. When he reappeared, we had already seen smoke in the area of the lean-to. This was a joyous thing. We put most of the remainder of rice into a quarter of the water we had and it cooked rapidly over lively flames. Within ten minutes, we would be able to eat. At 2:00 in the afternoon, we could respond to the grumbling in our stomachs. We each had to be content with that hot meal, topped off by one mouthful of water and a squirt of toothpaste. This had been the main menu for the last few days.

We put the fire out just as soon as it had done its job because we needed to preserve the wood for a signal the next morning. We were not going to let them miss us tomorrow. If setting the fern patch on fire was our way out of that place, we had the inspiration and desperation to do it—strong winds, self-immolation, and smoke inhalation be damned.

★ ★ ★

The radio stations broadcast repeated bulletins, including a special appeal to Benjamin Gordon, the forest ranger we saw just before beginning our hike eight days earlier. "Mr. Gordon is being asked to contact the nearest police station," the announcer would plead, but Benjie Gordon never did call. Apparently he had gone into hiding. The broadcasts also carried instructions for us in the happy event that we could hear them. We never did.

There was also an updated headline that shouted our predicament in *The Star*, the afternoon tabloid published by the Gleaner Company:

SEARCH FOR MISSING FIVE INTENSIFIES

Helicopters of the Air Wing of the Jamaica Defence Force and units of the Police Mobile Reserve are continuing their search for five boys missing on a hike to Blue Mountain Peak, who up to press time had not been located.

A spokesman for the Police Mobile Reserve told the newspaper that more men from the Mobile Reserve will be going up to the Blue Mountain this afternoon to intensify the search.

SECOND TIME

It is the second time that five boys have been reported missing on the Peak, as 30 years ago, in [1939], a group of boys from Jamaica College, including [John Ennever, the brother of] the College's former Headmaster, and recent General Manager of the JBC [local broadcasting station], Mr. Harvey Ennever, were reported missing and a search launched.

The military and police were told that the five boys now missing on the Peak, after a hike which started on Saturday last week, were Gordon Cooper, George Hussey, Roger Bates, Cecil Ward and Geoffrey Haddad.

The noon and 6:00 p.m. radio broadcasts on the crisis were not encouraging:

The search continues for the five boys missing since Wednesday on a hike to the Blue Mountain Peak. A party of about fifty soldiers was sent out on foot this morning to search the area in which it is believed the boys traveled. The Chief of Staff Brigadier David Smith has said that a helicopter of the Air Arm resumed a search this morning but it was realized that it was difficult for those in the aircraft to spot people on the ground and so a team was sent out to blaze trail through the area. The hike was started at Clydesdale, and on Wednesday the boys were reported to have reached Penlyne Castle on the other side of the mountain, but no other report has been received about them. Brigadier Smith said that the investigation had revealed that an officer of the Forestry Department, Mr. Benjamin Gordon of Clydesdale, was the person known to have last seen the boys, and he was appealing to Mr. Gordon who was in Kingston today, to contact the military by telephoning 68121 and asking for extension 228 or 229. The 6:00 p.m. transmission ended with a personal appeal to us: The Jamaica Defence Force is also advising the boys if they are listening to this bulletin that a JDF helicopter will be flying over the area between 8 a.m. and 9:30 a.m. tomorrow and they should make every effort to reach a clearing or open space by that time so that the helicopter can spot them.

We were in a clearing. There was no doubt about that, but a clearing nowhere near our planned trail. Roger's father had gone up to Mavis Bank to learn anything that could be helpful. The other parents anxiously awaited his return.

★ ★ ★

"G. B., catch dat for me nuh!"

When George spoke again after some time, he was showing signs of desperation, perhaps bordering on delirium. He had already had his ants for an appetizer, and I figured he needed help from a genuine bush man to snare a bird or something we could cook for dinner, like a wild pig.

The croaking lizard (*Aristelliger praesignis*), is a nocturnal insect-eating gecko found in Jamaica. They are grayish to reddish in colour. During mating season, the males make a distinctively loud croaking call.

This was no pig. Without irony or humour, George gestured in the direction of a greyish-white creature clinging close to the base of the tree. He knew I had no fear of the animal, and if I could grab it, he would have been okay with eating it. I felt it was my duty to tell him that it was a white lizard, very similar to the despised croakin' lizard that terrifies Jamaican housewives and macho men alike.

My answer disgusted George enough for him to let the matter alone, and he climbed back to a higher point in the tree so he could pluck some more ants for snacking. It was Cecil and George that seemed to fantasize the most about fresh-boiled food, whatever they could catch. Cecil tried bringing birds down by flinging rocks at them; at other times, he had delusions of seeing another wild hog.

They say that the body starts to feel weak and confused after a short time without proper nutrition. Irritability and poor decision-making may then be followed by hallucinations and muscle spasms. Heart trouble and progressive multi-organ failure could then develop. Our minds, tested by hunger and fear, had begun to show signs of fragility.[1] The afternoon was remarkably clear, perfect weather for a rescue by air. The ridges around were not at all clouded by fog, but fears still persisted that we would not be found.

"Do you think they've stopped searching? No, not so quickly. Hope not. Parents wouldn't let it. But suppose…?"

The feelings and comments were universal.

We watched all day until, sure enough, we eventually heard the drone of a plane. It was flying too high and clearly not part of the rescue effort. We saw no other aircraft, but a Jamaica Air Service craft making daily crossover flights between Port Antonio to the northeast of us and Kingston to the southwest.

* * *

In my early teens as one of the Windsor 'inventors', we designed an airborne antenna which was, to our knowledge, the first one built in recent memory. It was 1965. I don't recall how Scope I was constructed, but it had failed.

Our one and only walkie-talkie set had a range of about 400 feet and the gang badly wanted to extend its range so we could keep in contact with base while roaming the immediate and extended neighbourhood. We were always on the move, scouting out or snooping around, sometimes without reason, just being curious and adventurous teenagers. Scope II was designed, built, and operated by me. It consisted of a properly constructed kite about two feet by three feet and was made in a conventional framework consisting of thin slender pieces of bamboo. That was a fairly standard form of construction. Before covering the kite with tissue, however, the entire frame around its perimeter as well as the radial pieces, were wired with a continuous length of copper wire.

Shameful to say, but the wire had been 'liberated' from transformers used in switchboards and the like belonging to the Jamaica Telephone Company. The wire was then led along the length of string from the kite to the flyer's end where it was connected to the antenna of one of the walkie-talkies. I flew the kite. Up she soared into an overcast sky in response to a strong, southerly Caribbean breeze. Off the other radio would go, carried by someone on a bicycle.

In a matter of minutes we had exceeded the range, 500 or 600 feet, and as far as about a mile, when disaster struck.

It was at this point that distant lightning, quite unnoticed by us before, 'struck' Scope II, causing the radio to emit a loud crackle. We were frightened as hell and I immediately let go of the wire attached to it. I also nearly released the main string attached to the kite. Down she came, to be packed away for another day.

With thousands of feet of copper wire on hand, our imaginations were never limited. By using our battery-operated mini reel-to-reel tape recorders, we discovered that we were able to create some kind of a telephone communication system. This was certainly the case in those days, when telephone calls were charged on a pay-as-you-go basis. By plugging a microphone into the recorder and a speaker, or another microphone at the other end, we made a one-way transmission by putting the machine into the record mode. For two way conversations, the same procedure was used at the other end. My system was connected to my adjacent neighbour using four sets of wires over 120 feet long. But the Crawford-to-Floro system necessitated running the wires above Windsor Avenue, so we installed it at night to avoid any suspicious onlookers. At twenty feet above the road and being very thin, it was unlikely that anyone passing by would notice them in the daytime. Alas, the set-up didn't last very long. A vehicle with a higher-than-expected payload came along the next day and brought the whole contraption down!

I can't recall what jogged my memory up there in the mountains; perhaps it was one of those incidences, but I suddenly recalled that I had both a radio and copper wire at hand.

Full of enterprise, I fished out the length of copper wire from my bag and attached it to the cutlass. Roger helped me rig it to the transistor radio, climbed the tree, and angled it until we were able to pick up an RJR (Radio Jamaica & Rediffusion) transmission, but there was only music, no news of any kind. We had to preserve the batteries in the radio, because unlike the flashlight, there were no replacements. I turned the radio off. Everyone who had a timepiece synchronized it at 4:25 p.m. I remember because I didn't have a watch.

★ ★ ★

To proceed down towards the river we would have had to follow the ridge that appeared to be only a few yards wide and which fell off at a very steep angle. It was as narrow as any we had encountered. On the other hand, to go down either side would be sheer lunacy, because the ridge had a double precipice we quickly deemed insurmountable given our physical and mental condition.

There was, naturally, another possibility: head back up onto the main Blue Mountain Ridge, now some 3,000 feet above us. Surely we would be seen there as all searches so far appeared to be concentrating in that area. If it were at all discussed, it was not with any passion. Where would the energy have come from?

George beckoned for us to help in the evaluation of the compass readings he had taken the evening before, and our map, on which we had plotted our trail thus far, showing the bearings:

facing north
- Peak of right hand ridge -- 100°
- Best way up right hand ridge -- 90°
- Position of settlement -- 0°
- Apparently shorter to n. coast -- 40°
- Position of mouth of river -- 10°
- Possibility of Mavis Bank -- 120°
- Three known ridges to -- 40°
- Steep gorge to settlement -- 10°
- Enclosed by mountains to south
- Two gaps to south -- 150°, 190°, best 150°
- Less rugged to-- 150°
- Big mountain ahead -- 30°

Using George's compass bearings, we created a rosette diagram in our minds in order to find the spot on our map that best fit its parameters. In unison with George, we settled on an approximate location.

With the search apparently over for the day, we marked Camp 9 on the map with heavy hearts.

We were now deeply troubled. Some of us were definitely contemplating the unthinkable idea, if only briefly, that we could be left on the mountain forever. Our entire world now consisted of a fern patch, a fifty-foot tree and what was left of five recently healthy young men, devastatingly out of food and water.

On the eighth day of our hike, we found ourselves trapped on a narrow ledge high up above the Swift River Valley in rugged terrain along the northern slopes of the Blue Mountains, perhaps where no man had ever trodden. So we had done something historic, perhaps, with no one and nowhere to tell the story.

Despite the flurry of activity, I was able to spend most of the day taking it easy or getting some sleep under the lean-to. As the sunlight waned, we made our way back to it from each of the lookout points we had staked out. We tried to make the coming night more comfortable by packing some more tree roots and fresh ginger lilies into the sleeping area. Cecil's sleeping bag was returned to the ground and was shared between Gordon and himself for the night's rest. Gordon's toothpaste was passed around for one ration each.

Not satisfied with leaving the firewood out in the open, we each curled up with a piece, hoping to keep it as warm and dry as possible.

We were plagued by the same answerless questions:

"So what if we know where we are? Will we be found tomorrow? What if we aren't? What will we eat? How will we keep going? Will we ever see our parents again? Could we all die here?"

It was enough mental exhaustion to make sleep easy.

★ ★ ★

Port Antonio, the largest town in the area, and located in the parish of Portland where most of the Blue Mountain Range runs, may not be among Jamaica's best-known tourist areas, even though British and North American tourism began there during the banana-boat era. There is a huge current thrust to elevate it to the status of the other better known tourist centres, as seen in the few resorts located there.

In the past, and despite its current troubles, Jamaica is considered, even today, a paradise. Perhaps this is true, though only in the major cities and tourist areas of Montego Bay, Ocho Rios and Negril where beautiful, secluded and traditional hotels have been replaced by an ever-increasing number of all-inclusive resorts that offer unlimited food and drink all day. Tipping is not permitted and is perhaps one of the reasons that the quality of service once enjoyed by patrons of such traditional resorts as Jamaica Inn, Tryall and Half Moon has fallen off. However, because of apparent (better value for your money) lower costs of these all-inclusive hotels, the island now benefits from increased visitor arrivals, well exceeding three million in 2009.

As late as the 1940s, little had been documented of the terrain in Portland, particularly the area of the greater hinterlands and the heavily rain-forested northern slopes of the Blue Mountains. To be sure, some topographical maps existed showing the more trodden regions of the area, but there really was no need to be concerned for mapping the inner regions until the ill-fated 1939 schoolboy expedition.

It was feared that the 1939 group could have been lost for good, but the hikers themselves at some point on their journey were in a jubilant mood when they recorded, "We will write a story!"

Suddenly, there was a need to describe in detail the enormity of the problems that could be faced by would-be hikers who ventured there. Some parts of these accounts were apparently based on imaginative reports and hypotheses, but most were grotesquely factual.

Newspaper reports during the 1939 crisis had carried sensational headlines:

WIDE JUNGLE SEARCH FOR FIVE LOST HIKERS

DRAMATIC SEARCH

Some excerpts from two of the reports are reproduced here from Hartley Neita's book *The Search*, describing the inhospitable deep interior of the mountains:

> It is no exaggeration to say that there are places in the island that the foot of man has never trodden, and are as inaccessible as any place in the world.

> Strange at it may seem, in a tropical island, these places so high up in the hills have a climate that is as near as it is possible for one to get in comparison to the colder regions of the world and when one adds to it almost incessant rain and mist of terrifying density one should be able to see what any one getting lost in there is up against.

> First of all, there is no food of any kind to be found at
> that altitude. You can see water and cannot get it and
> it means cutting your way through moss-covered veg-
> etation from which moisture is always dripping even
> at high noon. It is never dry. The sun appears only for
> a few seconds and then it is gone, might be, never to
> appear for the remainder of the day. [p.38]

and,

> Over a precipice dropping almost sheer for a thousand
> feet the five missing schoolboys went several days ago.
> They went over this precipice voluntarily, a deed of
> outstanding courage that the seasoned bushmen now
> on their trail will not emulate whether these lads are
> found dead or alive…They have either gone to their
> doom or else have reached a ledge* from which they
> dare not proceed, either downwards or upward. [p. 41]

Virtually nothing had changed for us between 1939 and 1967.
Hiking equipment was the same, as were affordable communications
systems. We were not prepared for what we had to overcome, and so the
very same thing that was feared for them now awaited us. In fact, the
weather conditions in our case were much harsher (more dismal, wetter
and much colder, 4°C, not taking into account the windchill factor)
and consequently, the probability of finding edible fruits/berries more
unlikely due to the time of year—December in our case vs. April in
theirs. Compared to us, the '39 group was much better prepared (and, in
fact, consisted of 'seasoned hikers'); however, they chose to carry a single
axe but no machetes. They even took along material for constructing
hammocks to keep themselves elevated from the cold and damp ground,
and perhaps for protection from wild boar and any other animals.

There was no meal that night. Instead, we held back the few remaining grains of rice for another day.

---

*   Our precise situation, perhaps presaged nearly thirty years earlier.

END NOTES

1   Excerpts from *The Outdoor Edge Magazine*, July/August 2013 – "LOST: Your Guide to Surviving in the Bush", by Dragan Uzelac, NIKO Wilderness Education:

The bush is neutral—it's neither for you, nor against you. What happens to you in the bush depends entirely on you. What you put into it is what you get out of it.

There are two kinds of 'lost' – the first you have simply become disorientated or walked off your intended trail.

In this case, the first thing you must do is stop, sit down and try to relax. This may sound like an easy thing to do, but most people run, believing that they're just steps off the trail. This can lead to death by exposure, which is a combination of dehydration, chilling, and fatigue. People have been found dead within the first 36 hours of being lost, with dry matches in their pocket and all the necessary gear to make it through the episode.

The best way to remain calm is to spend time, prior to any adventure out in the bush, developing the skills needed for this type of situation and being prepared and practiced with all the tools you carry; this will help you stay calm and survive, more so than having all the latest and greatest gear that you don't know how to use......

Mark the position where you first became lost. Make sure all of your marks are at eye level and you can use wads of moss, handfuls of grass, broken branches or blazes. And then pick the direction you believe is right. As much as possible, put up a marker when the last two are visible.. Use three marks to indicate a sudden change in direction. Such a trail will also provide large targets for searchers.........

No way out

The second kind of lost is much more serious. In this situation, you don't know where you are, how you got there or how you might get back.

If this is the case and you cannot find your way out using the above method, you will need to stay in one spot and wait to be rescued.

It is important to admit to yourself that you are truly lost. Continuing to wander around in the bush, hoping to find your way out, will only get you more lost.

Fire

Learning how to build a fire, ignite it in numerous ways and fuel it and to keep it going under all conditions takes years of practice. The ability to build a fire in a hurry can be the difference between life and death. A good warming fire should force you to stay one step back.

You should never venture into the bush without three ways to light a fire. These ways could include a metal match – a single rod can strike over 10,000 fires before you need a new one, and this is a tool you should carry on every outing. Matches/and or lighter, as well as cotton balls coated with petroleum jelly, sealed in a waterproof case, are also good backups…

Water

The importance of staying hydrated trumps the need for food by about 40 days……..
There is a real possibility that you may be lost for four or five days, but it is quite unlikely that you won't be found for 40 days.
Within your first 24 hours of being lost, water is something you should spend the time and energy to find……..
No matter what, in our environment you've got four days without water before irreversible damage is done to your body and brain. When you become dehydrated, your blood starts to thicken and it slows circulation and the transfer of warm blood to your fingers, toes, and brain.
A few tell tale signs of being properly hydrated: your urine colour should be slightly yellow and you must be passing about one litre of fluid a day.

Clothing and signs of hypothermia

Clothing is the single most important factor in your survival, above all else, and oddly it's most misunderstood and underemphasized of all topics. Clothing in the bush is just as important as a space suit is to an astronaut……

For hunting season, hypothermia is our greatest enemy, as opposed to hyperthermia. Most cases of hypothermia are reported from -1 to + 10 degrees Celsius [30 to 50 degrees Fahrenheit] daytime temperature, because people go out undressed to be able to handle the evening temperatures, which are dangerously different.

One good test to tell if your core temperature has dropped to a dangerous level is to try touching your pinkie to your thumb. If this is difficult, you must stop what you are doing and start a fire immediately and get warm. When you have trouble touching your pinkie to your thumb, this means that your fine motor skills are almost gone. At this point, lighting a match might be impossible, but the metal match uses gross motor skills. If fire isn't an option, do your best to force yourself to exercise and bring up your core temperature – you're entering a dangerous state at this point, so you must do whatever is necessary.

Just like you won't learn to hunt or fish by simply reading an article, effective and survival techniques need to be studied and practised.

Rescued five say thanks

A letter of thanks to all who had played a part in their rescue was sent to the Gleaner yesterday by the five Jamaica College boys who were missing in the Blue Mountains during last week.

Written from Jamaica College on Christmas Day, the letter was signed by all five boys who were involved in the adventure — Gordon Cooper, George Hussey, Roger Bates, Cecil Ward and Geoffrey Haddad.

Said the letter:

"We, the five boys from Jamaica College rescued in the Blue Mountains, would like to express our appreciation publicly to the Jamaica Defence Force, the Forest Rangers, Radio, Press, Clergy and all who prayed for us, and Mr. Jack Biscoe, who played such a large part in our rescue.

"We were indeed in difficulties and seriously short of food. Without this help we certainly would not have made it out and been home for Christmas, about which we thought so often.

"Thanks to all who helped specially to Mr. Biscoe and his crew who spotted our smoke trail.

"It was good to be home for Xmas."

SAFE AND SOUND: The five boys at Camp on Sunday, after they had been rescued from the Blue Mountains. They are (from left) Gordon Cooper, Cecil Ward, Geofrey Haddad, Roger Bates and George Hussey. Behind them is one of the helicopters of the Jamaican Defense Force which took part in their rescue.

After intensive two-day search...

5 boys rescued from Blue Mtns. ravine

Spotted by light plane, taken out by 'copters

Anxiety for the five 'choolboys from Jamaica College who were lost in the Blue Mountains when they did not return from a hiking trip to the peak that was due to end last Wednesday, was relieved on Sunday morning when they were found, safe and sound, in a ravine in the mountains, and were brought out by helicopter.

Climaxing an intensive two-day search of the mountains by the Army and the Police, the missing five — Gordon Cooper, George Hussey, Cecil Ward, Roger Bates, and Geofrey Haddad — were found by a private plane piloted by Mr. Jack Tyndale-Briscoe, well known amateur pilot and aerial photographer.

They were in a defile in the mountains, about five miles down the Swift River, north of Portland Gap. The time was 9.25 a.m. and in the plane was Mr. Leslie Ward, father of one of the boys. Smoke from a fire built by the boys in a clearing which they had made in the heavy bush attracted the attention of the circling plane, and brought about their rescue.

Two 'copters

Two helicopters — one military, the other private — were used to take the boys out of the mountains. They were flown to Ken Jones Airport, in Portland, and from there to Kingston. The two helicopters brought three of the boys to Jamaican Defence Force headquarters at Up Park Camp, while the other two were flown to Palisadoes Airport in Mr. Tyndale Biscoe's plane and driven from there to Up Park Camp, where they joined their comrades-in-distress and were welcomed by their anxiously waiting families.

By noon on Sunday, the near-tragedy which had gripped the island and created national concern was over. The boys were in reasonably good shape. They were cold and wet and thirsty, but none the worse for their adventure. In fact, they said almost in unison, to answer to the inevitable question, that they would "do it again."

Telling the story of their adventure, the boys said that after leaving Clydesdale last Saturday, they climbed Sir John's Peak and were on their way to Blue Mountain Peak on Tuesday when they ran short of water. They started to search for a stream and found the bed of the river course, but because of foggy conditions, took a wrong direction and headed north instead of south.

Wrong direction

When they realised from the flow of the river, that they were headed in the wrong direction, they also discovered that they were in "bad country." The terrain was rugged, with dense bush and grass through which they had to hack their way. So they decided to remain where they were, in a ravine, and wait for rescue.

There was a tall tree in the clearing, and they climbed to the top of this, clearing its leaves and top limbs, so they could be seen from the air. They took turns as lookout, and by Friday, heard the planes and helicopters circling overhead. They were not spotted until Sunday morning, however, when the smoke from their fire, lighted that morning, caught the watching eyes of Mr. Ward and Mr. Tyndale-Biscoe.

One of the boys, Hussey, had a transistor radio, but he said he could hear nothing on it at first — "only screeches." Later he was able to hear music being broadcast, but no 'news' or any announcements concerning his colleagues and himself.

Food ran out on them. "We were down to our last two packs of rice, and we were unable to cook it because of the damp conditions," they said. But hunger had not yet become a serious problem.

Visibility

Climatic conditions in the mountains made visibility difficult from the ground as well as from the air. Just as the boys were unable to see the aircraft which were searching for them, so the aircraft were unable to see the boys. A low cloud-ceiling in the area — especially in the afternoon, reduced visibility considerably.

A combined Army and Police operation conducted the search for the boys. Also sharing in the search was Mr. Tyndale-Biscoe and Mr. "Tinker" Berrie whose helicopter was one of these used in the rescue operation. Foresters from the Forestry Department also took part in the search. Attention was concentrated on the south side of Sir John's Peak, where an Army patrol was stationed to maintain contact with other Army and Police patrols which were out on search along the various tracks in the area. These patrols concentrated on the ridges, while the Forestry Department concentrated their efforts among the foothills.

Intensified search

Following abortive searches on Friday and again on Saturday, the search was intensified on Sunday morning, when a planned 90-minute search from 8 a.m. to 9.30 was carried out. It was this intensified search in which the light aircraft and the two helicopters were engaged, that brought success at 9.25 a.m. when the boys were spotted.

When the discovery was made the plane signalled to the helicopter which had been concentrating on the south side of Sir John's Peak. The helicopter flew to the spot, located the boys, returned to base for refuelling and then flew back with the other helicopter. Both helicopters picked up the boys and flew them to Ken Jones Airport.

Meanwhile, at the Air Wing section of Camp, the anxious families of the boys awaited keeping vigil there from early in the morning. As the two helicopters flew in and came to rest on the ground, a subdued cheer rose from the tense gathering. Then there was the joy and poignancy of reunion with parents, sisters and girl friends. There were even a few unashamed tears of joy.

For the waiting parents, it was the end of a long ordeal of agony and uncertainty. Perhaps the parents who showed the greatest emotion were the Haddads. It was Mr. Haddad who on Wednesday when the boys were unreported from camp, took steps to find out what had happened to them and who contacted the other parents, the Police and eventually the Military, leading to the big search. Mrs. Haddad put it graphically: "We have had three sleepless nights."

Mr. Charles Cooper, father of Gordon, was not at Camp. He was over at Swift River, in Portland, organising a search of the area, working along with the foresters. "I felt certain that the Swift River area was where we were to look for them," he said. He heard by radio the news of the discovery of the boys and returned to Kingston later that Sunday, a happy man.

THESE ARE THE MOUNTAINS
(SOUTH SIDE)

THESE ARE THE MOUNATINS **PANORAMA: The sweep of the Blue Mountain Range** from left to right: 1) Morces Gap, 2) Bellevue Peak, 3) Sir Johns Peak, 4) High Peak, 5) Main Ridge Gap, 6) Mossman's Peak, 7) Portland Gap, 8)Two Claw in the distance behind, 9) Blue Mountain Peak, 10) Sugar Loaf Peak. *Photo courtesy of J.S. Tyndale-Biscoe..*

Note: The boys entered the Blue Mountain Ridge at 3—Sir Johns Peak. By the time they got to Main Ridge Gap (5), their water and food supplies were dwindling. Rainfall, heavy fog, and dense cloud formation coupled with the raging cold north-east winds resulted in poor visibility causing them to become disoriented. Then and there they were forced to abort the mission of conquering the Peak (9) and instead looked for a trail which would lead them back to Kingston. Whilst searching for a source of water they made the almost deadly mistake leading them over the Ridge to the north side (opposite side to which this photograph was taken) to one of the densest jungles in the world, next to Myanmar (once Burma). *-Jack Tyndale-Biscoe.*

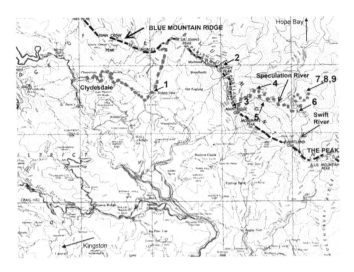

Top: The actual route taken on the way to Blue Mountain Peak, showing campsites numbered 1–9. Poor visibility, bad weather conditions, inadequate preparation and bad luck conspired to take the expedition off course to the north in Portland and left us trapped high in the woodlands, far from a living soul. The Speculation River, which is the largest tributary feeding into the Swift, was mistaken for the Swift for the majority of our time while descending into the jungle.

Bottom: Army Air Wing officers c.1966, a number of whom were involved in the search and rescue operations. *Left to right:* Captain John Dent, Captain 'Bunny' Stern, Major George Brown, Captain Dennis Walcott, Captain Andrew Bogle and Major Robert 'Bob' Neish. *Photo courtesy of JDF Air Wing Commander Lieutenant Colonel George Brown (ret'd)*

Top Right: Shown is one of the three compasses. Once we lost our bearings on the mountain, the device became useless because we no longer had a reference point from which to take a reading and correctly determine a target.

Centre Left: My military-surplus canteen (acquired from American WWII forces in Jamaica). By day four of the trek, December 19, our water supply went dry. After refilling at a river and moving on, we found ourselves trapped on a Blue Mountain ridge. By December 21 (day six), our water was almost depleted .

Bottom: My Bulova Accutron watch, serial #M7-1 591524, given to me by my parents at Christmas 1967, after the Blue Mountain ordeal.

Year 1967		AIRCRAFT		Pilot, or	2nd Pilot, Pupil	DUTY
MONTH	DATE	Type	No.	1st Pilot	or Passenger	(Including Results and Remarks)
—	—	—	—	—	—	—
						Totals Brought Forward
DEC	10	CESSNA 185	A1	Self	Plc Hudson	B - Santch - B
	11	Cessna 185	A1	Self	Maj Alwright	B - Mo Bay - B
	11	Bell 47 G	H1	Self	Casualty	B - New Castle - B
	12	Cessna 185	A1	Self	- TR	Tattoo Rehearsal
	13	Cessna 185	A1	Self	-	Tattoo Rehearsal
	13	Cessna 185	A3	Self	-	Air Test
	14	Cessna 185	A3	Self	3 + 3 JR	B - Mo Bay - B
	14	Bell 47 G	H2	Self	Capt Ogilvie	B - Pal - B
	18	DHC-6	T1	Self	Plc Lyons	B - Pal - B
	18	Bell 47 G	H2	Self	Maj Thornton	B - Caymanas - B
	20	Bell 47 G	H2	Self	Sgt Hall	B - Troy - B
	21	DHC-6	T1	Self	Cpl Dean	B - Pal - B
	22	Bell 47 G	H1	Self	Maj Cave	B - Blue Mtn - B
	22	DHC-6	T1	Self	Ch Campbell Air Cood	B - Mo Bay - B
	23	Bell 47 G	H1	Self	Maj Cave	B - Blue Mtn - B
	24	Bell 47 G	H1	Self	Capt Dent	B - Blue Mtn - B
	27	Cessna 185	A1	Self	-	B - Pal - B
	28	DHC-6	T1	Self	Maj Elkridge	B - Mo Bay - B
	29	Cessna 185	A1	Self	-	Cont. TRG
						JAMAICA AIR WING
						Summary for DECEMBER 67
						Date 3rd JAN '68
						Signature

FIXED WING (S) : 537.55   GRAND TOTAL [Cols. (1) to (10)]

CLYDESDALE AT START
OF HIKE. SATURDAY 16th DEC 1967
TIME 3.45pm.
FROM LEFT:

1. Gordon Cooper
2. Ronald George Hussey
3. Roger H.M. Bake
4. Geoffrey B Haddad
5.

Top: Capt Anthony 'Bunny' Stern's Log Book for December 1967, provided by Lt. Colonel Jaimie Ogilvie of the Air Wing of the Jamaica Defence Force in 2014.

Bottom: Signatures of four of the five boys attached to the back of last photograph of the boys together at the start of the hike on Saturday, December 16, 1967. The missing signature is that of Cecil Ward, a working man who was not available for the signing, which took place at Jamaica College in January, 1968.

Top: Me with Men's Doubles partner Keith Palmer (a multi-All-Jamaica triple champion) receiving our trophies from the Hon. Hector Winter (Minister of Sports) in 1969. President of the Jamaica Badminton Association, Mr. Frank Parslow, is at right. *Photo courtesy of The Gleaner Company*

Bottom: Panchacharan 'Punch' Gunalan (world badminton champion) and me at the IXth Commonwealth Games in Edinburgh, Scotland in 1970. Gunalan became head of the Malaysian Olympic Association and sadly passed away in 2012.

Top: Governor-General of Jamaica, Sir Florizel Glasspole, toasting the brides-maids at my wedding on October 5, 1974. Left to right: B. S. and Norma Haddad, me, the bride Susan Middleton, John (Commissioner of Police) and Phyllis Middleton, Jennifer Haddad (my sister) and Karen Goodson.

Centre: July 20, 2001: More than 150 attend B. S. Haddad's funeral held on the front lawn of his home at 25 Windsor, a place he seldom left. At right, I pay tribute to my father at the farewell. Note my 'Willys' jeep in the foreground at left.

Bottom: Front row, left to right: My wife Susan, sisters Jennifer and Beverley, Norma Haddad and me.

THE HADDAD FAMILY – FOUR GENERATIONS

Four generations of the Haddad family have been avid hunters and men of the outdoors. *Clockwise from top:* Shukrella Michael at a White Belly shoot, circa 1905; Badia Shukrella with a rack of White Wings, 1962; me, Geoffrey Badia, high in the Blue Mountains in 1986, and Neil Geoffrey (left) and Philip Geoffrey, my sons, after a White Wing shoot in Mexico, 2001. The advancements in the family's mode of transportation over a 110-year period are easily recognizable (i.e., bicycle, automobile, helicopter and by jet aircraft).

CHAPTER 14

FOUND

Sunday, December 24, 1967 (Day 9)

We headlined the *Daily Gleaner* again. This time it was the Christmas Eve edition, and our story comprised a substantial portion of the newspaper's front page and next news page. As with this sort of drama anywhere in the world (but maybe particularly so on a small island), people's emotions were caught up with the turn of events. The nation waited anxiously for news of our safe return.

Beneath the headlines were innocent-looking individual photographs of each boy.

The headlines warned:

Army, Police Comb Blue Mountain area
AIR, LAND SEARCH FOR MISSING BOYS
90-minute helicopter hunt planned this morning
Hikers last seen at Clydesdale on Wednesday.

The body of the article was another amalgam of the history of the hike from the perspective of several 'informed' parties:

ARMY AND POLICE patrols combed the Blue Mountain range yesterday in a search for the five Jamaica College schoolboys who left last Saturday on a hike across to the Peak—and have not returned home.

At press time last night, a patrol of soldiers from the Jamaica Defence Force were resting at Sir Johns Peak, preparatory for a further search in the Blue Mountain area—after an all-day search which produced no clues as to the whereabouts of the missing boys.

At the same time, a similar patrol of men from the Mobile Division of the Police rested last night at Mavis Bank after another all-day search of the Blue Mountain area, fanning out in all nearby sections where it was thought that the boys might have gone. Air and land search for the missing boys was intensified yesterday with all officers of the Forestry Department, whose territory covers the Blue Mountains, being called into the search.

An officer of the Forestry Department, Mr. Benjamin Gordon, is reported to have seen and talked with the boys on Wednesday the day on which, according to the reports, they should have completed the trip and returned to Kingston. Mr. Gordon is reported to have seen the boys on Wednesday at Clydesdale—the point from which, incidentally, they took off last Saturday. Whether, in fact, he saw them there or at some point in the mountains is not established as up to late last night the Army was trying to get in touch with Mr. Gordon to get more definite information from him.

Mr. Gordon is said to be based at St. Peters, near Newcastle.

An Army helicopter is going up again this morning to search the area in which it is believed that the boys are, and it is hoped that by this time the boys have heard— one of them is said to have a transistor radio—that a search is being made for them.

A 90-minute search—from 8 a.m. to 9:30 a.m.—is planned for the helicopter, which will circle the area around Sir Johns Peak in the hope that the boys, having heard the radio broadcast concerning the search, will look out for the helicopter and signal it.

Yesterday the JDF continued its search by air and land for the missing boys. A helicopter of the Air Arm flew over the mountains hovering low in an effort to locate them.

A team of foot soldiers was also sent out to search the area, following the trail, which it was said that the boys were to have followed, and to find out, if possible, where they may have deviated from the trail.

According to earlier reports, the boys were to have reached Penlyne Castle a well-known point on the Blue Mountain Peak climb, on Wednesday last. They had obviously not done so.

A report last night that they had reached Buff Bay, on the Portland side of the mountain, was not confirmed.

Mr. Charles Cooper, father of one of the missing boys, said last night that he took the boys to Clydesdale, near Chestervale in St. Thomas, at about 3:30 p.m. last Saturday, December 16. They took with them food, compasses, cutlasses, sleeping bags and methylated spirits.

Mr. Cooper said, when the boys left, it was estimated that they would have completed the trip by Wednesday last and returned to Kingston. He said it had been figured that they would have arrived at Mavis Bank that day, and would have returned to the city by land transportation from that point.

Another source said that, although the boys thought they could have completed the journey by Wednesday, it had not seemed likely that they would have been able to have done it by yesterday (Saturday), having regard to the round about route that they had planned.

Also mentioned in the report was the irony of my high school being involved once more:

JC boys again!

Missing in the Blue Mountains, on the Peak hike that started last Saturday and should have ended on Wednesday last, are: Gordon Cooper, George Hussey, Roger Bates, Cecil Ward and Geoffrey Haddad.

They are students of Jamaica College and are in the Sixth Form. They are between 16 and 17 years of age.

Their parents are:

Mr. and Mrs. Charles Cooper of 1 Plymouth Avenue, Kingston 6, Mr. and Mrs, R. O. Hussey of 13 Rochester Avenue, Kingston 8, Mr. and Mrs. T. P. Bates, 3A Richmond Avenue, Kingston 10, Mr. and Mrs. Leslie Ward, 13 Norbury Drive, Kingston 8; Mr. and Mrs. Geoffrey [should have been B. S.] Haddad, 25 Windsor Avenue, Kingston 10.

Mr. Cooper is an executive of the Bank of Nova Scotia, Jamaica Ltd. and Mr. Hussey is a businessman who operates a seafood sales enterprise.

Mr. Bates is an officer of the Ministry of Finance and Planning. Mr. Ward is also a businessman, and so is Mr. Haddad.

And:

Flashback

Around Easter, in 1939, another five Jamaica College boys hit the headlines and created concern throughout the island when they were missing in the Blue Mountains for over a week.

Those missing then were: Eric Gray, Douglas Hall, Donald Soutar, Teddy Hastings, and John Ennever.

They left on a trek across the Blue Mountains range and were unreported after they had been due to return home. A search was organized for them, and they eventually turned up, safe and well, in the foothills of the Blue Mountains, near Buff Bay, in Portland.

They had lost their way, had run out of food and had had a difficult time in the last two or three days of their highland adventure.

★ ★ ★

The search was now consolidated at maximum effort. Personnel comprised some 200 soldiers, numerous policemen, officers of the Forestry Department and civilian search parties. Three helicopters and a number of private planes had been commissioned.

Incredibly, we awoke after a good twelve hours' sleep that night. If I couldn't know where I was exactly, I at least wanted to know what time it was. It made me feel I had some facts on my side.

"What's the time, Rog? " I inquired.

"Blasted watch stop!"

"Cecil, what time yu have?"

He wasn't going to be helpful, either.

"Coops, what's de time?" I persisted.

Gordon rolled over and consulted his timepiece. His watch worked. He mumbled gruffly that it was eight o'clock.

This was no time to be sleepy and apathetic. We tried to rouse each other into getting up right away. Someone started describing his dream of the night before and it was weird to discover that our dreams had been frightfully eerie, as if there might indeed be a sort of telepathic communion between distressed minds. Every one of us had dreamed of being rescued while encountering a person or path heading to Mavis Bank. This was understandable, since Mavis Bank is a well-known spot from where we could easily get home. What was peculiar was that in each dream, we all had to pay the person to be led to safety. In exchange for money we were not only being promised 'passage to safe haven' but also a cold Pepsi and some bulla cakes. It was utterly improbable that this sort of mercenary thing would happen, but our fears and fantasies were powerful storytellers.

In reality, I again awoke with one of my ears filled with cold water, most likely the result of condensed moisture from our tattered raincoat 'roofing' material.

But we didn't dwell long on this because we were no longer dreaming. The bright promise of our dreams had been cruelly extinguished by the real light of day.

We were still under the porous lean-to. Our constant companions, the mosquitoes, were already awake and stood watch with us while we were obscured from the outside world. I noticed that Cecil was up and already busy. He was at it again, trying to get a fire going under the shelter. Bless his soul, he was being good-natured and optimistic. He got a fire going so well that I had to move myself from the lean-to as the flames threatened my feet with fresh embers. My toes had felt ticklishly warm, and my plastic bag almost caught fire. That got me up quickly enough, even though I hadn't wanted to at all. My body pains were no joke; my back was in agony. A persistent cough kept coming from my sore and painful throat, nagging signs of bronchitis.

★ ★ ★

The fire was transported out to the middle of the fern patch and we got it to blaze again. We finished not a moment too soon, because just a few minutes later we heard the new hum of a plane's engine. We piled green, wet ferns onto the flames, but the atmosphere was already so hot that they just browned. Unknown to us at the time, several plants in the forest will not burn or produce smoke, but rather only smoulder. We couldn't make a smoke signal no matter how much fire we applied.

Our surroundings had begun to fog over and a large cloud moved into the area of the main ridges encircling us. When we saw the plane, it was Cecil and Gordon who took to the tree and combined their waving with signals from the front of our now battered metallic flashlight.

★ ★ ★

While we were being frustrated by humankind's most basic technical chore, radio communications were being made between a plane and the air traffic control tower at Palisadoes Airport in Kingston. The aircraft was about six miles due north-northwest of us above the rugged northern slopes of the Blue Mountains. Aboard Delta Yankee, now descending from 8,300 feet and heading towards the Palisadoes Airport was pilot J. S. 'Jack' Tyndale-Biscoe, with co-pilot and spotter David du Mont, Biscoe's long time friend, who was on holiday from work in the Bahamas.

In the rear of the four-seater aircraft sat an anxious and perplexed passenger. Les Ward, Cecil's father, was not accustomed to being tossed around by turbulence in a tiny flying machine. He was also suffering from a serious bout of motion sickness. Ward was screaming bloody murder, demanding to be returned to the ground. The strongest constitutions, perhaps, may not have fared any better in a small, single-engine aircraft fighting airflows while trying to manoeuvre along the ridges and valleys of the Blue Mountains, especially after having eaten a traditionally hearty Jamaican Sunday breakfast.

Du Mont felt for the sickly dad sitting in the rear of the plane, but he was focused on the ground.

"Jackie, you have got to check it out," du Mont insisted.

"There is definitely smoke, not fog this time!"

"Alright boss, let's take a look," Tyndale-Biscoe said, more hopeful again. The C180 Cessna Skywagon came skimming the top of the ridge towards the south, making her way at a very steep angle down in our direction. This was our chance! Cecil had suggested we gather leaves from the cut limbs of the tree. I gathered them frantically now. As the plane headed into the dive to get below the dense enveloping cloud, I threw them into the roaring fire. There was a glorious burst of smoke. We waited with pounding hearts until Gordon shouted in exhilaration:

The Cessna 180 was 'Jack' Tyndale-Biscoe's airplane of choice for his transportation and aerial photography operation.

"G. B.! Rahtid, de plane turn!" he shrieked. "De plane turn, dem see us. An' we did t'ink say we lost to rass!"

He was screaming like a madman from his perch in the treetop. The uppermost limbs had been lopped off in order to lay out the sleeping bag. Gordon, with all of his antics, was fortunate not to have become entangled in it, otherwise he would have toppled in an instant.

George, Roger, and I were overcome with emotion. Our voices trembled softly as we dared declare to each other that we were found. With great excitement and anticipation, we scrambled to the middle of the fern patch next to the tree.

Then there was silence. Nothing. The plane disappeared out of sight behind the mountain ridge* to the north of us. Seconds passed before the echo of the airborne engine came again to our ears. Was it the same aircraft? Another one? Two? But there was still nothing to see. Was it a sort of auditory and visual hallucination? Did we imagine that first manifestation of an aircraft? Had we finally lost our minds?

Our hearts sank. But within minutes, the Cessna shot by low overhead, passing what seemed to be within feet of Gordon and Cecil in the tree. That scared them to death. The engine was cut three times. We took this as confirmation that we had been seen. We knew we couldn't be heard from the ground, but we kept on shouting and waving because we couldn't stop ourselves.

The plane circled back and now came a message from the pilot who had opened the window of the aircraft and shouted down. It was a measure of how acclimatised we had become to the sounds of isolation

---

*   It was the ridge facing us on the opposite side of the Swift River Valley.

that his words sounded as if they were coming through a megaphone. They came loudly, but not clearly:

"Stay where you are!"

"Stay...RRR...are!"

"RRR...to call the helicopter!"

Delta Yankee, now circling at an altitude of about 6000 feet, was one of two aircraft belonging to Airways Charters, a company owned by Jackie Tyndale-Biscoe and managed by his wife Marjorie. At about the same time, another aircraft of his was reconnoitring the northeastern area of the Blue Mountain Ridge at altitude 8,500 feet, more or less. This aircraft, a Beechcraft Debonair with the markings 6Y-JFC, was being piloted by Ian Jacobs, an Airways Charters pilot. Biscoe radioed Ian Jacobs the pilot of his other aircraft, the Beechcraft Debonair 6Y-JFC:

"Foxtrot Charlie, Foxtrot Charlie: Delta Yankee do you read?"

"Delta Yankee, Foxtrot Charlie: go ahead."

"Found the boys...a tiny clearing on a near vertical ledge...high up on a ridge deep in a ravine...Swift River...some of them are in a tree..."

"Delta Yankee, confirm you found the boys."

"Affirmative, Foxtrot Charlie."

"Foxtrot Charlie Roger," Biscoe answered gleefully, "...appears to be no major injuries...now seeing two in a tree and three on the ground."

"Delta Yankee...Thank God!" Jacobs exulted.

"Foxtrot Charlie, David saw some smoke, spotted them...and confirmed with binoculars...what a Christmas gift for the parents...all those thousands of anxious souls . . ."

"Roger, Delta Yankee...am I to call base?...Does Marjorie have the air-to-ground radio on?"*

---

* Howard Nugent, the principal of Audiofon at the time, recalls installing two-way VHF – EF Johnson radios in each of Airways Charters aircrafts; 6Y-JDY and 6Y-JFC for communicating to each other and the Base Operations, managed by Marjorie Biscoe. The main aircraft radios were factory installed. In order to communicate with the Control Tower at Palisadoes, the aeronautical frequency used was 118.1MHz.

"Delta Yankee, Roger, she's as anxious to relay any news, but I'm too low, we have to stay in this gorge in the Swift…dense clouds moving in…making sure we don't lose sight of the boys. One blink of the eye and they're gone! Advise Palisadoes of my new plans…not able to contact the Tower at this altitude."*

"Delta Yankee: Roger, go ahead."

Tyndale-Biscoe had a major concern. "Delta Yankee, if that fire goes out… I don't know what we'll do…dangerous as hell…experiencing major turbulence…now circling a bit to gain some altitude…up to 6,500 feet…come in Foxtrot Charlie."

On the ground, Marjorie Tyndale-Biscoe was already in contact with Captain Bunny Stern, who was standing by helicopter JDF-H1 at Army headquarters. In addition, a number of ham radio operators, including Ernest DeSouza (who lived across the road from Tyndale-Biscoe) and Lloyd Alberga were on hand to pass on the good news.

"Roger Ian, please stand by; we must stay in contact, line of sight; I cannot afford to go high enough to be in contact with Palisadoes…do you copy, Foxtrot Charlie?"

"Foxtrot Charlie, check your fuel, Jackie…I only have forty-five minutes left."

"Roger on that, Foxtrot Charlie. We have a little," he said, pausing to curse. "Get the choppers here ASAP. That's the only way out for them. It will be very difficult though—not much space to work with. I may have to refuel before they get here. Taken many photos and noted co-ordinates in the meantime. Let's hope that the weather holds."

"Foxtrot Charlie, standing by Delta Yankee—keeping this channel open."

From the posture of the aircraft, with its nose pointing straight up, it looked to us that they were going off to radio the message that we had been located. It was about 8:55 a.m.

---

* At the time, there was no real-time photography, so it was therefore impossible for Biscoe to relay precise information about the topography to the JDF to decide whether ground extraction was possible. He had no option, therefore, but to continue reconnoitering the area as low as a few hundred feet above our location.

But the Cessna did not leave. It circled around for roughly half an hour, sending down messages primarily related to our welfare. Were we alright? Was anyone injured? In our elation, and not being able to properly make out what was being said, we gesticulated broadly in response to whatever we imagined was being communicated.

The search was over. Nobody could begin to understand the severity of the problems we now faced. How would we ever be rescued from this dense and treacherous terrain? We were perched on one of the untrodden ridges deep in the bowels of the Swift River after all, encircled by a dense forest of tall trees.

CHAPTER 15

RESCUE OPERATIONS

From our little opening to the sky, we could hear the popping rotors of a helicopter coming at us from the north under the dense clouds now descending onto the surrounding mountainside. As soon as it came into view, the plane returned to the south, leaving those in the chopper to do their work. Gordon was still in his tree. The rest of us were down in the ferns.

The helicopter came through a clearing to the north, with its pilot busy trying to keep it airborne and away from the tree cover while Captain John Dent was making signals that we couldn't read properly. There were two stretchers aboard on the out riggings. I hoped they would be as happy as we were that none of us would have to be carried out of there.

The pilot swung the helicopter back around to hover over the clearing. The engine revved steadily as the giant insect-like craft balanced on a pin point. It rocked back and forth, but there was no noticeable vertical movement. This time, we could clearly see Captain Dent inside the bubble cockpit. He was writing something.

The chopper approached a further five feet down in our direction. A box was lowered to George and Roger, who literally floated through the ferrel to bring it to the rest of us, watching from a safe distance. From there, we managed to let Captain Dent know that none of us had been injured, at least, not with any broken limbs. We were eager to see what the box contained, and were delighted to find:

14 lb. of rice,

2 quarts of 'whites' (proof rum)

1 quart of syrup,

3 lb. of sugar,

2 lb. of powdered, pre-sweetened Kool-Aid

1 large can of pre-cooked meat,

some soap

and a few rolls of toilet paper.

The supplies were literally manna from heaven. We later discovered that the contents of the box were enough to sustain a squad of soldiers for two weeks. When it arrived, all we had left among us was one handful, no more, of rice. There was also a note in the box:

ARE YOU ALRIGHT

WE HAVE A PATROL IN THE AREA

STAY WHERE YOU ARE

OUR PATROL WILL GUIDE YOU

We didn't understand how the words 'Our patrol will guide you' would play out and we puzzled over it. We concluded that perhaps we were closer to a road than we thought and soldiers would be sent to escort us out. We weren't sure how likely that was, though.

"I don't think however close a road is, we will get out by foot today," someone muttered, "especially if it's an uphill journey."

Assessing the situation, Roger took the optimistic view.

"Well, we'll have Christmas dinner anyway," he exulted, "my grandmother cooks rice and peas just the way I like it."

While unpacking our survival rations we found a second note which read:

DO YOU NEED WATER

CUT AS MUCH BUSH AS POSSIBLE

FOR HELICOPTER LATER ON.

Both notes were written by Captain Dent. We were going to need water and we signalled 'Yes' to the second message. A five-gallon tank was put over the side and let down by rope. Amazingly, George had strength enough to not only support the tank on his own, but also to bring it up from the centre of the fern patch to where we had gathered.

We cooked a pot full of rice and opened up some of the beef. It was ice cold! Before the water could even come to a boil we flung ourselves at the rice; the beef we ate right out of the tin. To wash the whole concoction down, we also mixed a too-sweet drink using some of the white rum and syrup. After a few minutes of assaulting our stomachs in this way, we were all sick. But we simply allowed the nauseating feeling of the accumulated gas to dissipate somewhat and then it was back to the box. Again, we ate to our heart's content. Again, we made ourselves ill while the helicopter had been away. We spent an hour doing nothing but rejoicing and overindulging.

"Coops, wha' about de limbs dem want us chop down?" I asked.

Cooper had offered to chop two lower limbs off the tree, each six or more inches in diameter, to accommodate the return of the helicopter and to let it come in closer than the twenty-foot approach it was able to make before. He retreated to the tree when reminded, but upon getting there, settled into a comfortable branch, cutlass in hand, sunbathing. He didn't have much time to relax and joke around, because the helicopter soon returned, this time without stretchers, making a thunderous popping sound as it arrived from up the valley of the Swift River to the north.

He was galvanized into action, sliding down the tree and filling the fresh mountain air with flying wood chips as he slashed at the tree with the dull blade. By the time the chopper got into the clearing, Coops had felled the second limb with some kind of desperate Herculean strength and was gasping for breath, clutching the machete. For our part, George, Roger, and I battered the fern patch to the ground to make as much of a clearing as we could.

Due to the steep slope of the hillside as well as the proximity of the tail rotor to the ground, and with only inches between the tip of the main rotors and the tree line to spare, we knew that it would be impossible for the chopper to land. Now we were forced to wonder how we would get on board.

Captain Stern was deeply concerned. He had never attempted a rescue such as this. There was no way to approach our location from the north, south, east or west due to the tall trees on the perimeter. The only way in was by a perfectly controlled vertical descent.

JDF-H1 was still being piloted by Captain Stern. Army Sergeant Keith Hall, who had replaced Captain John Dent, was to now take part in the most daring aspect of our rescue operation.

As soon as the 'copter was centred in the opening, Sergeant Hall rappelled from the helicopter, then hovered at about twenty feet using the rope that had previously lowered the box of food to us. Hall held onto the rope, slowly using it to guide the chopper to a central point in the fern patch. With Captain Stern maintaining position, Sergeant Hall untied the rope from the chopper and released his hand from the skid. He then helped us in flattening the fern patch as much as possible, pro-viding an area from which we would be lifted. This action also allowed the chopper to get as close to the ground as was practical.

With the helicopter now within feet of the ground, the uplift force produced by the rebounding of the downward wash from the main rotor blades against the ground allowed Captain Stern to maintain his vertical position with reduced power but with a corresponding decrease in the stability of the heli-copter. Constantly adjusting power was critical. Since Captain Stern could not see either the trees or the ground behind him, he had to trust his skills and the judgment of Sergeant Hall at all times.

The Bell 47G-3 helicopter had a maximum capacity of close to

The JDF at the time had two Bell 47G-3 helicopters. JDFH-1 and JDFH-2 were built in 1963 and 1964, respectively. On October 11, 1963, the first regular commanding officer, Major Leslie Whittingham -Jones (along with his infamous dog ('Boots') arrived in Jamaica. He was a British Army Air Corps (AAC) helicopter instructor pilot whose task was to train pilots and organise the Jamaica Air Wing. Shortly thereafter, the first helicopter (JDF H-1, a Bell 47G-3B-1) was delivered, and it was assembled in the JDF workshop and pushed down the road to the Air Wing. The first two pilots from the Air Wing to be trained on these helicopters were Captains Robert Neish and Bunny Stern. Captain Neish had been the C.O. of the Air Wing up until October 30 1967. He had already joined the army at the time of our hike and was promoted to Major General in 1979. He served in that capacity until 1990.

1,100 pounds. The diameter of the rotor was approximately thirty-seven feet, leaving precious little room for error in a situation such as ours. It was now hovering precariously, about four feet above the ground over a very steep incline in the middle of the patch, with Sergeant Hall 'steadying' it by holding onto one of its skids.

Captain Stern was able to manoeuvre between the parameters of the rotor and the tree line. Sergeant Hall tried his best to hold on to the skid, thereby providing the pilot with a vertical and horizontal reference point relative to the ground. At times, it seemed that he was being lifted off the ground.

Over and over, the blades clipped small leafy branches. We could tell that climbing into the helicopter was not going to be easy, possibly endangering everyone's lives if there was a slip-up. In fact, it was the most daring part of the rescue. Had there been an accident of any sort, we would all have perished. If we had not succumbed to the direct force of the rotating blades of the two-ton-plus chopper, the ensuing fire would have done it.

The decision was that Roger and I would be the first to go out on the chopper. I had intended to go first, injured and all, but Roger beat me to the door!

He climbed onto the back of Sergeant Hall, made his way to the skid and then stepped into JDF-H1 next to Captain Stern. I followed suit, climbed aboard and got strapped in.

The skill of the pilot of JDF-H1 in lifting us from the ground cannot be overstated. That he was able to negotiate the north ridge slope and extract four teenagers from its tentacles justified the confidence that had been placed in him.

Biscoe reported that he had never seen another such opening at this elevation before. How we came upon it remains a mystery. Was it destiny, providence, or simply coincidence? Most likely, 'beyond coincidence'. According to an actuary, it was suggested that the best (highest) probability for us locating that patch was no more than 1 in 1,000,000, if we knew that it existed somewhere on the mountain. Obviously we did not know of its existence, infinitely reducing the probability of running into it.

Hurrying to chuck as much of my remaining belongings (and some of the others') into my now mostly empty haversacks, I took a few seconds to absorb the surroundings with the sincere realization that this was not only our final campsite but could very well have been our 'death camp'. The morbid thought sent shivers up my spine. All that was left, besides the structure of the lean-to, was our tattered and torn raincoats, pieces of which were strewn on the ground and on the roof.

CHAPTER 16

REALITY SINKS IN AT ALTITUDE 4000

I just sat there, relieved yet focused, strapped into the glass bubble heli-copter next to my hiking buddy and a pilot who had not yet introduced himself. There was simply no time for formalities. Sure, we had been found and were being taken out of the forest, but nobody told us where we were going or how long it would be before we would see our family and friends. My pulse skyrocketed. I felt faint and light-headed, as if the adrenaline itself were coming up and causing the bitter taste in my mouth. Reality was beginning to set in.

A few glances were exchanged between Roger and me. Terror was written in our eyes, with not a word to go along with it. I looked down and forward through the cockpit of H1, sometimes wrenching my neck backwards to look up and all around. Glancing downwards through the chopper's doorless side, I became embroiled in my emotions, as sick as I had been a few minutes before, but for a different reason.

I could no longer see the area in the trees from which we had just been plucked. Not the huge tree and not even the fern patch. I couldn't even make out the tree pattern, a landmark visible only a few seconds before that would have reminded me of our little opening to the sky. Was the tree pattern recently created by the vortex of a cyclone associ-ated with a hurricane, or was it created more naturally by ganja farmers preparing a long-ago plot?

The fire and ensuing smoke, which had saved our lives a few hours earlier, had long subsided. For the first time, I gained some larger per-spective into what would have happened had it not been for du Mont and Tyndale-Biscoe. There were only two possible outcomes without their actions—both of them very grim.

It's said that the human body, in general, is very hard to kill. Particularly in the case of nutrition and hydration, a person can, depending on climate, body weight and other factors, live for weeks without food. Several cases of men on hunger strike, such as Mahatma Gandhi, who went hungry for three weeks while in his seventies or shipwrecked sailors awaiting rescue, demonstrate that a strong will and a lot of luck can stave off death for a long time. Though holding on for weeks without food is possible, death is likely in far less time because of individual and environmental factors. If the individual is unfit, with average to high metabolism, suffering from cold and under stress, especially if water is scarce, the prospects for survival are slim, perhaps a matter of mere days, even hours.

There's no telling how much time each of us had left to live at that moment. We knew it was almost Christmas, but had no confidence that we'd be spending it with our families and friends, or how long we would have survived trapped in that place. As time passed, our health would have deteriorated rapidly and we would have remained there to starve...or we would have perished in our attempt to control-burn the hillside. Otherwise, while dying of thirst we may have attempted to access the gorge of the Swift River. In this case, if the treacherous mountainside approach did not do us in for certain, the pounding rapids and rock-faced sides of the Swift would have crushed and broken our bodies beyond recognition. Our remains would likely never have been found.

Overcome by emotion and trembling uncontrollably, I quietly thanked God.

★ ★ ★

As she had been from the day we were considered missing, my mother was at home. Based on all her normal daytime activities, she could have been classified as Jamaica's first informal commercial trader (ICT), a legal entity introduced in the eighties for persons to conduct commerce on a single-proprietorship basis. Twice a week during the evenings, she played badminton at the Rainbow Club at Half-Way-Tree. Tournaments could last as long as a week, and she did well in them, becoming an All Jamaica finalist in Women's Doubles on a number of occasions, with either Sheila Phillips (Nasralla) or Alice Rumsey as her partner. The season had ended by then so there was no opportunity to release some of the tension.

She had no career speciality and so, she dealt in a host of products and services, most notably as an Avon Lady. In the early days before she got her car, she took 'Jolly Joseph' (Jamaica Omnibus Service) buses downtown to the distributors Bryden & Evelyn, then worked on foot, lugging the bag of products she would deliver and taking orders all around the city. Later, once she had wheels, there were no limits, and she began serving uptown customers as well. She began handling airline reservations and ticketing, clothing, and jewellery. My mom persevered, despite being robbed on several occasions.

Now in her eighties, she continues to drive. As always, my mother is still very well liked, spending a lot of her time being helpful to others, often putting them ahead of herself. She was courteous and helpful to anyone she met, strangers, including the indigent, tourists and visitors at her synagogue.

All of these activities came to a halt on December 19th, 1967. As of that Wednesday, she had been answering the phone, which rang cease-lessly. Badly affected by false information about our rescue on more than one occasion, she had gone into panic mode, unable to handle any more calls. By Thursday, she thought that we were not only lost, but dead. She had to see Dr. Sleem for medication. By today's standards, she was very independent, but even though she was a strong-willed woman, she was beginning to break down.

A neighbour, Janet Delvaille, who lived at 16 Windsor Avenue, over-heard and later vividly remembered Norma telling the news media, "I can't say anything yet. I can't tell you anything until I see him," she said as news broke that a search party had located the boys.

According to Carlysle Hudson, who lived at 3 Windsor Avenue:

> Finally, we were relieved when we got the news that they were found in the mountains by the Jamaica

Defence Force helicopter, which was specifically searching for them. We happily, as a group, went to Up Park
Camp," he continued, "to greet the arrival of Geoffrey
who arrived safely as if nothing had happened, not realizing what we all went through, taking at least ten years
off each of our lives from worrying. In closing, I would
want to think that Geoffrey introduced the word 'stress'
into some of our lives at our young innocent and tender
age as a result of this much publicized event. This event
was possibly what triggered hypertension in my life, as
I was so on edge for those days, which at the time, felt
like months.

Five minutes after hearing that we had been found, my mother went
into denial mode. "I went crazy," she said. "I was running around the
house screaming but at the same time praying. I did not believe my
sister who telephoned me to relay the good news. I refused to speak
to her. Someone else called your father who was at the JDF command
centre from the first day. I don't think I slept in over three days. Shortly
afterwards, I heard someone speaking to the JDF, vaguely remembering
them calling the names Bates and Jackie Biscoe."

She was not clear about what happened next.

"I must have passed out," she surmised, "for how long is also uncertain." At about the same time, Richard Roberts, who knew the family
very well, arrived at Number 25 and managed to get her into his car,
then headed for the JDF. Being a Sunday, the trip was made in record
time. Oblivious to traffic laws, Roberts got her to Up Park Camp in less
than ten minutes. On arrival, she ran to my father for consolation and
to ask repeatedly if I had been found and if I was safe. Of course, no
definitive answer could be given at the time about my well-being. Alive
for sure, but what else?

The details about our present situation was later recorded as follows in my father's usually meticulous manner:

9:30 a.m. 24/12/67

Brian received message and Babs [my mother's sister] phoned me at the JDF, HQ.

Brian took phone message – Boys have been found – Mrs. Bates. I asked Barbara to phone Norma for Mrs. Bates number, which was not listed in the directory, to confirm, and ring me back. Babs phoned me back, 'affirmative'.

Billy Du Mont* and Mr. Biscoe found the boys in Portland and that a JDF helicopter was standing by.

Babs phoned me back, 'affirmative'.

We were flying steadily along the river course, with JDF H1 bearing ahead at full speed. Now several minutes away from Camp 9, high above the gorge of the Swift River and still buffeting in the turbulent currents along the Blue Mountains, the river became wider but the dense forest persisted. At this elevation, however, the Bell 47G helicopter with its Lycoming six cylinder engine was operating somewhat below its maximum capability of 105 miles per hour and 270 horsepower. A few minutes later, the landscape changed drastically into the beautiful rolling hills more typical of the lower slopes of the mountains. The meandering Swift River was still directly below us.

I began to wonder why we were not making a turn for Kingston, when Captain Stern, gesticulating rather than speaking, began his descent towards the delta of the Swift. *What next?* I thought.

---

* It was in fact his brother David du Mont, who had spotted us.

CHAPTER 17

ANOTHER NARROW ESCAPE

The helicopter approached the rock-covered delta of the river, and I could see people waving in our direction and cheering from a bridge in the north-coast town of Hope Bay. As Captain Stern's instructions were being deciphered in my weary brain, a second helicopter appeared on the scene and was coming straight at us, almost at ground level. Stern was one of the few qualified pilots sufficiently trained to do such high-risk manoeuvres in the terrain, and he had been specifically assigned the task of extracting us.

Now hovering at about ten feet, Stern spoke while directly looking at us.

"Not landing…stones…getting off."

For my part, I was only interested in one thing: putting my feet on ground that was not the Blue Mountains. We were going to be handed over to the other highly skilled pilot, Captain Andrew Bogle, as Captain Stern had to return and pull out the remaining hikers along with Sergeant Hall. Getting us onto the ground at the delta was not going to be as simple as I imagined. His parting words did not register with me, unfortunately.

Stern had specifically told us that it was too risky to land the helicopter because one or both of the skids could lock into and fasten between the rocks, making his take-off both difficult and unstable. He was going to hover the craft one to two feet above the ground, allowing us to 'step off'.

None the wiser, and in too much of a hurry I jumped off, gratified to be on land again.

My unexpected premature jump from the aircraft caused an imbalance to the chopper, and it rose rapidly to about fifteen feet, rolling to the right with the main rotor blades at such a steep angle that they came very close to my head and the ground. Indeed, Captain Stern had anticipated my side of the aircraft to rise on my departure, so he was prepared to respond. But he was not ready for what transpired and probably overcompensated. I almost put the mission in jeopardy.

Stern apparently changed his mind about not landing the craft. In his displeasure, he landed it and gave me a round scolding before allowing Roger to disembark.

Notwithstanding the aforementioned, had it not been for the quick reaction of Captain Stern, it would have been catastrophic. The result would not only have been a severe setback to the mission but possibly cost three people their lives.

CHAPTER 18

TO KEN JONES AND KINGSTON

Captain Bogle advised us that he would now take us to Ken Jones Aerodrome, just outside the town of Hope Bay. That was the end of the conversation. The relatively short and smooth ride just above sea level was a welcome treat, with the serene blue waters of the Caribbean on our left and the foothills of our cloud-covered mountains to our right. We were also greeted with brilliant sunshine and unusually dry Portland weather.

Within minutes, Bogle was settling JDF-H2 on the tarmac adjacent to the office building at Ken Jones. Unknown to us at the time, another aircraft (which had not been involved in the search) was standing by to take us to the Flying Club★ at Palisadoes where they were stationed.

The pilot, Freddy Ramson, along with long-time friend, Terrence Bates (Roger's father), had just landed there to await our return. Roger and I were ecstatic, to say the least. The flight to Kingston over the Blue Mountains was anticlimactic. I managed to look down with great respect for the ominous and perilous terrain in which we were trapped only a few hours before, unashamedly shedding a tear or two. I was strapped in at the back along with Roger. I don't recall a word that may have been spoken. Just as things were in our various interpersonal relationships, so were we rescued as well. Roger and I boarded together;

★ At the time, the Jamaica Flying Club had four aircrafts of its own. The members had another twenty or so. Members wanting to rent aircraft could do so either directly from the club or from one belonging to a member.

Gordon and Cecil (who were genuinely inseparable, 'like batty and bench' as we say in Jamaica) were picked up together. This meant that George, the original leader, like the proverbial skipper at sea, was the last to mount up and get off the mountain.

I must have dozed off, glad that we were now safe and on our way home. The next thing I heard was the communications between the aircraft and Palisadoes Tower. As we taxied toward the club house, my mind drifted to the few occasions I had been there to swim and on one occasion when I was scheduled for my first plane ride as a young boy. Now a decade or so later, I was in that very place for a very different reason. I was immediately reminded why.

As I entered the clubhouse, I found myself staring straight at the front page of the *Gleaner*. The reader was a friend of mine, Francis Cooke (later a hunting and fishing comrade) who heard the commotion and pulled the papers from his face to gawk at me.

"I can't believe that's you, Geoffrey," he said as if he'd seen a ghost. "We really thought that you guys would never be found." He got up, shook my hand and continued to stare in total disbelief.

CHAPTER 19

TERRA 'FIRMER'

After the news that we were found and were being rescued shot over the airwaves, a host of family, well-wishers and the press descended upon the grounds of the Air Wing division of the JDF. At around midday, family members and friends were invited by Rudolph Green (later Major-General in 1973) to the Officers' Club for refreshments and to relax in anticipation of our arrival. They had been through a lot, but everyone who had hoped, prayed and waited was now dealing with feelings of elation tinged with anxiety.

Other notable members of the JDF who were involved but were not visible at the time were Brigadier David Smith (1965–1973), who oversaw the search and rescue mission and was occupied elsewhere directing search parties, and Major George Brown, Officer in Command of the Air Wing (1967–1970), who was responsible for selecting the personnel for the rescue operations at the Swift River.

★ ★ ★

Gordon and Cecil were next to be extracted from the bush by Captain Stern. They were also taken to Ken Jones airstrip in Portland after being trans-shipped by Second Lieutenant Bogle from the delta of the Swift River near Hope Bay. By all accounts, their transfer from H1 to H2 went according to plan. Delta Yankee had refuelled and departed Up Park Camp (JDF-HQ) to retrieve them. They arrived at army head-quarters at precisely 12:35 p.m.

An hour or so later, Roger and I arrived, and before we could join
the gathering, we were greeted by my mother, Aunt Freda, my long-
time friend Richard Roberts, and a gleeful Robin Crawford. I distinctly
remember my mother's state as we walked to the centre of the tarmac.

"Is this really you?" Mom asked, hanging onto me as if I might
evaporate. Not to be left out of the excitement, my Aunt Freda suddenly became attached to Roger, to the extent that in a later interview
with JBC Television's Consie Walters, the reporter thought that he was
speaking to Roger's mother (who was not present)!

At about the same time, three helicopters arrived in formation. H-1
was manned by Captain Stern and his passenger, Captain John Dent;
H-2 was brought in by Captain Andrew Bogle and Sergeant Keith Hall;
and a Hughes 300 flown by American super-pilot Bill Passaretti, with
passenger George Hussey. H1 and H2 also brought our gear lashed to
its out-riggings. While H1 and H2 took a direct approach, the Hughes
300H buzzed in and did a circle before landing with George and our
survival box of food retrieved from the fern patch. Missing was a few
pounds of rice, some Kelly's syrup, white rum and whatever else we had
consumed when the rescue started.

Passaretti (to whom I will come back later regarding his connection to Tinker Rerrie and the movie *Dark of the Sun*) was more than a
daredevil. He was a serious pilot who used his skills for work in transportation, movie stunts and agriculture, but he did enjoy being in a
chopper. It was no wonder that George, who looked the most ragged of
the group, was as sick as a dog due to the bunny hopping Bill did over
the mountains just to satisfy his love of challenges. Later on, we all wondered: Had it not been for Capt. Rerrie's chopper with Bill Passaretti
at the stick, which was able to enter the clearing safely (rotor diameter
twenty-seven feet, compared with that of H1 and H2 of thirty-seven
feet) and was able to manoeuvre low enough to the ground so that
George could hop in (without taking any guidance from the military)
how would George have been extracted?

Unloading H1 and H2, with rotors still turning, took place very
quickly. Our now frail-looking bodies were hunched over to avoid the

rotors. A bolt of adrenalin must have rushed through us simultaneously, because according to one observer, Roderic Crawford:

> Although it was obvious that the boys had pain on their faces, bruises and scratches over almost all of their exposed areas (hands and faces), seeing them in motion moving away from the helicopters, one would not believe that they were the same ones who only hours ago faced the stark reality of being lost forever and paying the ultimate price.
>
> Now, seeing them in person, I felt like I had to get reacquainted again after that experience…the sudden rock-star fame had a natural but temporary distancing effect.
>
> It had taken me days to sink in that they were really seriously lost…may have been just my upbeat outlook…

George, ably assisted by Bill and Roger, retrieved our survival box of 'delicacies' from the H-300. Within minutes, as we stood there on the fiery hot tarmac, looking somewhat unkempt (and somehow nonchalant), we nevertheless eagerly answered everyone's questions. Then came the formalities, such as the on-the-spot press conference and posing for photographs, neither of which we could have imagined only a few hours before. The gravity of the situation had not yet set in. After all the debriefings and picture-taking had died down, we were allowed to collect our belongings and head for home.

Shortly after a brief flyby, the choppers left without much fanfare, except for the daring Passaretti in the H-300. He treated the audience to a direct dash at the hangar/maintenance building going full speed at roof height, before suddenly pulling the chopper upwards to execute what appeared to be a 360-degree (barrel) roll. Everyone gazed in amazement as the gathering roared in appreciation.

Top: The interior of the Shaare Shalom ('The synagogue in the Sand') in down-town Kingston

Bottom: The Centenary — 1985: A portrait of the directors of the Shaare Shalom Synagogue in Kingston during the 1985 centenary. *Left to right, seated:* Ainsley Henriques, Ernest de Souza (acting spiritual leader and secretary); Solomon de Souza (president), Edward Ashenheim. Standing: Wallace Campbell, Lloyd Alberga, Charles Alexander, Ursula Ashenheim, Geoffrey Haddad. Top: Samuel Henriques (honorary past president), Dr. Ronald Delevante (vice-president), David Henriques (treasurer): Frank Myers, David Matalon.

Top: The typical gathering for Christmas at the Haddads, circa.1960. The celebrations, which usually lasted all day and featured firecrackers (clappers and thunderbolts), children's gifts, food, and drink, were cancelled in 1967 because of that year's anxious holiday events. I am in the front row at right.

Centre: 25 Windsor Avenue in August 2001. The inaugural cricket match with players consisting of family and friends of B. S. Haddad, one month after his death. In this photo, I am in the centre with bat in hand; my sister Jennifer is to my right, and friend Richard Roberts and uncle Danny DaCosta are to my left, respectively.

Bottom: In this photo, third from left is Dr. Astley Smith, Consul General for Jamaica at Vancouver.

Top: I and my family visit the old homestead at Windsor Avenue, St. Andrew, Jamaica in 1985.

Centre: 25 Windsor Avenue became home to a modern three-story office complex, appropriately named 'THE ROSWIND'.

Bottom: By 2013, the building had been redesigned and repurposed for use by the Embassy of Trinidad & Tobago.

Top: Mamee Bay, Ocho Rios, Jamaica, December 21, 2013: I present W. Donald Soutar with an advance copy of the book for his review. At age ninety-three, he is the sole survivor from the 1939 hike.

Bottom: December 21, 2013, Mamee Bay, Ocho Rios, Jamaica. *Left to right:* Gordon Cooper, W. Donald Soutar, Geoffrey (G. B.) Haddad, Cecil Ward, and Donnie Soutar, who became ill the day before the hike, allowing my last-minute participation.

Top: John Allgrove, civil engineer and mountaineer with me in December, 2013. He is the owner of the Hostel at Whitfield Hall, where hikers to the Peak regularly stop overnight on their way to witness the sunrise. He was not involved directly with the search, but we became good friends because of our common interest in engineering and love for the mountains. (He provided invaluable information based on his extensive knowledge of the mountains and which was used throughout the book).

Bottom: With internationally acclaimed jazz musician Monty Alexander, OD, in Vancouver, February 24, 2014, presenting him with an advance copy of *If I'm Not Back by Wednesday*.

Top: David du Mont (*left*) played a crucial role as spotter for famed pilot/photographer Jack Tyndale-Biscoe (*at right*) *Photos courtesy of David du Mont and Jack Tyndale-Biscoe*

Centre: Jamaica 1966—Bill Passaretti aboard one of three Hughes 300 helicopters which he helped to reassemble in Jamaica. Bill was one of the designers and lead test pilots while working for Howard Hughes in the '60s on the 300 series. *Photo courtesy of Glen Passaretti*

Bottom left: Me and Tinker Rerrie (owner of the Hughes 300 rescue helicopter flown by Bill Passaretti) rafting on the Rio Grande, Portland, Jamaica, August 1966. Bottom *right:* On scene filming *Dark of the Sun (The Mercenaries)* are co-stars Rod Taylor and Yvette Mimieux with Passaretti's H300, which was used to transport the actors to/from various locations in Jamaica.

Top: Left: David du Mont and I dine at a wedding in Vancouver of May 2006. It would be the first time that I would meet the person who saved my live nearly forty years before. We spent the evening and days afterwards sharing the details of that event.

Centre: Roger Bates and I at the Capilano River, North Vancouver, Canada, November 2012. This was one of a number of times that we met since the 1967 ordeal.

Bottom: Helicopter rescue pilot Colonel Anthony 'Bunny' Stern, OD, at his home in St. Andrew, Jamaica in 2014.

Top; Left: Making my first trip along the beaten 14.5 mile trail to the Peak, August 1969, with fellow hiker Roderic Crawford on the banks of the Yallahs River, which provides a substantial portion of the city's water supply. *Centre:* With Mr. John Allgrove Sr., owner of the Whitfield Hall hostel, a 'must-stop' on the way to the Peak. *Right:* After a night at the Peak, we return to the pre-arranged pick-up point. B. S. Haddad and Robin Crawford are on the spot to greet and transport us to Kingston.

Bottom: En route to Blue Mountain Peak in 1986, I (*left*) act as guide to a group of Japanese engineers. On this occasion we returned the same day, perhaps forego-ing the opportunity of seeing Cuba and watching the spectacular sunrise, visible on some occasions. This was my eighth journey to the Peak.

CHAPTER 20

AFTERMATH

As was customary, everyone in my family looked forward to the holidays, especially my father, a secular Christian with a Jewish wife and children, who had established the observance as family tradition. But there would be no Christmas at 25 Windsor Avenue in 1967. Once December 20 rolled around, and I had still not returned from the mountains, our favourite family day was never going to happen. It was the first celebration the Haddads had cancelled in over fifteen years. The reason was simple; my mother had no time to prepare.

My mom was great at entertaining, and for months in advance she had all sorts of dried fruit soaking in a mixture of white rum and wine for making her plum pudding. For my dad, who rarely went to church and spent most of his time at home, Christmas was the only time he went 'all out', supporting my mom's preparations and making sure that a real Christmas tree, the largest he could fit in the living room, was adorned with all the right ornaments and lights for the festivities. He did all this not only because he loved to have family over and entertain them but most of all, he wanted to keep the children happy and busy all day.

We would typically start at 10:00 a.m. and keep going until well after 6:00 p.m., with the entire family, including grandparents, uncles, aunts and cousins, numbering up to fifty at times, in attendance. The only thing that could end the party prematurely was if we ran out of food, if the bar went dry, or when the supply of firecrackers, or the big herd of kids was entirely exhausted. I cannot recall an event at which either the food or the bar went dry at my house.

Sorrel or roselle (*Hibiscus sabdariffa*) is known by many names worldwide, but is definitely the official Christmas drink in Jamaica. The rich red petals, which take about six months to develop, are boiled in water, ginger and other spices then strained, sweetened and spiked with rum or wine to produce a spicy drink served cold.

At 10:00 a.m., family members would start arriving. My mother, siblings, and I would welcome them while my father was still getting ready. Sorrel was the drink of the day. At 11:00 a.m., the kids who were five to twelve years old were given packs of 'clappers' (firecrackers), one pack at a time, along with a lit Four Aces cigarette to ignite the clappers at the north end of the lawn.

It turned out that the cigarettes had a higher value for the older kids, since theirs would somehow burn all the way out before they could finish setting off their clappers. My father soon caught on to the fact that the kids were not only using the cigarettes for ignition, but also for furtive inhalation, and soon substituted the cigarettes with mosquito destroyer coils.

The thirteen-and-over group got 'bolters' (larger-sized firecrackers), in rounds of ten at a time, to set off at the south end of the lawn.

For the next several hours, 25 Windsor was something resembling a battlefield, with the lawn covered in paper wrappers and hardly a blade of grass to be seen. Remnants of the firecrackers were typically left out there until New Year's Day, a time for setting off whatever recreational explosives were left over.

There was only one serious mishap during these Christmas extravaganzas. One year, an older boy, 'Pigoo' (the nickname my dad imposed on him, as he did to everybody), ignored Uncle B's strict instructions that rounds of ten bolters were first to be placed on the ground, then picked up one by one for firing. Instead, while igniting a bolter, this kid kept the other nine in his hand. The remaining fireworks were set off seconds apart, with some of them landing on the roof and verandas of the house where the women and gentlemen at the bar were located.

Fortunately, no one was seriously hurt. Needless to say, my dad lost his cool, and bolters were suspended for most of the remainder of the day.

My uncle Danny DaCosta remembers the entertainment this way:

> B. S. kept them supplied with 'clappers' and 'bombs' all day. He seemed to have a larger stock of these noise-makers on hand than the proverbial Chinaman's shop. His energy was fantastic and he seemed happiest when he was keeping all the children happy. It was a sight to behold.

At around noon , lunch, consisting of rice and peas, potato salad, roast beef, chicken, ham and turkey, was served in abundance, along with a whole host of soft drinks, hard liquor and liqueurs. Of course, plum pudding covered in a delicious wine-and-cream sauce would follow.

By 2:00 p.m., everyone was assembled in the living room for gifts distributed to children and adults alike, from a cardboard suitcase or two that my father carried, containing some of the wrapped gifts. The others were put under the tree. Before this however, Dad, dressed in a Santa outfit, would hand an envelope containing a ten-shilling note (worth about US$1.50 at the time) to each of the children. After he called a child's name, and handed over the cash, he would again call them all in turn and give them a present.

At 4:00p.m., clappers and bolters recommenced.

When it was 6:00 p.m., dinner was available (for anyone who had room) with more plum pudding and sorrel. Norma's plum pudding sauce was to die for.

When I was twelve years old, the duty of playing Santa Claus fell to me.

★ ★ ★

Within fifteen minutes of arriving at JDF Headquarters for debriefing and interviews, I started to feel somewhat woozy, thinking that I might faint. Only two hours before, we were all digging into the food, rum, and syrup our bodies would take in a short time. Certainly, the rice had no chance to be cooked, and the combination of the other assorted items led to feelings of nausea; in some cases, there was violent vomiting.

Standing on the hot concrete tarmac at the Air Wing Division of the JDF was uncomfortable, but just as irritating was the reflection of sunlight from the surface for anyone who wasn't wearing sunglasses. Unavoidably, the noise from the three helicopters quickly proved to be an eerie reminder of our earlier encounter in the forest. Still scratching those aggravating mosquito bites and the bruises inflicted by branches, rocks and prickles, I became aware that my head was pounding.

Up to this point, my father was still so elated and I was still so scared of what he would say that no meaningful exchange took place between us.

"Rest," he said to me as soon as we came in contact at army head-quarters. There was none of the legendary rage, only concern and relief. The only other thing I can recall him saying was that he was concerned about my obvious loss of weight.

By the time I got home it was about 1:30 p.m. I made a beeline for the kitchen table and sat on the only stool in the room. My vision began to blur. For the moment, it felt impossible for me to collect my thoughts, but as I tore into the chicken meal my mother hurriedly placed in front of me, everything started flooding back. Just ten days ago, I had been seated in this same spot, unable to gather my thoughts, stuffing my belly, watching the clock and yelling at any and everyone who crossed my path as I madly prepared my haversacks to make it on time to the Coopers. Still working on the chicken, I did a double take when I saw my mother putting lovely fresh fruit and some ice cream on the table. Now I was home and alive.

I vividly remembered that while sitting on the stool I felt something soft wrap around my feet, which were by now badly blistered. The pain seemed to dissipate almost instantaneously, and I could see that the cure was my four year-old black Labrador, Rex, who happily accepted pats on the head and food from the table. Another glass of water and a few more strokes on Rex's dark coat, and I was fully back in the present.

The voices I could hear sounded like ten to twenty people in the house, enough for a party, but there must have been some kind of 'buffer zone' established, quite likely at my father's insistence, to ensure that I'd be left alone for the time being.

The next thing I remember, I was lying down, drifting in and out of consciousness. The bed seemed so soft and comfortable that sometimes I felt that it was moving up and down.

Later, I was awakened by a familiar voice. In his deep, authoritative baritone, Dr. Sleem was saying, "Well young man, you almost gave your parents heart attacks. I hope you won't have any such ideas for a long time to come."

After checking my vital signs he continued, "Your asthma may come back, so I'm leaving a prescription for that, and by the way, you have a serious case of bronchitis. I'm sure you know what that means: no cricket, football, badminton or feeding the fish until I give you the OK…you hear what I just said, B. S.?" he asked scoldingly of my dad. "Make sure that the boy follows my instructions."

Turning to something he had seen during the exam, the doctor added, "Now, this blasted black and blue on your backside really looks nasty." After poking around the wound, which was still oozing some-what, he covered it with gauze and tape, instructing my father to take me for an x-ray the following week.

"Finally," he told my dad, "the boy must have some healthy food. He seems to have lost about twenty pounds!"

Throughout Dr. Sleem's visit, my mother was nowhere to be seen. She was either on the front verandah serving refreshments to the guests or in her bedroom in total disbelief.

"Is this you?" she had asked when she first met me on the tarmac at the Air Wing. "I can't believe it, you've lost so much weight. Your father was a raving lunatic, especially to anyone who crossed his path over the last six days. If it weren't for him, only God knows what would have happened."

I remember going alternately into my bed, to the bathroom and back again. I felt as if I were being purged and reborn. Laying there was more comfortable than ever, surrounded by three pillows; one under my head, another over my head and the third between my legs. I eventually fell asleep. Every now and then I would awaken, but dared not open my eyes for fear of what my surroundings would be. I gradually accepted that I was down from the mountains. After all, it was quite warm, the way Kingston is for most of the year.

My mosquito bites and scratches were covered with calamine lotion; my head was sopped with white rum to alleviate any stuffiness; my throat and nostrils were alive with the fumes from Tiger Balm rub. My hip area, which was sore, discoloured, and mildly infected, reeked of iodine or some other ointment.

I was unaware of time passing. Now and then I would feel as if my entire body was being elevated and I grimaced in pain, bravely bearing discomfort from the bruise in my back. One of the first voices I heard was that of my girlfriend and her father.

They stood there blurry at the doorway, but did not come in. They spoke, but their voices were inaudible. Perhaps my ears were still clogged with mountain rain or the roar of aircraft; maybe it was the vibrations and pressure differential caused by the helicopter bouncing around. Before I could solve that great puzzle, I fell dead asleep.

For the rest of the afternoon and early into the evening I could hear a flurry of activity on the front porch, but couldn't make sense of what people were saying. It seemed at the time that there was tremendous laughter and noise, but I couldn't quite reconcile why. I was overcome with fatigue, as well as restlessness, but was too lethargic, not strong enough to even sit up in bed, much less walk. A urinal of some sort had to be provided because I kept downing syrup and water non-stop.

That first night back, I awoke numerous times and looked up and out the window for stars, there were none. There was no moon, no rain, no wet clothing saturated with the smell of smoke, nothing to directly connect me to the ordeal, yet my body shook violently at the thought of it all happening to me all over again.

Sometime later that night, my mother came to see me. With tears in her eyes, she handed me a gift-wrapped box. She said she really believed that she would never have seen me again after not turning up on Wednesday (December 20th) and so wanted me to have this gift.

It was a watch, an 18-carat gold Bulova Accutron, one of the first made with a tuning fork. Along with the date, the inscription read:

TO GEOFF, FROM MUM AND DAD.

Then she hugged me for a very long time. I burst into tears. I memorized the serial number and can still recite it on demand: M7 – 1 591524, the 'M7' signifying the year it was made. I recently found that watch and had it refurbished. It is once again in good working order.

★ ★ ★

Once we were used to the idea of being safe and sound, we noticed there were whisperings about the authenticity of the harrowing ordeal. Some of the mischief suggested that we all conspired in a massive hoax after taking the safer, more well known route to the Peak, though no one bothered to ask how we could have done so yet had to be rescued on a desolate ridge well away from the main track. Some of the boys thought that our adventure never took place at all.

Quite to the contrary, *some* suggested that our survival was heroic, devoting much time to proposing theories of how we acquitted ourselves so far from the popular way up the mountain. The suggestion was flattering, but none of us wanted to be labelled as heroes.

Without appearing ungrateful, we all disavowed any claim to such a title, with the hope that this book will show that common sense and determination, not heroism, were our redeeming characteristics.

★ ★ ★

As in most Commonwealth countries, December 25 and 26 are designated public holidays in Jamaica. The *Gleaner* was not published on those days. For all persons interested in our well-being, the only sources of information were via JBC television and radio, the older radio station RJR and of course, the telephone.

Most Jamaicans awaited the arrival of the newspaper on Wednesday, December 27, 1967 that was sure to shout the fate of the five missing teens.

Instead, the grim December 27 *Gleaner* headline read:

6 INFANTS DIE IN CHRISTMAS DAY BLAZE

> Hostel for displaced children razed in early morning blaze. Cries awaken attendant; heroic rescue operation—PM on early scene, takes personal charge.
>
> Six children between the ages of one and six years—five boys and a girl – lost their lives horribly on Christmas morning, when they were burned to death in a fire which razed the children's home in which they lived and where they had been sleeping soundly in their beds.

A photograph of Prime Minster Hugh Shearer was centred on the page, carrying the coffin of one of the six children to the graveside. The nation was in shock. The story of our rescue, quite appropriately, was placed instead on page two. Above the story of our adventure was a photograph of us, sitting on JDF–H2 minutes after arriving at the army base:

> After intensive two-day search, 5 boys rescued from blue mtns. ravine spotted by light plane, taken out by 'copters.
>
> Anxiety for the five schoolboys from Jamaica College who were feared lost in the Blue Mountains when they did not return from a hiking trip to the Peak that was due to end last Wednesday, was relieved on Sunday morning when they were found, safe and sound, in a ravine in the mountains, and were brought out by helicopter.
>
> Climaxing an intensive two-day search of the mountains by the army and the police, the missing five— Gordon Cooper, George Hussey, Cecil Ward, Roger Bates, and Geoffrey Haddad—were found by a private plane piloted by Mr. Jack Tyndale-Biscoe, well-known amateur pilot and aerial photographer.

They were in a defile in the mountains, about five miles* down the Swift River, north of Portland Gap. The time was 9:25 a.m. and in the plane was Mr. Leslie Ward, father of one of the boys. Smoke from a fire built by the boys in a clearing which they had made in the heavy bush attracted the attention of the circling plane, and brought about their rescue.

Two 'copters

Two helicopters—one military, the other private—were used to take the boys out of the mountains. They were flown to Ken Jones Airport, in Portland and from there to Kingston. The two helicopters brought three of the boys to Jamaican Defence Force headquarters at Up Park Camp, while the other two were flown to Palisadoes Airport in Mr. Tyndale-Biscoe's plane and driven from there to Up Park Camp, where they joined their comrades-in-distress and were welcomed by their anxiously waiting families.

By noon on Sunday, the near-tragedy, which had gripped the island and created national concern, was over. The boys were in reasonably good shape. They were cold and wet and thirsty, but none the worse for their adventure. In fact, they said almost in unison, in answer to the inevitable question, that they would "do it again."

Telling the story of their adventure, the boys said that after leaving Clydesdale last Saturday, they climbed Sir Johns Peak and were on their way to Blue Mountain Peak on Tuesday when they ran short of water. They started to search for a stream and found the Swift

---

*   It was two miles, not five.

River.* They decided to follow the river course, but, because of foggy conditions, took a wrong direction and headed north instead of south.

Wrong direction

When they realized, from the flow of the river, that they were headed in the wrong direction, they also discovered that they were in "bad country." The terrain was rugged, with dense bush and grass through which they had to hack their way. So they decided to remain where they were, in a ravine, and wait for rescue.

There was a tall tree in the clearing, and they climbed to the top of this, clearing its leaves and top limbs, so they could be seen from the air. They took turns as lookout, and by Friday, heard the planes and helicopters circling over head. They were not spotted until Sunday morning, however, when the smoke from their fire, lighted that morning, caught the watching eyes of Mr. Ward and Mr. Tyndale-Biscoe.

One of the boys, Hussey,** had a transistor radio, but he said he could hear nothing on it at first—"only screeches." Later he was able to hear music being broadcast, but no news or any announcements concerning his colleagues and himself.

---

*   The details contained in the report came from someone close to if not within our party, but I emphasize salient portions of it and present the following notes to correct the record: At the time we did not know that the river would lead to the Swift River (We later learned that with the exception of our final location (Camps 7, 8, and 9) we were not traversing the Swift but the Speculation River (which changed directions frequently). We had no idea in which direction the river would be flowing until we got to it. The Speculation is the largest 'tributary' flowing into the Swift. Also, it was David du Mont, not Les Ward, who saw the smoke.

** It was I who had the transistor radio.

Food ran out on them. "We were down to our last two packs of rice and we were unable to cook it because of the damp conditions," they said. But hunger had not yet become a serious problem.*

Visibility

Climatic conditions in the mountains made visibility difficult from the ground as well as from the air. Just as the boys were unable to see the aircraft, which were searching from them, so the aircraft were unable to see the boys. A low cloud ceiling in the area especially in the afternoons, reduced visibility considerably.

A combined army and police operation conducted the search for the boys. Also sharing in the search was Mr. Tyndale-Biscoe and Mr. "Tinker" Rerrie whose helicopter was one of those used in the rescue operation. Foresters from the Forestry Department also took part in the search.

Attention was concentrated on the south side of Sir Johns Peak, where an army patrol was stationed to maintain contact with other army and police patrols which were out on search along the various tracks in the area. These patrols concentrated on the ridges, while the Forestry Department concentrated their efforts among the foothills.

Intensified Search

Following abortive searches on Friday and again on Saturday, the search was intensified on Sunday morning, when a planned 90-minute search from 8 a.m. to

---

* We had no more than a couple handfuls of rice at this point, so hunger was becoming a very serious problem.

9:30 was carried out. It was this intensified search, in which the light aircraft and the two helicopters were engaged, that brought success at 9:25 a.m., when the boys were spotted.

When the discovery was made the plane signalled to the helicopter, which had been concentrating on the south side of Sir Johns Peak. The helicopter flew to the spot, located the boys, returned to base for refuelling and then flew back with the other helicopter. Both helicopters picked up the boys and flew them to Ken Jones Airport.

Meanwhile, at the Air Wing section of Camp, the anxious families of the boys awaited keeping vigil there from early in the morning. As the two helicopters flew in and came to rest on the ground, a subdued cheer rose from the tense gathering. Then there was the joy and poignancy of reunion with parents, sisters and girl-friends. There were even a few unashamed tears of joy. For the waiting parents, it was the end of a long ordeal of agony and uncertainty.

Perhaps the parents who showed the greatest emotion were the Haddads. It was Mr. Haddad* who, on Wednesday, when the boys were unreported from, took steps to find out what had happened to them and who contacted the other parents, the police and eventually the military, leading to the big search.

Mrs. Haddad put it graphically: "We have had three sleepless nights."

---

* I will be forever indebted to my father whose foresight and swift actions resulted in our being spotted and rescued in time; and my mother who suffered through, amongst other things, sleepless nights.

Mr. Charles Cooper, father of Gordon, was not at Camp. He was over at Swift River, in Portland, organizing a search of the area working along with the foresters. "I felt certain that the Swift River area was where we were to look for them," he said. He heard by radio the news of the discovery of the boys and returned to Kingston later that Sunday a happy man.

I vaguely remember going to our high school on Christmas Day to pen the following letter which also appeared on page two of the *Gleaner* on the 27th. I do not, however, have a recollection of arriving at the home of Jackie Tyndale-Biscoe shortly after our return with my mother to thank him for his help. I was reminded of this many years afterwards.

Also, we were requested to attend a meeting at the JDF headquarters shortly after the event. After discussing our near-fatal experience, the army offered to provide us with radios and other necessary equipment, should we again wish to attempt the mission. Naturally, we were in no condition to do anything about their offer there and then. We needed to get back to our families and friends and to get some much-deserved rest so that we could enjoy what was left of our vacation.

A letter of thanks to everyone who had played a part in our rescue was sent to the *Gleaner* and signed by the five of us:

Rescued five say thanks

We the five boys from Jamaica College rescued in the Blue Mountains would like to express our appreciation publicly to the Jamaica Defence Force, Jamaica Constabulary Force, the Forest Rangers, Radio, Press, Clergy and all who prayed for us and Mr. Jack Biscoe who played such a large part in our rescue.

We were indeed in difficulties and seriously short of food. Without this help we certainly would not have made it out and been home for Christmas, about which we thought so much. Thanks to all who helped, especially Mr. Biscoe and his crew who spotted our smoke signal. It was good to be home for Christmas.

Sincerely,
George Hussey
Roger Bates
Cecil Ward
Gordon Cooper
Geoffrey Haddad

AFTERWORD

CONNECTIONS, COINCIDENCES, AND REFLECTIONS

I think it was at about 9:00 p.m. on a Tuesday night in 1966. The Rainbow Badminton Club was having one of its usual biweekly practices at the warehouses of Jamaica Transport Ltd., located along Spanish Town Road in Kingston. The All Jamaica tournaments for both seniors and juniors were played there, as well as the island's annual inter-club championships. I was fortunate enough to be allowed to play with senior members of the club, if only for a few minutes at a time, in between one of the match breaks. In fact, this tradition of attending the club with my mother had been going on for more than five years.

Without warning, there was a loud bang. The ensuing heat was so intense that we all had to evacuate the building. No one had any idea of what was going on.

A tanker truck had just erupted violently and was on fire. As we exited the building, we quickly realised that the explosion had been designed to take place and was being filmed for an international movie at the warehouse owned by Captain Tinker Rerrie. The thought that we were actually there during production provided much more entertainment than badminton at the time.

My first memories of Rerrie, affectionately known to all who knew him as 'Tinker' or 'T.R.,' was in his association with badminton, specifically the Rainbow Club and the Jamaica Badminton Association (JBA). That was in about 1965. I am not sure whether T.R. found the sport of badminton or whether the sport found him, but I rather believe it was the latter.

His contribution to badminton as one of its greatest benefactors will never be forgotten. By sponsoring tournaments, providing a venue for clubs and showing eagerness to please, he gave his all to the sport and persons associated with it.

For certain, he provided a place for the Rainbow Badminton Club shortly after they lost their facility of many years at the Rainbow Club in Half-Way-Tree, which had been owned and operated by Ivan (my mother's uncle) and Hazel Galan; that was T.R.

On Saturdays, T.R. opened his facility to upcoming badminton juniors so they could practise there. One of the coaches was my father. The space, electricity and the coaching lessons were provided free of charge to the budding athletes.

Playing host and entertainer was one of T.R.'s natural gifts. I believe the occasion was the Thomas Cup (equivalent to the Davis Cup), Jamaica vs Canada which was played at the University of the West Indies at Mona, after which T.R. arranged for the entire contingent, family and friends, to go on a rafting trip and a picnic on the Rio Grande in Portland. I have no recollection as to why I was selected, but I had the honour of sitting in front with TR in his Mercedes Benz on the trip from Kingston. Perhaps it was because I was the youngest of the group. I recall that he had a loudspeaker mounted on the roof of the car power-ful enough for the six-car party to hear and that the tune he seemed to play continuously was Peter, Paul & Mary's 'Puff the Magic Dragon'.

The next thrill I had was to accompany him on a raft down the Rio Grande for the two-and-a-half-hour trip, stopping for a scrumptious lunch, no doubt also arranged by T.R. I'm not sure if it was only his love for badminton that he loaned his helicopter and pilot Bill Passaretti to take part in the Blue Mountain search. Rest assured, getting George out of his predicament on the treacherous mountainside above the Swift River, on the last planned day of the search, would have been next to impossible without the inclusion of his small chopper, and the skill of his trusted and experienced pilot Bill Passaretti. No money ever changed hands for that act of bravery and humanity.

Did my spending the day in his company shortly before my escapade have anything to do with his involvement? All I know is that we are deeply indebted to both Tinker and Bill.

Bless them both.

It would be a great injustice if I ended without this anecdote regarding Bill Passaretti, obtained from a dear friend of his family, and to whom I am most grateful.

"Bill and Peggy Passaretti, with their three children in tow, arrived in Jamaica around 1966. Bill was a pilot and licensed chopper mechanic, who looked after the two Hughes 300 helicopters* at Jamaica Transport Limited (JTL), and kept them serviceable mainly for business travel.

Bill also spent many hours working with MGM during the filming of 'The Mercenaries', much of which took place in Jamaica in 1967. The movie was the dramatization of Wilbur Smith's *Dark of the Sun***, set in the Belgian Congo. The Hughes 300s were three-seaters, with a payload of 500 lb., I think. His regular passengers at the time were action stars Jim Brown (the NFL legend) and Rod Taylor, who both probably weighed that much, combined. With Bill's 165 pounds, therefore, they were overloaded.

---

* According to Glenn Passaretti (May 8, 2015):

Island Helicopters had 3 Hughes 300 Aircraft. Originally it was called Trans World Helicopters (TWH), then changed names to Island Helicopters later on. The new choppers were sent to Jamaica in wood crates in pieces and my father, Bill Passaretti, and other engineers working for Tinker built them in a hanger at Palisadoes Airport. My father was intimately familiar with this helicopter because he was one of the lead designers and test pilots while working for Howard Hughes in the early 60s in Culver City, CA. It was the first small business class helicopter to hit the market and was a two-seater originally then redesigned into a three-seater.

** *Dark of the Sun* (a.k.a *The Mercenaries*, UK 1968) starred Rod Taylor, Yvette Mimieux, Jim Brown, and Peter Carsten. Shot partly in Jamaica, the film is based on Wilbur Smith's 1965 novel, *The Dark of the Sun*, in which a group of mercenaries sets out on a rescue mission in the Congo. Its high-octane sequences and violence rattled critics at the time of its release, but the movie went on to become an action classic.

I was lucky that I often flew with Bill when I needed to get somewhere in a hurry on business. He did his best to instruct me in flying, but I was going to be a problem pupil who had his mind focused elsewhere.

Once on the way home with him from a trip, we landed at the Caymanas airstrip to refuel. At the time, the 'strip' was just a grass track mainly used by crop dusters. With fuelling complete, I was about to take off when a Snow Aeronautical crop duster appeared and headed straight for us. Snows have a huge radial engine in the front and the pilot has almost no forward vision, which is why he didn't see us. I tried to take off, but would never have made it. Quite likely we would have been minced by the propellers, but Bill grabbed the controls on the right-hand side, allowing us to lift just high enough for the Snow to pass inches below. I didn't need lessons for a while.

While flying with Bill, he would often practice 'auto rotations', a manoeuvre in which one selects a distant clearing as an emergency target. Bill would simulate an engine failure and we would try to land in the selected spot. Coming from the north coast, Bill would cut power over Stony Hill and we would try to make it to his base at JTL on Spanish Town Road.

On one occasion Bill, Tinker and a British Leyland sales director were going to visit a customer in Mandeville when Bill had a genuine engine failure. Tinker was not worried because he knew the drill, but Keith Maddox, the Leyland man, positively freaked out and tried to climb over Tinker from the middle seat to get out. Tinker was quite badly scratched on his face and arms.

I would guess that Bill and Peggy left Jamaica in 1969 or so, and an Irishman, Barney, took over.

The couple went to Washington State where Bill continued helicopter flying. Tragically, he was killed while crop dusting early one morning in July 1971 when he turned into the sun and was blinded, hit a high-voltage power line and went down."

Tinker Rerrie's friends agree that he lived his life with a passion for doing what he loved. He passed away in January 1976 in Victoria, Canada.

★ ★ ★

Vancouver, Canada, May 2006

My wife Susan and I were guests at the wedding ceremony of the daughter of good friends we've had for about forty-five years. After the ceremony, we moved, as is custom, to another venue to continue the celebration. It was a late spring evening and the beautiful campus of the Simon Fraser University seemed particularly enchanting. We faced the pristine view of Vancouver's rugged, still snow-capped coastal mountains. On the ground, it was time for delectable food, witty speeches and a special treat of live-band music. I was prepared for good times, but nothing could have adequately prepared me for what happened next.

We took our places at a table for eight; Susan was on my left and on my right, an unknown gentleman. Short in stature and blonde with a receding hairline, I figured him to be about sixty. He had an affable and relaxed way about him, and it wasn't long before we were engaged in conversation. We spoke of this thing and that, of the island we both came from, of our interest and connection to flying and it was then that memories of a mutual experience converged. The gentleman turned out to be David du Mont, the man responsible for saving my life some thirty-nine years before from the rugged, uninhabited terrain of Jamaica's Blue Mountains. I was staggered; du Mont was amazed that this-boy-turned-adult was his actual table companion so many years later. I laughingly assured him that I seem to have a way with life events that defy probability. He was of course puzzled at this. I told him of a sequence of peculiar improbable events that I had witnessed unfold since the time we had been found.

Three persons of different families, living on the same street as my family, had seen their lives in dire peril, each incident happening within a short time span of the others. One had been missing at **SE**a, one in an **A**ircraft and I, on **L**and. Our trials had been thereafter referred to as the 'saga of the SEALS'.

Martin Plimmer and Brian King documented 'stories of amazing coincidences and the mystery and mathematics that lie behind them' in their best-selling book, *Beyond Coincidence* (2005). They may well consider the incidents of the SEALS and the meeting between David du Mont and I as that sort of happening. What I know is that a genuine relationship and mutual respect grew out of the latter, when almost forty years later, destiny played its hand. I explained the incident of the SEALS to du Mont this way:

INCIDENT A

The Haddads lived at 25 Windsor Avenue—son, Geoffrey. Between December 16 and 24, 1967, five Jamaica College boys were trapped in the Blue Mountains of Jamaica, one of whom was the author. (sea**L**s)

INCIDENT B

The Atallas lived at 39 Windsor Avenue—father, George. Four months later, in April of 1968, George Atalla and either one or two others left Kingston for Grand Cayman in a Mooney aircraft and never made it. Neither their bodies nor the aircraft were ever found. They apparently met with foul weather and ran out of fuel. (se**A**ls)

INCIDENT C

The Delvailles lived at 16 Windsor Avenue—father, Stuart. Some years later, Stuart Delvaille and two others went fishing south of Jamaica and were reported missing. Families met at homes and prayed for their safe return. They were found a short while afterwards, exhausted but thankful. (**SE**als)

That two of the three young men beat the odds and went on to live successful family lives is miraculous. That they all lived on Windsor Avenue in Jamaica's capital city and went through what they did within a relatively brief period of time is even more so.

He shook his head, looked at me incredulously and started on his account of my rescue. It happened that his own story was fortuitous and his memory in perfect working order:

"I'd just got back to Jamaica for the Christmas holidays from the Bahamas, where I had been working in aircraft maintenance and heard that my nephew Roger was one of the boys whose return home from their hike to Blue Mountain Peak was overdue. It was all over the news by then," he said.

"I had been in aviation in Jamaica for so many years before that and I knew those mountains from the air like the back of my hands".

My excitement grew. Here I was, in an unexpected time and place, being fed first-hand information of the rescue that had been planned for us all those long years ago. I sat engrossed, transported across the years while du Mont continued:

"I immediately went to my good friend and mentor Jackie Tyndale-Biscoe* and by December 22nd, we were airborne. We had studied the map of the trail you boys had intended to take for an entire day before and we knew you couldn't be on the south slopes. That area is cultivated

---

*   Jack Tyndale-Biscoe once told an interviewer that his wife had a fear of flying, so he took to the air with a camera to show her what she refused to experience herself. And so his sterling career in aerial photography was born. He was employed with Pan American's Clipper Service in 1944 and was a licensed private pilot by 1949. In 1963 he parted ways with Pan Am to start a business which he named Airways Charters. It was based at Palisadoes, a peninsula close to Port Royal, and the site of Jamaica's principal international airport (now Norman Washington Manley International Airport, NMIA).

In1967, when he played such a major role in our lives, he had a Cessna 180 (6Y-JDY) and a Beechcraft Debonair (6YJFC), both of which were stationed there.

Problems ensuing from loose security obliged Tyndale-Biscoe to relocate his business twice. His first move was in 1969, when he moved to one section of Caymanas Estate, a large tract of land planted in sugar cane and expansive enough to accommodate a golf club, a field manicured for polo-playing and the airstrip that housed his aircraft. The other section of the estate, which is divided in two by a highway linking Kingston to the old capital of Spanish Town, is the site of Caymanas Park, home to Jamaica's horse racing industry and a hub of excitement on race days. He made his second and last move in 1987 from the Caymanas airstrip to the Tinson Pen Aerodrome, the most established of the island's aerodromes after its two international airports.

Sadly, Jack Tyndale-Biscoe passed away on September 30, 2003, but not before I came to know him very well and obtain from him many of the photographs he shot on that memorable day in 1967, plus several others which capture a unique bird's eye view of the island's topography. Some of these photos are prominently displayed throughout the book. He continued to love and play music. After his days with Hugh Coxe's band where he played the deep bass, Jackie taught himself to play the electric organ and was an inspiration and advisor to me on numerous occasions. I would sometimes visit him just to listen to him play and to learn a new tune.

and doesn't have much vegetation. Those slopes are sparsely populated, but populated nevertheless. If you had been there, you would have been seen by that time if you hadn't already found your way out. So we knew we were in for it. You had to be on the north slopes; everybody knows the north slopes are uninhabited and densely forested."

Jackie knew the area well from the air, but in his many years of flying and taking photographs, had never been faced with a situation like this. I vividly remember him saying,

"David, I really hope to hell that the boys are not down there! We'll never be able to see them and likewise, they won't be able to see us. It's jungle down there! We can't even penetrate it by ground rescue!' But the rest is history," he mused.

We spent a great deal of the evening telling story after story of how we saw events unfold on both sides of that gripping story. Conversation continued the next day and I came to a more profound understanding of the slim chance our rescuers had had of success. I think today of how providential the seating was at that wedding banquet!

Robin Crawford, who was also at the event, wrote the following in an e-mail shortly afterwards:

> Geoff, It was especially surreal (and emotional) to witness the moving encounter between you and your life-saver after forty years. That alone was worth every penny of the trip. I still can't believe I was a witness to, and minor participant in, that piece of Jamaican history.
>
> Nuff respect,
>
> Robin.

★ ★ ★

Thirty years later—December 22, 1997

Whether or not we wanted a reminder of our expedition, it would be prominently recalled by none other than Hartley Neita, sometimes two or three times during the week of the anniversary, in the *Gleaner* features, "Interesting Historical Highlights" or "This Day in our Past". The article, or variations thereof, would read:

> 1967 – Five Jamaica College students, Gordon Cooper, George Hussey, Roger Bates, Cecil Ward and Geoffrey Haddad are reported missing in the Blue Mountains.
>
> The group left Clydesdale for the Blue Mountain Peak...and were due at Penlyne Castle two days ago. Planes from the JDF Air Wing begin a search for them. It is the second time in 30 years that five Jamaica College schoolboys have been lost while on a hike to Blue Mountain Peak.

Hartley Neita always ended his articles with, "Today's Gem". I am sure he would not be unhappy if I quoted the following two written in December 1997 and 2006, respectively:

> In life we rise and fall,
> and we struggle to our feet,
> the world is fraught with twisting,
> and the sour and the sweet.
>
> —George B. Wallace

and

> For love is God and man's one masterpiece
> The only common link with time and space
> Mystery, infinity and earth.
>
> —George Campbell

★ ★ ★

Kingston, Jamaica – September 2013

Geoffrey Haddad's *If I'm Not Back By Wednesday* gives his account of his adventure in the Blue Mountains of Jamaica, and it is gripping! I know the Blue Mountains, and without reservation, can say that he has captured the essence and intrigue of these mountains, the spirit and traditions of the Jamaica College schoolboy, and the 'never say die' will of our Jamaican people.

With our mutual love for the outdoors, it is not surprising that our paths crossed repeatedly over the years. My home from 1937 to 1955 was Torre Garda in Pennlyne Castle, and I have leased/owned Whitfield Hall since 1964. Coincidentally, my mother helped arrange for the search for the five Jamaica College (JC) boys who, in 1939, were lost in the Back Rio Grande Valley north of Blue Mountain Peak—a different area from Geoffrey Haddad's group.

Like Geoff, I went to JC and am a Civil Engineer. We first met in the 1980s when he was the project director responsible for the Expansion, Modernization and Coal Conversion of the Caribbean Cement Company's plant here in Jamaica, and became good friends thereafter.

I have hiked extensively in the Blue Mountains, and indeed know well the area where Geoff's group got lost. They were indeed very close to established trails and surely crossed the trail from Portland Gap to Butterfly Gap/Shirley Castle at about 5,500 ft. elevation. But the vegetation there is very thick.

Quite clearly, they went north at Main Ridge Gap before getting to the established trails (including the alternate route they had planned), and went down the Speculation River instead of south as they believed—easy to do in the thick ferrel (bracken) and bamboo grass (Japanese Bamboo) on Main Ridge. The Speculation River would have been flowing heavily after our traditional October/November rains that year.

The greatest piece of good luck they had was that at this time of year we usually get north winds which cause this area to be shrouded in fog and clouds, sometimes for weeks, with no let up, together with cold, driving rain. That they got the breaks in the weather, allowing them to be found, is the greatest miracle of all. When they reached the Swift River, following the river became treacherous, and climbing out of the valley was the best thing they could have done, leading them to the other miracle, the only ferrel patch in the area [visible from the air].

Geoff's book also provides some flavour of middle class Jamaica in the 1960s, but above all demonstrates once again that people have to be extremely careful about venturing off the beaten track in these rugged mountains with dense tropical forests and often very cold and variable weather conditions. We at Whitfield Hall have had to search for and rescue many lost hikers, some, including wild pig hunters, have died here too.

John Allgrove, PE
Owner, Whitfield Hall, Jamaica

★ ★ ★

Vancouver, Canada — November 17, 2013

If I'm Not back by Wednesday is an amazing true story, well researched, well written and a great read! Geoffrey

Haddad recounts an ill-conceived and harrowing adventure from his childhood in Jamaica. He and four other 17 year-old fit-worthies from Jamaica College, got hopelessly lost in the vastness of the rainforest jungle on the wet side of the Blue Mountain range. They were lucky to survive. They had set out to find a new way to the Peak, the highest mountain on the Island, Blue Mountain, and thence to the north shore. They never made it. Beset by rain, fog, cold and by mosquitoes and wasps -and with no trail to follow-they ran low on food, fuel and water. They would not have lasted much longer when they were spotted from the air and then rescued by a Jamaican Defence Force helicopter.

Having lived in Jamaica as a boy, I too ventured to the Peak, but on horse back and with a guide. I can't imagine trying to hike to the Peak and down again through the jungle without a clear trail to follow.

Fortuitously, a good friend of mine and Geoffrey's parents, David du Mont, persuaded a photographer-pilot friend to take him along on one last flight just as the air search was winding down. David spotted the boys just as his pilot decided to turn back.

It took forty years for David and Geoffrey to actually meet. By an odd coincidence, they found themselves sitting beside each other at a wedding in Vancouver, Canada, just a few years ago. They exchanged stories and were astounded when they discovered their small-worlds connection. Geoffrey took that as a sign that he had to finish the book that he had been working on all those years. We are glad he did; I give it five stars.

Darcy Rezac,
Managing Director Emeritus
The Vancouver Board of Trade

★ ★ ★

Ocho Rios, Jamaica—December 21, 2013

On December 1, 2013 I was contacted by Donnie Soutar and was informed that he would be in Jamaica from December 20th for three weeks. *So what*, I thought? I was scheduled to be in Jamaica from the 17th to the 21st, anyway.

Donnie was the fellow who became ill the day before our hike, and I took his place. Next he informed me that he would be bringing along his ninety-three-year-old father and wondered if we could all meet at Mamee Bay, a beautiful secluded beach area on the island's north coast close to Ocho Rios. His father was W. Donald Soutar, the only living member of the Jamaica College five lost in the Blue Mountains in April of 1939. I was stunned at the opportunity of meeting Donald Sr.

I decided to bring along a copy of the advance version of my book which I would show to him.

But Donnie had other surprises. He had also invited to visit and enjoy a sumptuous lunch Gordon Cooper and Cecil Ward, both members of my 1967 group.

The date, December 21, was exactly forty-six years and five days after we had begun our infamous hike into the mountains. It was surreal to have had this unexpected meeting.

The next day I visited W. Donald in Kingston and presented him with the last copy I had of the advance version of *If I'm Not Back By Wednesday* as we exchanged memories of our trips.

★ ★ ★

Fort Lauderdale, Florida, USA—February 21, 2014

This serves as a review for the book *If I'm not back by Wednesday: Trapped in Jamaica's Blue Mountains, December, 1967* by Mr. Geoffrey B. Haddad by me, the sole living survivor of five Jamaica College schoolboys "Lost in the Blue Mountains, in the Easter of 1939 for thirteen days".

It was a great privilege for me to read Geoffrey's new book and, yes! "from cover to cover". Once I started I found it more and more difficult to put the book down, not only because it was a specific and exciting adventure of these five boys who ventured as they fought their way to their destination, but also constantly reminding me, now ninety-three years of age, of very similar experiences my other four companions and I suffered in 1939.

Geoffrey's description of the terrain they were forced to travel, conquer and subdue twenty-four hours a day, awake and/or asleep but never forgetting the extensive growth of bamboo grass, prickly tree ferns, other heavy undergrowth, dense mountain forest, rivers and constant rainfall which rarely discouraged the explorers, is a masterpiece.

The description of the boys' rescue by helicopters and David du Mont first spotting Cecil and Gordon in the top of a tree, literally kept me on the edge of my seat. All are to be greatly congratulated, as they risked their lives to succeed. I found it quite touching that Geoffrey did not actually meet David until some forty years after he had been rescued.

Over 208 pages of excellent and exciting reading with a wonderful collage of photographs, completing a wonderful book, well prepared and beautifully written and also intertwined with historical information of Geoffrey's family, his life at Jamaica College and also among other things, the worried families and general public left back at home.

Well done, Geoffrey. I wish you all the success and I am very proud of you.

Sincerely,

W. Donald Soutar

(A member of the five boys from Jamaica College who were lost in April 1939)

★ ★ ★

Toronto, Ontario, Canada—May 8, 2014

I twice read the advance copy of Geoffrey Haddad's book and devoured every page, each time.

As a lifelong professional journalist and a person with a passionate, life-long love affair with my homeland, Jamaica, it always amazes me when I read a non-fiction work that speaks to an event that took place in my life-time. I can remember and know of it intimately because I watched and listened in rapt attention when the event was unfolding; I know, or know of, the people involved.

But the amazement is normally about how inaccurate, incorrect, inflated or under-inflated is the account and how it differs so completely from the events as I remember.

Geoffrey's biographical account of five boys lost in
Jamaica's wild Blue Mountains is a great, great read. It
is a historical document, attention-holding and accurate.

He and I share an alma mater—the 200-plus year old
Jamaica College—and myself and every other past or
present JC student know that because of the psyche of
that particular school, we could easily have been part of
that five, or in another five, who nearly died in the Blue
Mountains. We were encouraged at JC, and the men of
that school still are, to be leaders and adventurers and
to take the attendant risks and have the cool heads and
self-control that makes leaders.

Great work Geoff. I would unhesitatingly urge Jamaicans
in the Diaspora, and we are everywhere in this world, to
read the book. It is a necessary historical document.

Philip Mascoll OD,
Founding member, Jamaican Diaspora Board
Toronto, Canada.

★ ★ ★

In Memoriam—W. Donald Soutar (1920–2015)

William Donald Soutar was born April 14, 1920 in Kingston, Jamaica.
After leaving Jamaica College in 1938 he worked for the Bank of Nova
Scotia. He later trained with the British Army in the Jamaican Battalion
and the Royal Signal Corps in electronics, particularly communications,
for which he had developed a passion from age 12, building a radio
using his homemade blow torch and soldering iron.

He gained a scholarship in the USA to be trained at RCA (Radio
Corp. of America). On his return to Jamaica he worked as Asst Eng.
for the very first Radio Broadcasting Station ever to be on the Air in

Jamaica, called ZQI with an Englishman, Denis Gick. He then joined Excide Battery Co. which later became Wills Battery Company, in 1950. In 1962 he became the General Manager and was the Manager Director before leaving for the USA in 1975. His last years at Wills, saw him managing 89 permanent staff, 120 salespersons and numerous agencies throughout the island. During his time at Wills he was also able to assist persons with their ham radios, hi-fi sets and even hearing aids, whenever they required servicing. He was affectionately known as Dr. Soutar to his hearing aid 'clients'

In the USA, he managed two vegetable oil tankers and provided several shipping companies with parts and technical training under his company Island Shipping Agencies. He retired in 2002 and continued to reside in South Florida.

Sadly he passed away after a battle with cancer in Florida on January 24th, 2015. He is survived by his younger brother Farren (Jamaica), elder sister Yvonne (Trinidad), his wife Audrey (Jamaica) the mother of his children Donnie and Carolyn, and grandchildren Sarah, Joseph, Lauren, his second wife Patsy (USA), her child Lisa, and grandchildren Tiffanny and Lindsey.

I was fortunate to have met Donald Soutar nearly seventy-five years after his encounter with the Blue Mountains and nearly fifty years in my case. The chance meeting took place at Mamee Bay in December 2013 where we shared our experiences over several days. The meeting was arranged by Donnie, his son, and surprisingly included two of my 'almost lost for good' hiking buddies, Gordon Cooper and Cecil Ward. W. Donald graciously accepted my request to review my book *If I'm Not Back by Wednesday: Trapped in Jamaica's Blue Mountains, December 1967* and I for one am happy that he did. In May of 2014 I was able to share with him his contribution as it stood.

It was indeed an honour and a privilege to have known him and to have shared many of his life experiences.

On the last day of his hike in 1939, along with his four other JC lads, it was he who spoke the first words to persons who they had encountered.

According to his fellow hiker Douglas Hall: "The man who had called now appeared from behind the trees. Needless to say we were surprised.

'You the five buoy dat lost in de bush?' 'We are,' Soutar shouted and the rest became history."

Hartley Neita, one of the island's prominent historians and communications consultants, had penned a book called *The Search* which chronicled the misadventure of Soutar and his other 4 Jamaica College colleagues in April of 1939. He frequently wrote, in *The Gleaner*, excerpts from newsworthy items under "This Day in our Past" or "Interesting Historical highlights". One such item dated December 23, 1997 read as follows:

> 1967: Army and Police patrols, assisted by the Air Wing of the Jamaica Defence Force, are searching the Blue Mountains for five Jamaica College Schoolboys* who left Kingston six days ago to hike to the Peak and have been seen since. Five Jamaica College boys were also lost in the mountains at Easter in 1939 and were found after nearly three weeks (actually two weeks) of search by the army, police, scouts and citizens. They were Eric Gray, now working with Times Store, Donald Soutar at Wills Battery Company, Douglas Hall, now a Professor at the University of the West Indies, Teddy Hastings who is in business in British Honduras and John Ennever who has since died.

Thus connecting the two adventures nearly forty years apart, forever.

Hartley Neita would end each one of such writings with "Today's Memory Gem". On this day he wrote:

> There is a morning in all human night
> And life and birth and beauty beyond death.

> May Donald's memory be for a blessing and his soul rest in peace.

> *The author*

---

* Those five boys were Roger Bates, Gordon Cooper, Cecil Ward, George Hussey and Geoffrey Haddad.

★ ★ ★

Synergies: A Link to the Past
Miami, Florida, February 12, 2015

Geoffrey's book could only be a very entertaining, inspiring and, historic account of a most unforgettable experience. It has got to be an enjoyable read.

I will bet that Geoffrey Haddad did not know or realize that he spoiled my first Christmas back in Jamaica after attending the Royal Military Academy Sandhurst, and other Courses at The School of Infantry in England for a few years.

It was a most unforgettable time for me as I had returned a few days before from England and was thoroughly enjoying my first Christmas Party at The Jamaica Officer's Club that night in 1967, when at about 0130 hrs, the late Maj. Trevor McMillan, my Company Commander at the time, came and told me that some school boys had gone missing on a trek through the Blue Mountains. With a drink in each of our hands while having a most enjoyable time at the Club, he instructed me to leave at 0500 hrs, with my platoon, in search of the boys. The mission was simple: Find the boys!

Early that morning we got up to the start point in the mountains close to 'first light' and off we went on foot with my soldiers, in search of them. I decided that it was best not to use the normal tracks as I imagined them to be adventurous boys, so I endeavoured to retrace their steps in uncharted wilderness.

A couple days later we got the message over the radio that they were found and we all breathe a breath of fresh air as we were so very pleased out of sheer concern for them. By this time we were deep into the dense wilderness cutting our way through the thick forest. It is not a very nice experience for them being lost in the jungle without water food and most of all warm clothing, especially during the winter, that season. Once the elevation got above 2,000 feet one can easily feel the change in temperature. So as we got higher, there was a radical change in temperature. Up on the Peak the temperature usually got down in the range of about 33–34 degrees Fahrenheit, close to freezing on a cold night.

It may seem simple but Jamaica is known to have some of the densest jungles in the world, next to Myanmar which was once Burma in South East Asia. Among other things, this is the reason why the Canadian and British troops came to Jamaica for their jungle training.

Anyway, after a few days they were spotted from the air and taken out by helicopter while it took me and my soldiers a few days to return from the jungle. So there went my Christmas and I got back to Up Park Camp, the Military base and HQ of the Jamaica Defence Force, just in time to enjoy the rest of the Season.

This was certainly one of my many memorable experiences. Kudos to Geoffrey and his friends; it's nice to be alive.

Oliver H. Jobson, Capt (Ret'd)
Jamaica Defence Force. 1965–1976
Author / SPeaker / Facilitator - *Expanding
the Boundaries of Self* and *Saved from
Suicide by The Lord's Prayer*

★ ★ ★

California, USA, April 26, 2015

The main reason that I vividly remember the rescue in December of 1967 is because when my dad, Bill Passaretti, was searching the Blue Mountains for the five JC boys in 'his' Hughes 300 helicopter, he noticed a small clearing and a banana tree with a big bunch of bananas that were almost ripe. A few days after the rescue he said to me, "Come on, we are going on a mission." I was thirteen at the time and was working with my father during Christmas break helping with maintenance on the 'copters. He got a machete and we flew off way up into the mountains. I remembered that the forest was very dense and flying just above the trees was dangerous. For sure, if you went down in there they would never find you. He found the banana tree and told me to jump out with the machete and climb the tree and to chop down the bananas. I got the bananas and strapped them to the cargo platform just below the passenger door and back to Kingston we went. My brother, Bill, remembers the huge bunch of bananas we brought home. Due to you and your buddies, we got a few hundred bananas!

The owner of the helicopters was Tinker Rerrie. I remember how special I felt on payday. He would come personally to the hanger and pay me in cash. He was very generous to my family. Tinker provided us with a company home, cars, polo ponies and drivers. He took us river rafting just like he took you. I also remember being in his car at a time when we were spending the weekend at Silver Sands. On one occasion we went to town to get some patties and he had the radio blaring with his outside speaker as we drove through town. I clearly remember the Beatles song, 'OB-LA-DI,

OB-LA DA' was playing and everyone on the side of the road just loved it.

I have to tell you, Geoffrey, that all of us (my brother Bill and sister Kathy) have been deeply touched with your story, and it bought us all to tears hearing about your unbelievable experience, and seeing our father just so briefly in the video. We lost him when we were all so young that we are all still deeply traumatized from it, and it is almost impossible to talk about him without totally losing it. He was truly a special guy and was loved by everyone who met him; he had that kind of charisma.

Glen Passaretti, son of rescue pilot Bill Passaretti
Orange County, California
V.P. Sales and Marketing, Direct RM

★ ★ ★

Where Are They Now?
My 'Blue Mountain Five', some of the persons involved in the search and other connected parties listed below, are all alive and well, living either in Jamaica, Canada, USA or Australia. We've all had varying degrees of contact with each other, but in some cases, hardly any at all:

Roger Bates is married to Anne (née Cadien) and lives in Edmonton, Alberta, Canada. He worked as the senior technician at NCR, Edmonton branch and retired in 2007. He has three children and seven grandchildren.

Gordon Cooper is married to Laura (née Facey, sculptor and artist extraordinaire) and lives in Saint Mary, Jamaica where he practises, *inter alia*, animal husbandry.

George Hussey is married to Carmen (née Chang) and has two children. They live in Mississauga, Ontario, Canada. I am informed that he is still involved in pest control management.

Cecil Ward is a professional photographer, an amateur artist and actor. He continues to reside in Jamaica.

Major George Brown joined the JDF Air Wing in July 1963 and became officer in command in November 1967. He retired from the Air Wing as its CO in December 1970. He continued his flying career with local internal airlines as a pilot and training captain, in which capacity he is proud to have imparted some flying skills to many young first officers who ultimately became senior Air Jamaica captains. Following a few years of crop spraying, he joined Alcan Jamaica Company as their flight department manager, pilot and maintenance engineer. Compulsory retirement age caught up with him in 1996, just when he was getting really good at what he was doing, and enjoying it. He moved with his family to Atlanta that year to concentrate on his golf game.

Robin Crawford moved to Florida in the mid-1980s with his wife, Christine, and family. He is the father of three daughters. He works for an international firm providing enterprise application and IT information services to many corporations, including GE. Robin is still an avid videographer, and enjoys foreign vacations with his family when time permits.

David du Mont emigrated to Florida, where he is still an avid aircraft enthusiast, attending conferences and rebuilding contemporary aircraft as well as 'warbirds'. No doubt he is currently working on something interesting.

Ian Jacobs, who joined Airways Charters in 1967, was involved along with Jackie Biscoe on many searches. This was in addition to the company's main business of shuttling persons around the island to one of its forty-three airstrips, at the time; and aerial photography. They were also involved in transporting actors for movie productions, sometimes using their aircrafts as props. On occasions, scheduled flights were cancelled to attend to urgent calls for aerial searches. Airways Charters donated pilots' time and fuel and never charged for any of these SOS calls. He moved with his family to Australia in 1974. Ian retired from the government forestry department after twenty-three years and currently lives on the West Coast in the town of Bunbury.

Donnie Soutar was the person who became ill the day before our hike; I took his place. He moved to the UK in 1969 where he studied Business then Law. As a solicitor he specialized in Maritime and Admiralty

Law and worked with what became the largest law firm in the world, Clifford Chance. In 1989 he moved to Florida where he now lives with his wife, son, and daughter. He is an in-house contracts manager for a large regional maritime company.

Captain Anthony 'Bunny' Stern left the Air Wing of the JDF in 1976 as lieutenant and returned in 1978 for a year as lieutenant colonel. In that same year, he obtained the Order of Distinction and left office in 1979 with the rank of colonel. In 1982, he went to London as defence advisor (military attaché) for the Government of Jamaica, where he was responsible for training 100 military personnel. He continues to maintain a keen interest in aviation and has been the secretary general of the Jamaica Aircraft Owners and Pilot Association since 1997. He resides in Jamaica.

Major Stephen Cane, an English Officer, went to Barbados to assist his family in the operation of a fairly sizeable property. Major Cane passed away a few years ago. It is understood that the property may still be a tourist attraction.

Captain John Dent, who was also an English Officer, returned to the UK and continued his career in the British Army.

I, *Geoffrey B. Haddad* continued playing badminton and was the Junior triple champion until 1969. I won the Jamaica mens' doubles championship in 1969 and represented Jamaica in international events on a number of occasions. I was nominated for the Sportsman of the Year award in that year, competing against such luminaries as Olympic sprinter Donald Quarrie. I and my sister were the youngest participants in the Commonwealth Games in Edinburgh 1970 in the sport. I am a registered professional engineer in British Columbia and Ontario, Canada, as well as in Jamaica. A 1974 graduate of McMaster University in civil/structural engineering, I subsequently earned a master's degree in 1975, specializing in structural engineering. I have practised as a consulting engineer, a product development and divestment consultant, project and construction management consultant, and other related fields, including forensic engineering for over thirty years. I currently live in West Vancouver with my family, including four grandchildren.

ACKNOWLEDGEMENTS

It was an immense privilege to have been in contact with Hartley Neita, but sadly, he passed away before we had a chance to meet in person. Out of my tremendous admiration for him, I have referred liberally to his thoughtful documentation of the 1939 boys' trip into the mountains, and I am deeply heartened to know that his book is currently required reading in history at first-form level at Jamaica College.

On a more personal note, I am also gratified to have discovered that the worthy gentleman and I shared the habit of holding onto every scrap of information gleaned over the years, a practice that eventually contributed to what I have finally put together. I do hope that my paper-weary family will now forgive me for all the time I felt compelled to spend away from them as I collected material. I also trust that they can now understand the chronic disarray of their husband's/father's library.

The participants in both incidents and Mr. Neita himself were graduates of Jamaica College. I would like to salute that outstanding institution for the pivotal role it played in our lives. To the late Mr. Neita and his family, I record my deepest thanks for the inspiration I needed to pursue the writing of this book to its end.

Thanks to David du Mont for his eagle eye, and Jackie Tyndale-Biscoe for his remarkable abilities as a determined pilot and photographer. I'm thankful for the several aerial pictures he shot, which so graphically show the location and nature of the severe peril we faced on the mountain. I am also grateful for the photographs taken and provided to me by Messrs. Dowie and Valentine of the *Daily Gleaner* and the *Jamaica Broadcasting Corporation* (JBC), respectively. For the other photographs, I thank my relatives and friends for having the presence of mind to take them at the time. Particular thanks to Robin Crawford for the 8mm film he shot at Army Headquarters, Up Park Camp, and for delivering my famous last words to my father, precipitating the great search of 1967.

I am indebted to Captain Anthony 'Bunny' Stern of the Air Wing Division of the Jamaica Defence Force (JDF), one of the army's most experienced helicopter pilots, who was ably assisted by Sergeant Keith Hall and Captain John Dent (JDF HQ). In our case, their intervention was of necessity a daring rescue, carried out by determined and highly skilled pilots who put their own lives at considerable risk to reach and extract us from nearly impenetrable terrain. Without a doubt, it is to the determination and ability of all these men that I owe my life.

A special thanks to Roger Bates for his review of an earlier manuscript and for his and Gordon Cooper's recollections, stories, diary excerpts and photographs; which are included here.

Special recognition is owed to Tinker Rerrie of Jamaica Transport Ltd. for the contribution of his private aircraft, a Hughes 300 chopper flown by experienced pilot, helicopter designer/constructor Bill Passaretti; as well as to all the owners and operators of independent search vehicles and aircraft who participated, including those of the Jamaica Defence and Constabulary forces.

Thanks also to David Coxe, who remembers searching in a plane (most likely a Piper Cherokee), rented from the Jamaica Flying Club. He paid for his own fuel, joined the search effort at a very early stage, and remained with the search parties for the duration.

Thanks to Dudley Delapenha, who recalls searching for the boys with Jackie Biscoe as the pilot in a high-wing aircraft.

Gratitude to Ian Jacobs, who piloted a Beechcraft Debonair belonging to Jackie's company, Airways Charters, and who worked in tandem with Jackie throughout the search. I'll always cherish the help of Freddy Ramson, who transported Roger and me to the Airport (now Norman Washington Manley Airport, NMIA) and who sadly later lost his life in an aviation accident.

I would like to especially mention four officers whose attention to the emergency was constant and whose efforts were of the highest standard: Police Commissioner Gordon Langdon; JDF Chief of Staff,

Brigadier General David Smith, JDF Air Wing Commander Lieutenant Colonel George Brown (who selected the pilots for the mission) and Major-General Rudolph E. G. Green.

A million thanks to Ann Walters, for her dedication and assistance in the preparation and editing of the manuscript. To Myrna Allen, who made only minor errors in converting my hieroglyphics to the first printed version on her IBM Selectric II typewriter; without question, an admirable task.

In September 2012, I had the good fortune of meeting Michelle Neita, daughter of Hartley, who played formidable roles, including that of editor, in the production of *The Search,* other publications by her father, and for her review of my book. It was she who gave me the final push to go public. Thank you, Michelle

I am indebted to Michael Grant and his team at Kingston Communications for their assistance in the initial packaging of my book and for helping to bring my story to life. Their dedication to detail and accuracy was outstanding. Having to recount significant portions of the story after nearly fifty years required a great deal of patience.

I also wish to thank Kay Alexander Glanzer for her photo restoration and enhancement work, particularly on photographs dating over a century.

Thanks as well to Patrick Kitson for his meticulous work on the illustrations used throughout the book.

To my publishers and printers a big 'thank you' for their guidance, dedication, patience and perseverance in seeing this project come to fruition.

Thanks also to John Allgrove, for his in-depth knowledge of the mountains and the history of Whitfield Hall (a hikers' lodge in the Blue Mountains still owned by his family); Lloyd Alberga; Marjorie Biscoe; Susan Bloomfield (Biscoe); Captain Andrew Bogle; Major Stephen Cane; Professor Diana Cooper-Clark; Robin Crawford; Roderic Crawford; Janet Delvaille (Crawford); Ernest DeSouza Jr.; Dudley Delapenha, Michael Delevante; Dorothy Floro (Bates); Mr. Robert Hamaty, OD; Mary Olga Hanna, PhD, literary critic, Edward Charles Hanna; Heather Harvey (Jacobs), Victor Carlysle Hudson; Ian Jacobs; Rabbi Dana Kaplan;

David Langdon, Rudy Mantel; Michael Marley; Howard Nugent; Jennifer Nugent (Haddad); Len Moody-Stuart; Major-General Robert Neish CD; Lieutenant Colonel Jaimie S.A. Ogilvie, CO of the Air Wing; Rhona Panton (Banks); Glen Passaretti, Mr. Darcy Rezac CD; Richard Roberts, Attorney-at-law; Dr. Charles Royes; Donnie Soutar; Captain Dennis Walcott; Lilian Watson (Bates), Cecil Ward and Anthony 'Tony' Winkler.

To all the others who made this work possible; there are too many to mention. I apologize for any omissions and offer my undying gratitude.

My parents, B. S. and Norma Haddad, deserve a grateful son's eternal thanks, particularly my father, who first raised the alarm and initiated the search; who introduced me to those mountains and knew full well that time was of the essence; who relinquished the comfort of his home to set up watch at military headquarters for the duration of the emergency; who pored and plotted over maps to determine the most likely productive path of rescue. I treasure my mother, who matched him step for step in love and relentless determination while I was lost in our bewitching but merciless mountains. Thank you, Mom and Dad.

Finally, I thank everyone who prayed and lived without sleep for all those uncertain days and those who mounted the determined search. There is no way to ever repay your generosity.

Geoffrey B. Haddad
West Vancouver, Canada
December 2015

Geoffrey B. Haddad was born in Kingston Jamaica. By the time he was five he had developed a passion for the outdoors. At sixteen he had hiked all the hills of the southern flanks of the Blue Mountains, either while on cub/scout outings or hunting with his father. Conquering the Peak, however, had always been a personal goal. Spontaneously accepting that challenge on December 15, 1967 almost cost him his life.

He graduated from McMaster University in 1974 (first class honours) and completed a master's degree in structural engineering in 1975. He is a professional engineer registered in Jamaica, British Columbia and Ontario, Canada He has worked in the consulting engineering and related fields since that time. He resides in West Vancouver, Canada with his family, including four grandchildren.

CPSIA information can be obtained
at www.ICGtesting.com
Printed in the USA
LVOW04*0412300916

506845LV00004B/12/P

9 781460 274385